Inequality, Crisis and Social Change in Indonesia

A mood of deep uncertainty has permeated Indonesian society since the collapse of the dictatorial regime of President Suharto in 1998. As new governments were formed in quick succession, by B. J. Habibie, Abdurrahman Wahid and Megawati Sukarnoputri, long-established patterns in the distribution of wealth, power and symbolic capital in Indonesia have been disrupted, modified or reasserted. This socio-political upheaval has affected even comparatively safe and stable regions such as the island of Bali, which serves as the focal example in this analysis of contemporary Indonesian society.

Times of crisis present a unique opportunity for research on social change and for uncovering social tensions and fault lines within society. This book describes how major economic and political crises combine with social aspirations at a grass-roots level to elicit shifts in local and regional configurations of power and knowledge. Special attention is paid to disadvantaged sectors of Balinese society including marginal ethnic or religious groups, rural populations and women.

Thomas A. Reuter is a Queen Elizabeth II Research Fellow at the School of Anthropology, Geography and Environmental Studies at the University of Melbourne.

Inequality, Crisis and Social Change in Indonesia

The muted worlds of Bali

Edited by

Thomas A. Reuter

RoutledgeCurzon
Taylor & Francis Group

LONDON AND NEW YORK

First published 2003
by RoutledgeCurzon
11 New Fetter Lane, London EC4P 4EE

Simultaneously published in the USA and Canada
by RoutledgeCurzon
29 West 35th Street, New York, NY 10001

RoutledgeCurzon is an imprint of the Taylor & Francis Group

Typeset in Baskerville by
Integra Software Services Pvt. Ltd, Pondicherry, India
Printed and bound in Great Britain by
MPG Books Ltd, Bodmin

British Library Cataloguing in Publication Data
A catalogue record for this book is available
from the British Library

Library of Congress Cataloging in Publication Data
Inequality, crisis and social change in Indonesia : the
muted worlds of Bali / edited by Thomas A. Reuter.
     p.   cm.
  Includes bibliographical references and index.
  1. Social change–Indonesia–Bali (Province) 2. Bali
(Indonesia : Province)–Social conditions.   3. Bali
(Indonesia : Province)–Civilization.   I. Reuter,
Thomas Anton.

  HN710 .B3 I54 2002
  306′.09598′9–dc21
                                                    2002031670

ISBN 0–415–29688–9

This book is dedicated to all the people who were disadvantaged, silenced or persecuted under the dictatorial New Order government of former Indonesian President, Suharto.

Contents

Figures

Maps

Tables

Contributors

Diana Darling is a free-lance writer and editor who has lived in Bali since 1981. Among her published work is *The Painted Alphabet: a novel based on a Balinese tale* (1991, 1994, 2001); 'Dispatch from Indonesia', an Internet column for CNET (1998–1999); and the translation (from French to English) of Michel Picard's *Bali: Cultural Tourism and Touristic Culture*. She is a regular contributor to *Latitudes* magazine.

I Nyoman Darma Putra lectures in Indonesian literature in the Faculty of Letters, Udayana University, in Denpasar, Bali. He is currently also completing a PhD thesis at the School of Languages and Comparative Cultural Studies, University of Queensland, Australia. His main publications to date are *Tonggak Baru Sastra Bali Modern* (2000) and *To Change Bali: Essays in Honour of I Gusti Ngurah Bagus* (Wollongong/Denpasar: University of Wollongong Institute of Social Change and Critical Inquiry/Bali Post, 2000. Co-edited with Adrian Vickers and Michele Ford).

Natalie Kellar completed a Bachelor of Arts at the University of Melbourne in 1994 and an Honours Degree in Indonesian at Monash University in 1995. She obtained a PhD at the School of Asian Languages and Studies at Monash University in 2000, for research on the politics of gender-identity in the classical Balinese dance-drama Arja and other contemporary Balinese theatre forms. Dr Kellar's main interests are gender relations and female identity in Indonesian society, the Indonesian and Balinese performing arts, and Indonesian literature. She is currently working in LOTE educational publishing as an Indonesian editor.

Graeme MacRae is employed as a lecturer in Social Anthropology in the School of Social and Cultural Studies at Massey University in Auckland. His main research has been in Bali on topics including the political economy of tourism, economics, ritual, spatial organization and history. He is currently working on a comparative study of social, economic and architectural aspects of temples in Balinese and South Indian cultures.

Ayami Nakatani is an Associate Professor in anthropology at Okayama University, Japan. She has published papers on the Balinese handicraft industry, Japanese fatherhood, and feminist anthropology. Her current research interests include the representation of Southeast Asian handicrafts in the Japanese market.

Thomas A. Reuter obtained his doctorate in anthropology at the Center for Advanced Studies, Research School of Pacific and Asian Studies, at The Australian National University in 1995. He subsequently taught for 2 years at the University of Heidelberg (Germany), before completing a 3-year Australian Research Council post-doctoral fellowship at The University of Melbourne. He has recently been appointed for a 5-year term to the School of Anthropology, Geography and Environmental Studies, The University of Melbourne, as a Queen Elizabeth II Research Fellow of the Australian Research Council. Dr Reuter has published widely on Bali, based on a decade of anthropological research with a particular focus on the people of the island's central highland region. A research project on new social movements in Java is still in its early stages. His major publications include: *Custodians of the Sacred Mountains: Culture and Society in the Highland Bali* (Honolulu: Hawaii University Press, 2002) and *The House of Our Ancestors: Precedence and Dualism in Highland Balinese Society* (Leiden: KITLV Press).

Adrian Vickers is currently an Associate Dean (Research and Graduate Studies) of the Faculty of Arts, University of Wollongong. He teaches Southeast Asian history and has published extensively on Indonesia, and especially on Bali. He is currently completing a study on nationalism and commodity relations in Indonesia. The most well-known among his numerous publications is *Bali: A Paradise Created* (Penguin Books 1989).

Acknowledgements

The contributors would like to thank the University of Melbourne for hosting the *Third Australian Conference for Balinese Studies*, on 24–26 September 1999, where the chapters contained in this volume were first presented. For financial support of the conference our gratitude extends to the Indonesia Forum, the Melbourne Institute of Asian Languages and Societies (MIALS), and the School of Anthropology, Geography & Environmental Studies, as well as to the individual institutions of the contributors for providing leave and funding for conference travel.

Special thanks to Ms Michelle Chin, Secretary of the Society for Balinese Studies (SBS), for her support in organizing and advertising the conference, and to Linda Connor, Raechelle Rubinstein and Helen Creese, for advice concerning the preparation of this edited volume.

1   Introduction

Thomas A. Reuter

Indonesia has been in a state of continuous economic and political crisis since the fall of former President Suharto's authoritarian government in 1998. The crisis persists as the current government of President Megawati Sukarnoputri struggles to rebuild a country torn apart by decades of corruption, nepotism and state oppression, as well as by interethnic violence, religious conflict and separatism.[1] Under the seemingly chaotic conditions of the last 4 years, social tensions and conflicts have surfaced that, for decades, had been simmering under a lid of political repression and remained hidden behind the veil of a culture of enforced silence.

While it may have been viewed and widely reported upon as a cause of concern for Indonesia and its neighbours, this continuing state of instability also provides an opportunity. People who had been silenced during the so-called 'New Order' (*Orde Baru*) period of Suharto's rule have become relatively free to voice their grievances and pursue their interests under the momentarily more equitable political conditions created by the social turmoil and major political restructuring since 1998. Indeed, some of the silences that are being broken in the current 'Reform Period' or *Era Reformasi* reach back much further still. Some contemporary struggles relate to patterns of inequity established in the course of Bali's pre-colonial or colonial history. A difficult time though it may be, the present period of uncertainty thus holds a potential for Indonesians and engaged Indonesianists to witness political and social change unfolding at a rather dramatic pace.

This volume presents case studies of social inequality, conflict and change on the island of Bali with the aim of illuminating some of the complex interactions between the local, regional, and national aspects of the current crisis in Indonesia (see Map 1.1). It incorporates contributions from eminent scholars in a range of disciplines, as well as presenting the innovative work of some younger researchers to a wider audience for the first time. The chapters in this collection were initially presented at The Third Australian Balinese Studies Conference, held on 24–26 September 1999 at the University of Melbourne and organized by the editor. The aim of this gathering had been to assess and discuss the dramatic changes in the

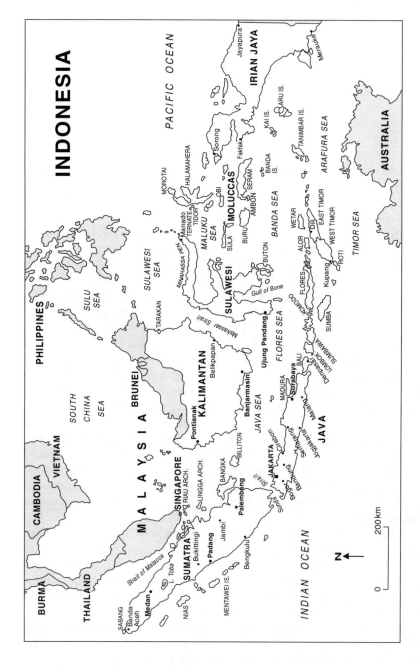

Map 1.1 Indonesia.

socio-political landscape of Bali emerging in the aftermath of the Asian economic crisis and following the collapse of former President Suharto's authoritarian government in Indonesia. Several revisions have been necessary to keep the contributions in pace with changing local conditions in Bali, and with the rapid unfolding of political events on a national level (see Map 1.2).

The contributors further examine how a 'global' economic and a 'national' political crisis are being experienced at a grass-roots level in Indonesia, with particular emphasis on interactions between local, regional and national structures of power and knowledge in a Balinese setting. Special attention is paid to disadvantaged sectors of Balinese society, including marginal ethnic or religious groups, rural populations and women, and to their efforts to renegotiate their social position during this moment of crisis. With their special focus on 'muted worlds' and social change, the authors are aspiring to add a new dimension to the study of Balinese culture, history, and society from a contemporary and critical perspective.[2] All contributions are based on original research findings.

INDONESIA'S NATIONAL CRISIS: A TWOFOLD CHALLENGE

A mood of profound uncertainty has swept Indonesia since the collapse of the 'New Order' regime of former President Suharto on 21 May 1998. After 32 years of systematic political repression of opposition parties, unions and individual dissidents, the sudden collapse of the regime came as a surprise to many. Subsequent events have shown that Indonesians were not very well prepared to capitalize fully from the opportunity to build a genuinely democratic society and government.

At first an unpopular interim government was established under the leadership of former Vice-President, Jusuf Habibie. Habibie took a number of important steps toward democratization and decentralization, notwithstanding the fact that he had been a prominent figure within Suharto's Golkar Party. During his brief time in office, the people of East Timor were given the opportunity to decide on their own future and promptly voted for independence. This decision precipitated widespread atrocities against Timorese at the hands of pro-integration militias, followed by a UN-sponsored, Australian-led military intervention and the separation of East Timor from Indonesia. After the first free parliamentary election in Indonesia in June 1999 and the rejection of his 'accountability speech' by the new parliament on 20 October 1999, Habibie was replaced by Abdurrahman Wahid, until then the leader of the largest and relatively moderate Indonesian Muslim organization, Nahdatul Ulama (NU).

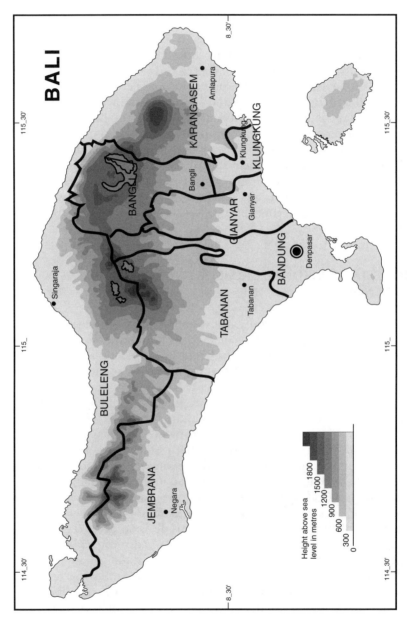

Map 1.2 Bali.

Megawati Sukarnoputri, the popular daughter of Indonesia's first president, Sukarno, had to content herself with becoming Wahid's vice-president, even though her 'Indonesian Democratic Party of Struggle' (PDI-P) had won the largest number of seats of any party in the house of representatives (the DPR). Sixteen months later, however, charismatic President Wahid or 'Gus Dur', as he is colloquially referred to, came under threat of impeachment on allegations of involvement in the 'Buloggate' and 'Bruneigate' corruption scandals and on accusations of erratic and ineffective government. On 1 February 2001, a motion of censure was issued by the DPR and, when Wahid failed to respond to the members' satisfaction, a second censure motion was issued on 30 April 2001. After a failed attempt to dissolve the National Assembly (MPR) and impose a state of emergency, Gus Dur was finally forced to step down on 23 July 2001, to be replaced by Megawati Sukarnoputri.

One year later, Megawati's government is again threatened by rising popular discontent in response to her failure to address Indonesia's growing economic woes, stamp out government corruption, and resolve widespread and violent inter-ethnic, interreligious and secessionist conflicts. Another major issue is the failure to establish supremacy of the law, which has encouraged the rise of militant organizations and the spread of 'organized crime' (*premanisme*), as well as increasing the incidence of vigilante killings of petty criminal offenders. In short, many Indonesians hold the current state, and particularly its security apparatus and legal system, to be dangerously 'weak' (especially in comparison to the Suharto state). Others, including the army and militant religious or political movements, take this weakness as an invitation to expand their influence and power. The popular sentiments working in the favour of militant movements stem from, among other issues, Indonesia's growing dependency on the IMF and other creditors and from wide-spread Muslim opposition to the US war on Afghanistan.

During this prolonged period of national economic and political crisis, local and regional patterns in the distribution of wealth, power and symbolic capital, which had become entrenched during the 32-year reign of Suharto, have had to be re-examined, modified, or reasserted, in Bali and similarly in other Indonesian provinces. In some places these negotiations have been accompanied by severe violence. In Bali and elsewhere, similar processes of change have unfolded under less dramatic circumstances and so have remained largely invisible to outsiders. Likewise, while some of the changes that have occurred relate to the country's formal political system and are thus readily observable (such as the new regional autonomy legislation that affords greater independence to Bali and other provinces), other transformations relate to more informal patterns of material and symbolic capital distribution and are less visible to the outside world.

In analyzing some of these obvious and less obvious changes, researchers involved in Balinese and Indonesian Studies have had to contend with two important questions that are of general sociological interest: What impact does a global or national crisis have on regional societies or local communities? And, how do such destabilizing external influences link up with pre-existing inequalities and tensions within these narrower contexts of social interaction?

One challenge lies in trying to tackle the general sociological issue of 'social change' from the angle of a concept of 'crisis'. In contemporary social science, few would debate that social change occurs continuously. It is anything but certain, however, how and under what historical circumstances social change may increase its velocity, or whether a major crisis may even transform a society completely. In order to address these questions in relation to an analysis of the current Indonesian crisis, the contributors emphasize that it is impossible to identify the form and degree of change taking place in Indonesia today without a proper understanding of the legacy of the New Order period, in all its local and regional complexities.[3]

A second challenge concerns the issue of the ethics of social science. If certain social groups who have been silenced in a given society, then we may have a responsibility to acknowledge and support their concerns. The voices of such disadvantaged people may become momentarily amplified during periods of great social instability and change, but this does not guarantee an improvement in their condition. The least we can do as social scientists is to lend some support by bringing the concerns of disadvantaged sectors of the societies we study to the attention of a broader audience.

In this context, it is necessary to acknowledge that many Western researchers were to some extent gagged by the New Order government as well, except for those who were willing to face a ban on continuing their work or imperil local informants with whom they could be connected. The present volume aims to take at least some steps – partially retrospective and partially proactive – toward exposing some of the inequalities and forms of oppression that characterized life in Bali under the rule of Suharto and his many local cronies and that still cast their shadow over the hopes of the current *Era Reformasi*.

It is a starting hypothesis of this book that long-standing social divisions, inequalities and associated tensions in a society, as well as the strength of its culture-specific mechanisms for peaceful negotiation, become accentuated and more visible at a time of major economic or political upheaval. The advent of such a crisis and of a period of dramatic social changes, however, presupposes an earlier historical period in which a normal process of continuous change was either stifled (by various means of oppression or silencing) or not fully acknowledged and accommodated in public discourses. Rather than promoting sensationalism or opportunism, the Indonesian crisis, is herein treated as a contemporary phenomenon with its roots in a history of three decades of oppression. Nevertheless, the new spirit of openness in the Indonesia of *Reformasi* provides unique opportunities for morally engaged social scientists to develop a more complete understanding of the local societies they have been studying, sometimes for decades already, without fully recognizing all of the hidden tensions and dormant potential for conflict within them.

It is proposed that latent social tensions can surface at critical historical moments in two fundamental and intimately connected forms; as practical rivalries over the redistribution of material wealth and power or as competing discursive claims raised in the context of a shifting symbolic economy of knowledge. Current social changes in Bali and elsewhere in Indonesia thus need to be examined from both a material and a symbolic perspective, and the contributors have endeavoured to do so. In terms of practical research, this requires exploration of the economic, political, and representational strategies employed by people from different sectors of Balinese society in the pursuit of a diversity of material and symbolic interests, as they seek to capitalize or protect themselves from the effects of the current turmoil.

HISTORICAL CONSIDERATIONS

Periods of dramatic social change are not unprecedented in the history of Bali's interlaced economies of power and knowledge. The island's society has been subject to several major transformations in the wake of colonization, Indonesian independence, population growth, modernization, and through active engagement with a globalizing world market and international tourist industry. In each case new conflicts arose and the discourse of conflict differed, as did some of the players and the stakes. But there are also some interesting parallels to, and resonance with, earlier crises, both at a national and a regional level.

Bali, for example, was one of the provinces worst afflicted by the mass killings in the wake of the violent anti-Communist purge of 1965–1966, which marked the collapse of the Sukarno government and Suharto's rise to power (see Darma Putra, this volume). In the present crisis, however, the idiom of social conflict is no longer one of competing political ideologies so much as an idiom of religious and ethnic difference. At the same time, however, the trauma of the 1965–1966 killings (not only of Communists but also of other 'undesirables', as defined by Bali's internal and local politics), which was a taboo topic in the Suharto years, features very prominently in current public debates. In part, this may reflect the fact that some of the underlying economic inequalities and related class issues in Balinese society, which had surfaced at that time, were never resolved and are resurfacing today.

The current crisis provides an opportunity for releasing different tensions that have been building in Bali for different amounts of time. Many of the more recent grievances certainly relate to the political silence imposed by former President Suharto's oppressive regime (see MacRae, this volume). However, other silences have been observed for so long – dating back to the pre-colonial and colonial periods of Balinese history – or are so fundamental – such as gender-related issues (see Kellar, and Nakatani, this volume) – that they have become almost intrinsic to Balinese society and culture and appear rather difficult to break. In any case, these grievances, new and old, have come to the surface to meet new opportunities for public expression and possible resolution.

Recent political events have precipitated a dramatic weakening of Indonesia's political and administrative establishment, with the instalment of new and fragile governments under presidents Habibie, Wahid, and Megawati in the place of the Suharto dictatorship. Amidst on-going complaints about widespread government corruption and nepotism, many previous alliances of high mutual profitability, within and between economic, political and cultural elites, have become untenable or at least unstable. Some past offenders have had to scramble for cover or reinvent themselves, and a few, including Bali's former governor, Ida Bagus Oka, have ended up in jail. The resulting uncertainty has encouraged people who have been economically disadvantaged, excluded from political participation, or culturally marginalized to call for social changes in their favour. In several of the following chapters, Bali's rising social tensions are examined from the perspective of such marginal groups or locations.

LOCAL ANATOMY OF A NATIONAL CRISIS

In Balinese society, open and physical confrontations between individuals tend to be avoided or concealed. When they do occur, and when the fact cannot be denied, social disapproval is usually extended to all of the parties involved, given that violent behaviour is classed as 'unrefined' (*kasar*), animal-like and, hence, dehumanizing. Studied social avoidance or 'maintaining silence' (*puik*) traditionally has been a much more common and legitimate alternative for showing opposition. A deep and widespread concern for sheltering the island's all-important tourist industry from the negative effects of violent political turmoil acts as a second and, perhaps, even more significant constraint. This does not mean that the idea of having a violent political and economic struggle on Bali is an inconceivable proposition, and there are some recent cases to illustrate that open and violent conflicts do occur.[4] Nevertheless, under the above constraints, Bali's symbolic economy is the most likely stage on which major social struggles are being played out, even though power and material resources may be an underlying concern in many cases.

Until now, a small and dominant elite within Balinese society has been able to create a compelling symbolic representation of the island's culture and history to which less privileged sectors of society have not been invited to contribute, and in which they have been depicted as marginal, or have not been acknowledged at all. Local politics of representation has drawn upon traditional idioms as well as those of the Suharto state to generate a specific language of social distinction, and a rationale for legitimizing an associated unequal distribution of 'symbolic' or 'cultural capital' (see Bourdieu 1986). Cultural knowledge has also become a primary economic resource in its own right due to the commodification of culture in the context of the island's highly developed tourist industry (Picard 1990).

Some of the most profound discursive shifts in the history of Bali's symbolic economy were triggered by exposure to colonial, global or nationalist discourses and interventions (Vickers 1996). Contemporary divisions and tensions in Balinese society are in part the legacy of such external influences (Connor and Rubinstein 1999). However, Bali also has a politics of representation of its own, through which these outside influences were and are channelled and accommodated, for example, by means of cultural brokerage and cross-cultural complicity. The beneficiaries have been a new Balinese elite who now wield their own local variety of a national state discourse of modernity to satisfy their own specific interests.

In recognition of this, the authors aim to take the critique of cultural knowledge in conventional post-colonial studies a step further, by exploring not only global and national but also local political discourses and associated, local fields of power. The contributors are thus moving away from a notion of the Balinese as passive victims of external interventions or portrayals (by the West, the Indonesian state, or the tourist industry) to a focus on their role as active and diverse agents of representation with conflicting agendas and a variety of practical strategies of self-assertion.

Local knowledge systems and associated representational technologies (e.g. ritual, literature, the arts, and the media) have been instrumental in legitimizing and perpetuating an inequitable distribution of material and symbolic capital in Balinese society. These same representational technologies, however, also provide some mechanisms for a collective reinterpretation of cultural knowledge, and for its contestation by minority groups. At this time of crisis, whatever cultural provisions there may be for negotiating change – by argumentation rather than by resorting to violence – are of crucial importance, and may be put to a severe test. The relatively low incidence of violence in Bali until now is somewhat of an anomaly for Indonesia, and the reasons for this deserve closer analysis. Some of the chapters reflect in particular on how violent social confrontations have been avoided in Bali, and at what cost.

The themes of 'crisis' and 'social transformation' thus provide a common focus for the discussion of current events and trends in Balinese and

Indonesian society in this volume. At the same time, the book also reflects a broad range of specialized interests among the contributors and thus caters to readers from a diversity of academic disciplines.

OUTLINE

Adrian Vickers' chapter on *Being Modern in Bali after Suharto* (Chapter 2) explores continuities and changes in public discourses on national and local identities by analyzing examples of Post-New Order journalism. His main focus are the significant problems faced by Indonesians and Balinese in their struggle to redefine nationhood and regional identity in the wake of *Reformasi*. An example is the ambiguous use of the term '*warga*', which has a range of meanings from 'clan' to 'citizen'. Vickers argues that the ambiguity of this and similar terms highlights Indonesia's new difficulties in reconciling local and national identities, which at times has had disastrous consequences. The major gulf in Balinese identity remains one between membership of, and loyalty to a local or pan-Balinese society, and a more precarious sense of citizenship within the Indonesian nation. This gulf, according to the author, has widened since the end of the New Order, and is due to a shift from a centralist model of the state to a new federalism with greater regional autonomy. Anti-Western sentiments temporarily served as a convenient way to boost a wavering commitment to Indonesian nationalism, but no stronger devices for nation building have been evident after the settlement of the East Timor conflict.

Graeme MacRae's chapter *Art and Peace in the Safest Place in the World: A Culture of Apoliticism in Bali* (Chapter 3) illustrates that – notwithstanding a widening gulf between national and regional identities in contemporary Indonesia – the national climate of political repression under former President Suharto has had a profound impact on Balinese society. Politics was generally avoided, even as a topic of conversation. This reaction, however, may have been encouraged by an underlying economic concern for providing a 'safe' environment in which the local tourist industry could flourish. The combined effect of the two factors has been particularly evident in the town of Ubud, where apoliticism has been ele-vated to something of a cultural value and become enshrined in cultural practices such as the visual arts. But the events of the past few years, MacRae argues, have brought overt political activity back into the fore-front of Indonesian public life in a way that neither ordinary Balinese nor local artists can ignore. The chapter first attempts to understand the 'culture of apoliticism' in Ubud during the New Order period, by placing it in a historical and tourist economy context, then examines the role of art in maintaining this culture of apoliticism, and finally, considers recent changes in response to the major crisis in the national politics of Indonesia since 1998.

I Nyoman Darma Putra highlights the differences, continuities and resonance among two political crises, past and present, in his *Reflections on Literature and Politics in Bali: The Development of Lekra, 1950–1966* (Chapter 4). One of the untold tales of modern Bali is the story of the artists and writers involved in the rise and fall of a left-wing movement between 1950 and 1966. The bloody massacre of 'Communists' in 1965–1966 was a traumatic event that has haunted Balinese memories, the more so because it was not allowed to be discussed during the Suharto period. In the wake of the current national crisis, however, Darma Putra's discussion on the role of left-wing artists in shaping ideological representation of Balinese society and art – in a specific idiom of class-conflict – touches upon matters that are once more of vital concern to many of his fellow Balinese. The author begins by sketching the development of Lekra (*Lembaga Kebudayaan Rakyat*) in Bali. This 'Institute of People's Culture' was a cultural organization affiliated with the Indonesian Communist Party (PKI). The development of Lekra in Bali from the early 1950s, its national significance, and key figures are discussed in some detail. Darma Putra illustrates how both right- and left-wing Balinese artists at the time employed literary works as a vehicle for the promotion of political ideologies, and used political ideologies, in turn, as idioms for reflecting on Balinese society and its conflicts. In view of recent government initiatives to legalize Communist parties and end the persecution of the children of 'Communists' killed in 1965, as well as a number of popular counter-initiatives, this dark chapter of Indonesia's past is now the focus of an important public debate on the nation's past and future. This study of the crisis that saw Suharto rise to power, in view of its very different idiom of political conflict, begs for a comparison with the current crisis, in the wake of Suharto's downfall.

The topic of discussion shifts to issues of gender with Natalie Kellar's chapter on *Transformations of a Genre of Balinese Dance Drama: Arja Muani as the Modern-Day Agent of Classical Arja's Liberal Gender Agenda* (Chapter 5). This chapter focuses on changes in Balinese artistic expressions before, during, and after the Suharto period. The popularity of the classic Balinese dance-drama Arja declined with the emergence of the modern theatre forms Drama Gong and Sendratari in the 1960s. Kellar argues, however, that Arja's marginalization was not just a result of changing popular notions of entertainment. Its competitors received active sponsorship from the political elite of the New Order state, on the condition of conformity to its various political and social agendas. One aspect of this conformity has been the more conservative gender platform of these modern dance forms. Unlike their predecessor Arja, Drama Gong and Sendratari employ a highly gender-specific form of representation, reflecting and reinforcing the discourse on gender espoused by the Suharto state. The more flexible code of gender identity embraced by classic Arja dance-drama, with its practice of cross-sexed performance was stifled, given that the images of female identity it offered were not only 'traditional' but also 'counter-hegemonic'. While classic Arja's broad conceptions of female identity and affirmation of gender ambiguity thus lost social legitimacy in the New Order context, the emergence of a modern and popular offshoot of Arja in the 1990s – the all-male troupe Arja Muani – provided a new artistic medium from which state discourses on gender could be reinterpreted and contested. Kellar examines how the new Arja Muani acts, to some degree, as a counter-discourse to New Order gender notions which persist until the present day, covertly by its use of cross-sexed performance and overtly by taking up themes of gender such as feminism, homosexuality and transvestitism.

A different perspective on changing gender roles is Ayami Nakatani's chapter on *Ritual as 'Work': The Invisibility of Women's Socio-Economic and Religious Roles in a Changing Balinese Society* (Chapter 6). The term for 'ritual', in refined or informal Balinese respectively, is *karya* or *gae*, but these same terms also mean 'work'. The author focuses on Balinese women's involvement in ritual-related tasks within the framework of their 'work' in general, by drawing on her research in a rural village in East Bali, where women actively engage in commercial cloth production as well as spending much of their time on the production of offerings. Nakatani reports on the women's open complaints about the burden of ritual labour and their simultaneous resistance to the idea of commercializing offering preparation; an increasingly common practice in urban areas. The analysis focuses on women's changing perceptions of their ritual obligations in contrast with other forms of work, such as house-keeping, child-care or income-generating activities. Marginalizing portrayals of women's role in ritual activities, and as workers in general, reflect broader renegotiations of the status of women in Balinese society. These changes in gender roles and gender politics are influenced by a general shift from traditional to modern means of production, as are Indonesian politics and society as a whole.

In his second chapter, on *The Value of Land in Bali: Land Tenure, Landreform and Commodification* (Chapter 7), Graeme MacRae discusses the escalating scarcity of land in Bali; a serious social crisis with a thoroughly economic foundation. While it is often assumed that land was a resource of little importance in the political-economies of pre-colonial Southeast Asian states, it certainly is no more. Land is now central to many major and minor socio-political conflicts in Indonesia and beyond. As population densities, standards of living, and the demands of commercial development all increase, competition over land is becoming fiercer. In Bali, with its traditionally intensive agricultural land-use and high population density, land has been a critical issue since at least the 1930s. More recently the leasing and disguised purchase of land by foreign expatriates, the rise of a wealthy indigenous middle class, and the development of large-scale tourism resorts have intensified this pressure. Despite its central place in local concerns, there have been few studies of land-use and land-tenure in Bali since the pioneering research of Dutch scholars in the 1920s. This important chapter documents the history of land distribution in the thriving tourist town of Ubud under variable local and national political conditions and the changing legislation of different governments. Elements of this process of change are a shift from collective control of land to individual private ownership, a progressive alienation of land and labour from subsistence agriculture to tourism and other commercial uses, increased state intervention in the form of systematic land registration and taxation, a loss of local control over land, and the growth of a new class of the landless and disempowered.

In my own chapter entitled *Mythical Centres and Modern Margins: A Short History of Encounters, Crises, Marginality, and Social Change in Highland Bali* (Chapter 8), I explore an alternative approach. I argue that studies of social change need to pay close attention to shifts in the distribution of symbolic, and not just material resources. I further aim to show how constructions of identity, as one specific mode of production of symbolic resources (i.e. 'social status'), were shaped by important historical encounters and by the social crises these encounters triggered. In support of this argument, I am drawing on my research among the 'Mountain Balinese' or *Bali Aga*, an ethnic minority widely assumed to be the original people of Bali who maintain a separate cultural tradition. While the Bali Aga may have been politically marginal for centuries, the idiom and implications of their marginality have changed continuously and are beginning to change again in the wake of the current crisis. The Mountain Balinese have traditionally enjoyed a separate and special status as the descendants of Bali's first settlers. The associated ritual privileges of the Bali Aga have been challenged as a modern and urbanized political elite began to redefine Balinese society and the place of the Bali Aga therein, especially during the Suharto period. Highland Balinese, who had been tolerated for being the island's original people, were increasingly portrayed as recalcitrant traditionalists and as an impediment to a New Order agenda of development and modernization. In the current climate of uncertainty and in the face of mass tourism and globalization, however, they and their traditions are beginning to be viewed, once again, as a repository of 'cultural authenticity' by a growing number of urban Balinese. The Bali Aga themselves have responded to changing outside portrayals of their identity by borrowing from the idiom of various dominant state or popular discourses to further their own causes. This chapter identifies continuities in these renegotiations of social status as they unfold in the wake of recent shifts in a Balinese and national politics of identity. I focus specifically on the continued importance of a traditionally pluralist value system, and an equivalently diversified symbolic resource economy, for regulating status competition and preventing social conflict.

That ritual or ritual authority can also do the 'work' of politics is shown in a chapter by Diana Darling, entitled *Unity in Uniformity: Tendencies Toward Militarism in Balinese Ritual Life* (Chapter 9). The famous collectivism said to be inherent in Balinese society and exemplified by spectacular ritual performances, she argues, is potentially ambivalent. In the absence of serious underlying conflicts, or in spite of them, this ritualized collectivism can be a stabilizing influence by fostering social cooperation in a wide range of creative and productive activities, from common ancestor worship to rice irrigation management. Under historical conditions of political inequality, however, it can also become a means of silencing opposition, and under the pressures of a national crisis, a vehicle of violence. The author suggests there has been an increasing trend toward militarism in Balinese culture – during and after the New Order period – that has been neglected, played down, or ignored in Bali's professional tourism image and which is likely to be overlooked in the perceptions that Balinese form of themselves. The author opens a timely discussion on whether this militarism is significant and what dangers it may entail, by suggesting that it can be detected in ritual contexts and in the social theatre of *adat* ('traditional') institutions. Examples show what appears to be a flourishing of 'uniformity' in new guises, resonating with a proliferation of militia groups elsewhere in Indonesia. Particular attention is given to the recent reappearance on the Balinese scene of so-called '*pacalang*', or '*adat* police'. The author asks what lies behind this incipient militarism, and what it may imply for Balinese society as it seeks to reaffirm its self-image in an era when Indonesian society as a whole is upgrading its civil expectations.

In the final chapter, *Indonesia in Transition: Concluding Reflections on Engaged Research and the Critique of Local Knowledge* (Chapter 10), I shall return to and develop some of the themes outlined in this introduction, in view of the research findings presented in this volume. With specific reference to the Balinese case, a tentative model for the analysis of societies and social change under crisis conditions is proposed. Assuming that crises are never completely imposed but also feed on local inequalities and lingering social tensions, the model is also of relevance to the critical study of societies under seemingly more 'peaceful' or 'stable' conditions. It is discussed how the influence of national or global political and economic change is modulated through local processes of cultural interpretation, and how its practical social impact depends greatly on the specific imbalances of local patterns of symbolic and material resource distribution at the time. Finally, some thoughts are offered on two related issues; the epistemology of social science and social scientists' ethical obligations toward people who have been silenced or made invisible, within their own local societies or by an encompassing nation state.

The present volume is thus of significance to scholars and students of Indonesian and Southeast Asian societies in a variety of academic disciplines,

including Anthropology, Asian Studies, Cultural Studies, History, Literature, Performing Art and Politics. Major topics include social change, the
manipulation of cultural knowledge and identities, marginality, gender,
and the politics of literature, ritual and art.

While the volume may be of particular value to those with a specific
interest in Balinese Studies, the contributors also endeavour to situate
Bali in the wider project of analyzing how the current Indonesian crisis
arose from the New Order period and how it takes effect at a local and
regional level. The book is designed to encourage and facilitate comparison with other Indonesian provinces, where the same national history
and subsequent crisis have precipitated different and often far more
violent types of confrontations. This raises questions as to the mediating
influence of specific, local (historical, political, economic, cultural and
social) conditions in different Indonesian societies on the local impact of
national or global processes of social change. It is therefore important
to anyone with an interest in the comparative study of social change,
especially in a contemporary Indonesian context.

Like other new nation states in Insular and Mainland Southeast Asia,
Indonesia is struggling with a legacy of colonialism, the advent of modernity and globalization, amidst popular aspirations for more democratic
and humane forms of government. The book thus may offer some new
insights on the development of modern nation states and democracy in
Southeast Asia and beyond.

Scholars in anthropology, cultural studies, history, politics and related
disciplines are also experiencing a crisis of their own. Theirs is a crisis of
confidence in relation to the task of promoting genuine understanding
between cultures in the face of accusations of subjectivity and collaboration in a continuing history of Western imperialism. Focused on culturally
marginalized and frequently under- or misrepresented sectors of Balinese
society, some of the chapters in this volume shed new light on this
sometimes insidious link between popular or scholarly constructions of
marginal cultural identities and associated systems of domination. Unlike
some post-colonial studies, however, the critical analysis of representational practices herein is focused not just on colonial and global, but also
on national and local systems of knowledge production. In attempting to
address a general crisis of representation in the social sciences – through
a strategy of moral engagement – the book speaks to all those who wish
to maintain their commitment to cross-cultural research.

Bali is visited by two million foreign tourists annually, and, notwithstanding the island's natural assets, the greatest attraction for visitors in
recent decades has been Balinese culture. While this book is not specifically
designed for a popular readership, an unnecessary complexity of language
and style has been avoided so as to make the text accessible to a wider,
educated audience with an interest in Bali and Indonesia. To raise awareness of contemporary Balinese concerns among members of this wider

audience is a matter of some importance, especially in view of the considerable impact the struggle to accommodate foreign visitors' security and
entertainment needs have had on Balinese politics and culture.

NOTES

1 'The present day' or 'today', in this volume, refers to the time of final editing,
in August 2002.
2 The Balinese themselves are familiar with use of the metaphor of 'muteness' in
describing a condition of social, cultural or political marginality. In the early
1990s, for example, the national television station TVRI broadcast the drama
Aksara Tanpa Kata ('Characters without Words'), which enjoyed immense
popularity and wherein the main protagonist was a 'mute' (*kolok* or *gagu*)
Balinese woman. The drama explored a range of salient social problems,
including the 'theft' of farmers' land by developers, the impact of contact with
tourists on Balinese morals, and discriminatory cultural practices relating to
women (see also Aripurnami 1996). The muted hero of the drama was
emblematic of a sentiment of having to 'suffer in silence' that many Balinese
could relate to very well at that time.
3 All of the contributors conducted the bulk of their research during the Suharto
era, and are thus in a position to identify the tensions that arose in that period
and to evaluate the degree and genuineness of the social change that has been
achieved since 1998.
4 Recent incidents of violent conflict include a major demonstration of disgruntled Megawati supporters upon her failure to secure the presidency, as well as
a number of conflicts at the level of the customary village community (*desa adat*) –
the so-called '*khasus adat*'. An example of the latter category, with economic as
well as ethnic and religious overtones, was the eviction at the hands of the local
Balinese community of street vendors in Kuta in April 1999, most of whom had
been poor Muslim Javanese migrants (see Vickers, this volume).

REFERENCES

Aripurnami, Sita (1996) 'A Feminist Comment on the Cinetron Presentation of
Indonesian Women'. In Laurie J. Sears (ed.), *Fantasizing the Feminine in Indonesia*,
London: Duke University Press.
Bourdieu, P. (1986) 'The Forms of Capital'. In J. G. Richardson (ed.), *Handbook
of Theory and Research of the Sociology of Education*, New York: Greenwood Press.
Connor, L. H. and Rubinstein, R. (1999) *Staying Local in The Global Village: Bali in
the Twentieth Century*, Honolulu: University of Hawaii Press.
Picard, M. (1990) 'Cultural Tourism in Bali: Cultural Performances as Tourist
Attractions'. *Indonesia*, 49: 37–74.
Vickers, A. (ed.) (1996) *Being Modern in Bali: Image and Change*, New Haven
(Conn.): Yale University Press.

2   Being modern in Bali after Suharto

Adrian Vickers

In April 1999, attacks were made on the street sellers of Kuta, who are mainly from East Java. These attacks were carried out by people dressed in Balinese costume, but local leaders would not admit that they were members of the traditional organization (*desa adat*) of the town of Kuta. I have since heard that this action was organized by the local Intelligence Bureau (*Intel*). The reporting of these events in the local Balinese media reflects what issues were at stake, and reveals much about the state of Balinese society in the wake of the national crisis that began with a run on the Rupiah and saw four changes of presidents in 4 years.

> **The Peace of Kuta is Disturbed** Denpasar (Bali Post) The calm of the atmosphere of Kuta, long praised as a place that is more than capable in guarding and keeping peaceful[1] its mix of occupants, was disturbed around 2 am, early on Thursday (29/4). Hundreds of market kiosks and pushcarts owned by members of the Kuta Foot-path Traders Association (PPKLK) which had been left overnight by their owners on the edge of and on the sidewalk along Jalan Melasti and part of Jalan Bakung Sari Kuta, were taken to the beach and burned by dozens of people in traditional costume (*pakaian adat*). Some were destroyed where they stood. [...] It is not yet known who carried out these actions [...] while the *Bendesa Adat* [Head of the traditionally-defined community] of Kuta, Made Wendra, emphasized that the traditional village (*desa adat*) he heads had never planned anything like this. The traditional village considered the members of PPKLK to be also people of Kuta (*warga Kuta*). But, he did not completely deny that those involved[2] were not also citizens of Kuta (*warga Kuta*). [the article goes on to explain that there had been attempts to reach an agreement to curb the operating hours of the street traders. The traders later protested to the office of the Head District Official (*Bupati*), wanting revenge, and asking for responsibility to be taken for the actions. The spokesman for the PPKLK was

Zainudin. The Bupati took part in the discussions, stressing that it was not clear that those who carried out the actions were from Kuta].

(*Bali Post*, 30 April 1999)[3]

Rumour has it that at least one of the Javanese was killed 'as a lesson'. The street sellers did not go away, however. A letter to the editor of *Bali Post* in September (by I Made Dwi Sukarya of Tegal, Kuta, 20 September 1999) indicated displeasure with the footpath sellers, who were described as 'dirty' and 'disturbing the view'. The author thought that the lack of on-going action on the presence of these sellers detracted from *Reformasi*, the process of reform that began with the fall of Suharto. At the same time, he wished Bali to be known as *Bersih, Aman, Lestari, Indah* [Clean, Peaceful, Conserving, Beautiful], an old slogan from the New Order (*Orde Baru*) days.

Later, on the same day as the attack on the sellers, one of many spontaneous strikes in Denpasar led to a demonstration in front of the Governor's office. As the *Bali Post* reports it:

Employees of the BGH Voice Their Feelings at the Governor's Office Denpasar (Bali Post) Thirty employees of the Bali Garden Hotel (BGH) 'voiced their feelings'[4] to the Governor's Office yesterday, Thursday (29/4). Their arrival took security personnel[5] by surprise, since they suddenly appeared in the Governor's Front Lobby. This group of employees claimed to represent 180 employees who had received the dismissal notices from the hotel.[6] They could be seen spreading out a number of 'posters' (English word used). Amongst other things these posters said 'Remove all military personnel at the BGH'; 'We are not Balinese dogs who can be abused'; 'Give legal guarantees to the little people'.[7] Only they did not scream out like others voicing their feelings, but firmly preserved the calm[8] in front of the Governor's personal office.

(*Bali Post*, 30 April 1999)

The two events themselves display some of the complexities of post-Suharto Bali, but representing them is even more difficult. After the fall of Suharto the language of belonging and the means to explain social change suddenly became more complex, not only to us observers, but to Balinese themselves. Here my main focus is on the language used by the *Bali Post* as the key medium of public discourse on Bali. In this language, we see a moment by which one hegemonic form – the rhetoric of the New Order – starts to be displaced, but very slowly. It was not just that the stilted, formalistic and opaque nature of Indonesian journalese has persisted, but that the related forms of obfuscation of social relations have also been maintained. The search for a new form is part of the need to find a new way of expressing concepts of civic participation. One

of the main problems faced is that of Indonesians defining for themselves a notion of citizenship that can incorporate a broad sense of
belonging.

NATIONALISM IN THE ERA OF REFORMASI

The language of discussing unrest in the two reports is both of the New
Order and not of it. This changing idiom raises questions about nationalism,
peace and calm, guarantees, actions and responsibilities. All of these
questions arise from the way the New Order defined its forms of modernity, and the contestation of those forms on Bali. In the Post-New Order
period, better known as *Era Reformasi*, the contest is a different one. The
events described above fit into a pattern that I would like to connect with
the sudden outpouring of anti-western and especially anti-Australian
feeling in Indonesia, which I see as another part of finding a new national
language. Events subsequent to those to be discussed below have seen
the objects of anti-foreign feeling change, especially to outpourings of
anti-Americanism, but the underlying mode of expression has continued
in the way described here.

One of the problems for scholars of Bali, and scholars of Indonesia in
general, is that in the *Era Reformasi* it has been much harder to 'read'
protest and conflict. Distinctions between the government and dissidents
are no longer clear. The events of East Timor showed most starkly that
outsiders cannot rush to make moral judgements about the roles and
aspirations of Indonesians. Is Megawati, who supports a centralized state
and would not have liked East Timor to be independent, the representative of democratic reform, while Habibie, the man who made East Timorese
independence possible, but who is also intimately linked to Suharto
corruption, a conservative? Megawati's supporters in Bali were more concerned with using the East Timor issue to attack Habibie than to attack
the military. Throughout the period that led up to her selection as president she played at alliances with different elements of ABRI ('The People's
Army'). Those of us involved in Balinese studies have all felt strong
sympathy for 'the Balinese' as a group oppressed by Jakarta's 'colonization',
as George Aditjondro (1995) puts it, but all is not necessarily sweetness
and light on Paradise Isle, as the first report makes clear.

Among the key issues of *Reformasi* is the creation of a new state and
society in Indonesia. Many groups, particularly from some Islamic sectors,
have continually called for a new kind of moral revival, and this is closely
related to the anti-KKN (Collusion, Corruption and Nepotism) campaigns
that developed spontaneously across the countryside (see Young 1999).
It is further related to general calls that have been coming from
commentators such as Arief Budiman from the early 1990s, for the
rebuilding of civil society in Indonesia.[9]

Debates about 'civil society' within Indonesia are more often based on liberal models that ultimately go back to a Weberian idea of the state. In Weber's analysis the state is taken as a given, which maintains itself by means of a monopoly on legitimized coercion.[10] In its simpler forms, the liberal version taken up in Indonesia sees the state as the enemy of civil society, and democratic reform as the triumph of civil society over the state. The terminology of such discussions is often not clear, however. While Muslim intellectuals may use the term *'masyarakat mardani'* to denote an Islamic vision of civil society, Balinese politicians and theorists have relied more on a dichotomy of *negara*, 'the state' versus *rakyat*, 'the people' or *masyarakat*, 'society'.[11]

A brief Australian–Indonesian 'Cold War' resulted from Australia's prominent involvement in the UN-sanctioned peace-keeping mission in East Timor. The way this was reported in Bali highlights problems of differentiation between nation, state, society and the Armed Forces in discussing the civil shape of Indonesia. The Australian jingoism and fear of invasion which seem to motivate Australian Prime-minister John Howard's 'back to the 1950s' approach is deserving of a separate study. The events following the 1999 Referendum in East Timor were presented by the Australian media through a combination of images that presented a death toll in the tens or even hundreds of thousands, and a revival of heroic images of the Australian military.[12]

What is of concern here is the sudden invocation of Indonesian jingoism and belief in their military at the same time, a belief at odds with popular opposition to the military during the demonstrations that brought down Suharto. In a variety of reports, and this extends to the reaction of Indonesian students at my own university, Australia is simultaneously seen as attacking the *bangsa*, the 'nation' or 'people' of Indonesia and its government. A lengthy Indonesian analysis of the reporting of East Timor has recently been produced by a group of media analysts (Siahaan *et al.* 2001). While it does not focus so much on the language of citizenship and belonging that interests me here, this study is important for its identification of the ease of mobilizing 'narrow nationalism' in Indonesia. This came, they note, because of the New Order representation of East Timor as a peaceful integration presented as being based on the whole island's ancient participation in the kingdom of Majapahit. This myth left the majority of Indonesians completely ignorant of the atrocities and exploitation that were being served up to the East Timorese people on a daily basis by the army.

Thus Indonesians from across the political spectrum genuinely could not understand the strength of East Timorese resistance, and saw the referendum of September 1999 as an act of ingratitude. The *Bali Post*, as one of the major regional newspapers of Indonesia, is one of the sources studied by Siahaan *et al*. They observe that even compared to other Indonesian newspapers (including *Bali Post*'s smaller Bali-based competitor *Nusa*), the *Bali Post* tended to favour the views of Indonesian officials over other sources. Only the *Surabaya Post* made less use of their own journalists as sources of information. They conclude that the *Bali Post* played down the use of strong force, especially murder, by the *TNI* and their militias. The *Bali Post* is thus seen as the most one-sided of the Indonesian newspapers, which were all partisan and unbalanced in their coverage. This coincided with a very limited working definition of democracy in terms of freedom of expression – rather than popular sovereignty or a number of other features (2001: 165–213).

The *Bali Post* depicted destruction and violence as being caused by East Timorese, not Indonesians. Once the vote had occurred, the Indonesian government hardly featured as an actor in such reports at all.[13] The *Bali Post* stuck with the line that all conflict in East Timor was the result of some form of tribalism, not of any direct TNI running of affairs. 'Foreign elements' are usually blamed for disturbing the situation, motivated by hostility to the Indonesian people. The *Bali Post* in its editorial of 18 September 1999 notes that

> In the midst of the disappointment (*kekecewaan*) resulting from the letting go[14] of Bumi Loro Sae (East Timor), comes another jolt (*goncangan*) which is even greater.[15] This jolt arises from Australia. Australia's attitude to the people (*bangsa*) and government (*pemerintah*) of Indonesia is extremely arrogant (*arogan*)...

The article goes on to explain that Habibie's aim had been to make Indonesia's role in East Timor *halal* or 'clean' in the eyes of the world, and he had returned the issue to a basic problem of humanity. What is extraordinary here is that, despite an editorial in the same paper 10 days earlier arguing that the period after the referendum would be a test for the Army, there is no attribution of blame to the Army (*Tentara Nasional Indonesia* or TNI) for the events.[16] This, however, is consistent with the earlier editorial, which describes the 'mental condition of the Indonesian nation (*bangsa*)' on hearing the results of the referendum. It also further questions what 'responsibility' means in Indonesian national discourse, and whether the TNI had the responsibility (*bertanggung jawab*) for security in East Timor.[17]

The anti-Australian feeling gave specific direction to the general outpouring of hatred for the East Timorese for daring to vote for independence. One letter to the editor in *Bali Post*, for example, expressed this ingratitude in terms that can be summarized as 'we gave them development (*pembangunan*), and this is all the thanks we get?'[18] This is a view I heard expressed in conversation by a number of Indonesians.

Later articles discussed the crucial issue, for tourism-reliant Bali, whether Australians would boycott Indonesia in the wake of union attempts to impose bans. These discussions moved from topics such as 'The Australian Government will not Prohibit its Citizens (*Warganya*) Going to Bali',[19] to an article on a speech by Pontjo Sutowo (head of the Indonesian Hotels and Restaurants Association, holder of Hilton franchise in Indonesia, and son of Ibnu Sutowo who is best known for his bankrupting of Pertamina in 1974, at the height of the Oil Boom).[20] Sutowo's speech was reported very much in the line of 'let them stay away, they need us more than we need them'. However I Gede Wiratha, head of the Bali Tourism and Restaurant Association, wanted to remind the world that 'Bali is part of an Indonesia which from its cultural side has a strength which is based and rooted in the people (*rakyat*); so that tourism on Bali is a grassroots tourism (*pariwisata kerakyatan*) with a basic concept of cultural tourism (*pariwisata budaya*).'

The terms raised here show a strong identification between citizenship (*warga*), the people or nation (*bangsa*) and the government (*pemerintah*). While an Australian audience finds absurd the idea of its government prohibiting (*larang*) its citizens from going to Bali, for an Indonesian audience this seems natural. Under Suharto, of course, we would all have expected censorship, but post-Suharto freedom of the press makes interpretation of this reporting more problematic. In tracing the discourses of modernity and citizenship at work here, we can begin to understand some of the contradictions and problems arising in the process of Reformasi. These are problems of redefining a modern identity as Indonesians, a modernity that is striving to differentiate itself from the New Order's orthodoxy of *pembangunan* or development as the only form of being modern (see also Reuter, Chapter 8).

NEW ORDER MODERNITY

There are clearly elements of New Order language in Post-New Order Indonesian journalism, and one might be forgiven for thinking that Suharto was still in power when reading that a criticism of the Indonesian government was identical to a criticism of the Indonesian people. I am reminded of the outrage in 1986 when the *Sydney Morning Herald* gravely insulted the Indonesian people through its report by David Jenkins that Suharto had corruptly milked the state of billions of dollars. The Australian government spent the next decade making apologies for this terrible lie, and are expected to do the same for the terrible lies they have been telling about the TNI.

Development or *pembangunan* as the New Order form of modernity also seems to be still important, at least for some Indonesians. This is despite the fact that it was this *pembangunan* that created or at least contributed to Indonesia's monetary crisis or *Krismon* through the heavy levels of corruption that were the subject of popular protests – including protests in Bali – during the 1990s.

In the same letter to the editor which describes the East Timorese as ungrateful, the author refers to those East Timorese *warga* who remain pro-Indonesian as *saudara* or 'relatives'. In general terms this view still fits in with the New Order's espousal of an 'integralist' theory of the state, as described by David Reeve (1985) and David Bourchier (1997). In this theory the family, *kekeluargaan*, is the basis of membership of the state; and we all know what the 'family state' meant to Suharto.

Warga, the word for 'citizen', is a key term, but an ambiguous one. In Balinese usage it refers to a larger family unit, or what in English is often glossed as 'clan'. The translation is not that accurate, but a common genealogical origin point is important. The East Timorese who stay loyal to Indonesia are simultaneously *warga* of East Timor and *warga negara*. But local communities can also confer *warga*-hood, as the opening article on Kuta showed. The Balinese of Kuta whose clothing confers *adat*-based *warga* status to them, are quoted as saying that they consider the mainly Javanese street sellers also as *warga* of Kuta. Common nationality may be phrased in terms of common *warga*-hood, but this usage is not to be taken for granted. *Warga* identity can be simultaneously local, regional and national, though never international. *Warga* and *bangsa* go together as terms for the national family. One is simultaneously a native of Kuta, a Balinese and an Indonesian.

The view of the state which emerges from these articles and from other aspects of contemporary Indonesian discourse is as a coercive force which tells its *warga* what to do, and in return confers development. During the New Order period this was self-evident. 'The people' under the New Order were conceived of us *wayang* puppets to be manipulated by the supreme puppeteer or *dalang*, Suharto, for fear that other *dalang* such as the Communists would come back and manipulate them. This *massa bodoh, rakyat masih bodoh* or 'stupid masses' view is sometimes more politely known as the 'floating mass' theory that was put forward by Ali Murtopo and other military minds. How does the mass move, in the *Era Reformasi*, to a more active and positive role?

Clearly it is difficult for some Indonesians to conceive of the masses as being responsible for their own actions. In the case of the East Timor vote, when it became clear the vote was overwhelmingly for independence, this was interpreted as due to manipulation from the foreign devils, either Australia or the United Nations, or both under United States manipulation. The writer of the letter about East Timorese ingratitude, however, does seem to move beyond this view, and I think it is here that we move into *Era Reformasi*.

ERA GLOBALISASI

Between the classic period of the New Order and the *Era Reformasi* there was a transitional period, begun with the '*Keterbukaan*' signalled by the New Order regime at the end of the Cold War (*c.* 1989), but more generally known in Bali as the Era of Globalization. In this period the idea of 'globalization' provided a new, more complex way of seeing development in Indonesia, which was no longer the exclusive property of the State, fathered by Suharto. Examples from the *Bali Post* can be most clearly seen in the letters the editors of the newspaper invited from their readers at the 50th anniversary of Indonesia's declaration of independence.

While expressing pride in the progress that had been made in the 50 years since Sukarno and Hatta declared independence, the readers generally noted that development had not delivered the elimination of poverty or ignorance, and that the Revolution's goal of equality had not been achieved.[21] The ideology of *Pancasila* (the five principles on which the Indonesian constitution is based) was appropriated by a number of the writers as a set of values to criticize the nature and course of development, and the problems of corruption and governance of the New Order state.

For example, A. A. Bagus Artha Negara of the suburb of Ubung Kaja in Denpasar (Bali Post, 16 August 1995) observed that freedom should involve popular sovereignty, and politics should be the arena in which the people (*rakyat*) exercise that sovereignty. Instead a small group were monopolizing power and blocking the achievement of equality. A number of other letter writers took up these themes and gave lengthy explications of how democracy should be achieved through alleviating poverty and eliminating corruption. Gst Ngr. Rai Sujaya of Peguyangan, Denpasar, observed (Bali Post, 24 August 1995) that poverty and ignorance were also forms of colonialism. A number of the letter writers identified the need to change modes of political and economic action in accordance with participation in the era of globalization (*era globalisasi*). Such participation, they said, should lead to social justice and a different type of 'development' than that offered by the government, namely, 'development initiated from the people, by the people and for the people' (Prakoso Kusprijatno of Denpasar).[22] The thrust of many of the letters is in accordance with this theme: Globalization is the key term of the present age, requiring a return to the ideal of equality and freedom of the Revolution, but in order to achieve the kind of justice that the New Order had not delivered. 'Asian Values' was not a relevant term to bring into play, since it did not provide any way to directly critique the corruption and collusion which many of the writers were objecting to.

The letters reintroduce a set of terms in which the 'indigenous nature' of Indonesian values is re-expressed. The return of 'the people' as a category is important, because the idea of popular sovereignty was not something that the New Order supported. In particular, under the New Order the idea of equality and the language used to express it, *sama rata sama rasa*, was considered to have connotations of communism. Under the New Order, *kekeluargaan* meant acceptance of the father figure (Suharto) as paternal authority governing an unruly and dangerous population. The constant unruliness was expressed through the anxiety about 'SARA' (ethnic, racial and religious) conflicts. Globalisasi in Bali at least began to undermine this discourse because it was a way of explaining how the tourist economy and direct contact with foreigners, not the state, created prosperity, and indeed, that the state was failing to manage and distribute that prosperity properly.

REFORMASI AND THE PEOPLE

After 1997, the term '*globalisasi*' is far less used in general discussions of a world in the flux of crisis. '*Reformasi*' has replaced it as the key to explaining the state of Indonesia to those who participate in it.

A crucial part of *Reformasi* has been the holding of real elections in 1999. These elections enact the ideas of popular sovereignty, and serve entirely different purposes to the elections held under Suharto. For that reason it has been important not to reject the principle of elections in discussions of the East Timor vote for independence, even if there is a suspicion of Suharto-style manipulation attributable to those running them. Gede Wiratha's speech as reported by the *Bali Post* establishes 'the people' as the basis of a new kind of state control. Indeed, his notion of 'people's tourism' as a way of interpreting 'cultural tourism' is difficult to translate into English because we have no precise equivalent to this notion of popular ownership without participation. If anything, the concept stretches back into the Old Order Indonesia of Sukarno, reminding us of LEKRA's *kesenian rakyat* (see Darma Putra, this volume), with the difference that 'art of and for the people' is easier to make sense of than 'tourism of and for the people'. The accompanying comment by Wiratha, that Australia is displaying 'Neo-Colonial arrogance' (*arogansi Neo Kolonialisme*) is pure Old Order-speak.

We should expect this on Bali, where Megawati's appeal is an appeal to Sukarnoism (see Suardika *et al.* 1998; Sawitri 2000). Megawati is a *warga* Bali because of her Balinese grandmother, and her then-hoped-for-presidency would have helped make the continuity between being *warga Bali* and *warga Indonesia* entirely unproblematic. Megawati, in as much as anyone can work out what her policies are, seems to stand for secular nationalism, and in particular national unity as advocated by her father's vision of Guided Democracy.

In this light, we might see anti-Australianism as a good thing for Indonesians, because it provides a focus for nationalism and national unity. Suharto had to use communism as an on-going enemy against whom the nation had to be on guard. Nowadays one does not have to turn the force of state coercion against an enemy within, since Australia and the UN provide post-Cold War enemies without. However, not all problems are thus solved.

Megawati's clear advocacy of the unitary state runs against the clear advocacy of a form of autonomy for Bali coming from most Balinese sources, especially the *Bali Post*. The experience of being a 'Jakarta colony' has meant that most Balinese want to see the wealth generated by the tourism industry to remain within Bali. Autonomy is a step toward achieving this aim, but this step could only be taken with the support of a national move toward Federalism.

There are other problems which are shown in the two newspaper items quoted at the beginning of the chapter. These are related problems of Balinese being Indonesians, but not wanting other Indonesians in Bali. The Kuta attacks seem to be generally applauded not only because the street sellers annoy tourists, but also because they are seen as having taken over Kuta. Balinese generally see themselves as under potential threat from Muslims, particularly Javanese, as shown by earlier incidents such as the temple thefts scare of the mid-1990s, and as raised in Balinese public discussions,[23] particularly after one member of Habibie's cabinet showed his Muslim credentials by saying that Megawati would not be a suitable president because she had prayed in a Hindu temple. The placard held up by a worker in the Governor's office, 'We are not Balinese dogs who can be abused', describes this feeling that other Indonesians (in this case the Javanese hotel owners) are treating Balinese badly.

For Balinese, the identification of the island with being *aman* or peaceful is a constant theme. The fall of Suharto was of course anything but *aman*, and the organized conflicts that have erupted across the archipelago reinforce the message. Bali's distinctiveness from the rest of Indonesia is its quality, real or imaginary, of being *aman* while everyone else is not. It was particularly threatening when seven Balinese were murdered in a political conflict in December 1998, and no doubt the Balinese tourist authorities were mightily relieved when this incident received virtually no overseas reporting, unlike the riots of 1999 in Bali following Megawati's failure to become president, riots that led to a tourist downturn.

Being *aman* during the New Order was the responsibility of one body; the Indonesian Armed Forces or ABRI, otherwise known as the *aparat* (apparatus) *keamanan*. In the editorial on the 'testing' of the army or TNI over East Timor, there is a clear recognition that the single entity ABRI is no more, and that in the case of East Timor the TNI and POLRI

(Indonesian Police) together are the chief *aparat keamanan*. This same editorial sees the East Timor vote as a 'king hit' (*pukulan telak*) to the Indonesian people (*bangsa Indonesia*). The implications of this are extremely ambiguous, since if the TNI did hit back, presumably this would be felt as only fair. The editorial closes with a prayer for peace by the 'people of Indonesia', over-determined as the '*rakyat dan warga bangsa Indonesia*'. The story becomes even more complicated with the knowledge that it was marines, and later special Air Forces, who were brought in to settle things down as the Australian-led UN forces came in.

To return this discussion to the topic of nation, state and society, it seems that in Balinese ways of talking about citizenship, nationality and being in the Indonesian state, the distinction between state and society is not at all clear. As Siahaan *et al.* (2001) show, after Suharto it is difficult to imagine what form democracy can take in practice, and how its form relates to processes of modernization. Likewise, the military as an apparatus of coercion is not seen to be a tool of the state or working in the service of society, but by implication a thing of the nation. It seems that those Indonesians who want to get the military out of society and removed from their position of control of the state have an uphill battle. That Balinese workers are struggling to remove *oknum militair* from workplaces is a good start, but the conceptual removal may take longer. The New Order left no language with which to construct a vision of a just society, and since its fall no new language has emerged.

NOTES

1 The word used here is a form of the Indonesian term *aman*, 'peaceful'. This was to become a key word in discussing the difference between Bali and more restive parts of Indonesia, and visitors to the island were continually reassured that 'Bali is still peaceful' (*masih aman*). *Diamankan* can also mean 'pacified', in the sense of forceful control.

2 '*Oknum pelakunya*', in the original. This rather officious term was often used by New Order officials to describe those who carry out the orders of people in authority.

3 All references to 1999 issues of the Bali Post are to the on-line version, which only contains a selection of articles. Reference from earlier years of the newspaper come from work carried out by Lyn Fisher as research assistant to an ARC Large project on modernity in Bali.

4 '*Unjuk rasa*' is the Indonesian term for a spontaneous (wildcat) strike or demonstration.

5 *Satpol PP* in the original. These security forces are not actually police.

6 Dismissal notices are referred to as *PHK* or *Pamutusan Hubungan Kerja*.

7 The original reads: '*Keluarkan oknum militer di BGH*'; '*Kami bukan anjing Bali yang bisa dimaki*'; '*Berikan jaminan hukum bagi rakyat kecil*'. It is rare to directly quote any workers or their representatives' views in *Bali Post* articles.

8 The Indonesian term used is '*ketenangan*'.

9 Arief Budiman is currently professor of Indonesian Studies in the Melbourne Institute of Asian Languages and Societies at The University of Melbourne.

10 My thanks to Andrew Wells for discussion of this point. The liberal model has been used in preference to a Gramscian one, which is advocated by some commentators, such as Siahaan *et al*. 2001.

11 One of the few Balinese public intellectuals to attempt to define these differences is the member of national parliament Dewa Palguna, whose writings from the late 1990s appear in his 2000 collection.

12 These comments are based on reading the *Sydney Morning Herald* and *The Australian* in September–October 1999. For the continuing fear of Asian invasion in Australia, see the timely appearance of David Walker's (1999) book which critically examines this fear of invasion. In 2001, the invaders shifted from Indonesians to Middle-Eastern or South Asian refugees coming via Indonesia.

13 See for example *Bali Post* of 9 September 1999, where the militia Aitarak is the major source of information. This article has an ambiguous sub-heading of 'Dili becomes a Sea of Fire', where the phrase used, *Lautan Api*, echoes the song of the Indonesian Revolution '*Halo Bandung*', which describes how the Indonesian scorched-earth policy turned that city into a *lautan api*.

14 *Terlepas*, the *ter-*, prefix avoiding any indication of agency.

15 *Yang tidak kalah hebatnya*.

16 Bali Post, 8 September 1999, 'Tajuk Rencana: Pasca-Jajak Pendapat Ujian Berat bagi TNI'.

17 On the differing interpretations of '*tanggung jawab*' or responsibility, and a summary of other main sources on New Order ideology, see Jackson 2000.

18 Surat Pembaca, Bali Post, 7 September 1999, 'Tak Usah Pusing Soal Timtim' Hasil jajak pendapat di Timor Timur sudah sah dan final, karena dijalankan oleh pihak-pihak (pro-integrasi dan pro-kemerdekaan), Pemerintah RI, Portugal, PBB, tanpa ada keberatan sebelumnya. Keberatan kemudian dengan alasan intern pihak (Indonesia tidak mendapat persetujuan DPR dan lain-lain) adalah kebodohan intern yang kalau ditampilkan di forum dunia, akan ditertawai. Sedangkan kecurangan pelaksanaan jajak pendapat adalah urusan PBB dengan pihak (pro-integrasi) yang merasa dirugikan dan bukan urusan Indonesia.

Indonesia tidak usah pusing-pusing lagi dengan Timor-Timur, serahkan saja kepada mereka dengan pilihan sebagai berikut: 1. Bagi warga Timor Timur yang merasa satu keluarga dengan saudaranya di Indonesia (pembangunan sudah 93% dari Indonesia dan lain-lain) untuk itu di tanah Timor Timur Anda tinggal minta bagian wilayah saja, dan mari kita kompak bersatu dan membangun lagi.

Bagi warga Timor Timur yang ingin merdeka (gabung dengan negeri lain dan lain-lain) silakan, tetapi jangan pongah. Anda sudah dikasi makan (baca pembangunan senilai 93%, mahasiswa diberi beasiswa, kepandaian, biaya hidup dan lain-lain), selesai makan silakan pergi, ucapkan terima kasih. 'Jangan makan di meja kami, berak di situ dan minta makan lagi'. Baik hatilah Anda pada kebaikan. I Ketut Artadi, S. H., SU. Jl. Sekarjepun V/14 Denpasar.

19 Bali Post, 21 September 1999, 'Bali' section.

20 Bali Post, 22 September 1999, 'Tourism' section: 'Industri Pariwisata Indonesia Siap Boikot Australia'.

21 The letters mainly appeared around 17 August (the date of the declaration of Independence), specifically from the 16th to 30th of that month.

22 Note that this author, as with a number of other contributors to this discussion, does not have a Balinese name, but from his name is probably Javanese. The majority of contributors were, however, Balinese, and not all from Denpasar, the capital.

23 The example I witnessed was the October 1998 Society for Balinese Studies conference, where discussions about caste conflict began to raise emotions, which then ran on into Hindu versus Christian antipathy amongst Balinese, and the threat of Islam.

REFERENCES

Aditjondro, George (1995) *Bali, Jakarta's Colony: Social and Ecological Impacts of Jakarta-based Conglomerates in Bali's Tourism Industry*, Perth: Asia Research Centre, Murdoch University, Working Paper No. 58.

Bourchier, David (1997) 'Totalitarianism and the National Personality: Recent Controversy about the Philosophical Basis of the Indonesian State'. In Jim Schiller and Barbara Martin-Schiller (eds), *Imagining Indonesia: Cultural Politics*, Athens and Ohio: Ohio University Center for International Studies Monographs, Southeast Asian Series, No. 97, pp. 157–85.

Jackson, Elisabeth (2000) 'The Politics of Pertanggungjawaban: Contesting the Meaning of Accountability in Two New Order Texts'. *Review of Indonesian and Malaysian Affairs*, 34(2): 29–60.

Palguna, Dewa (2000) *Parlemen Literer: Antologi Pemikiran*, Denpasar: Bali Mangsi.

Reeve, David (1985) *Golkar of Indonesia: An Alternative to the Party System*, Kuala Lumpur: Oxford University Press.

Sawitri, Cok (2000) *Mengapa PDI-Perjuangan Menang Mutlak di Bali?* Paper given at the Society for Balinese Studies Conference, Udayana University.

Siahaan, Hotman H. *et al.* (2001) *Pers yang Gamang. Studi Perberitaan Jajak Pendapat Timor Timur*, Surabaya and Jakarta: Lembaga Studi Perubahan Sosial and Institut Studi Arus Informasi.

Suardika, Gde Pasek *et al.* (1998) *Bung Karno: Saya Berdarah Bali*, Denpasar: Nusa Tenggara.

Walker, David (1999) *Anxious Nation*, St. Lucia (Queensland): University of Queensland Press.

Young, Ken (1999) 'Post-Suharto: a change of regime?' In Arief Budiman, Barbara Hatley and Damien Kingsbury (eds), *Reformasi: Crisis and Change in Indonesia*, Clayton (Australia): Monash Asia Institute, pp. 74–75.

3 Art and peace in the safest place in the world

A culture of apoliticism in Bali

Graeme MacRae

Returning to Bali in June 1998, a few days after the tumultuous events culminating in the downfall of President Suharto, I expected to find traces of these events in the form of economic stress and public apprehension, mixed perhaps with relief. I was surprised, however, to find most of my friends in Ubud hastening to reassure me that all was well. The trouble had all been in Java and other places, but Bali was perfectly 'secure' (*aman*). On further questioning it transpired that the explanation for this anomalous state of affairs was that the people of Bali and especially Ubud, unlike those of other parts of Indonesia, had been performing the correct forms of ritual with exceptional diligence. Indeed, they said, my arrival was fortuitously timed; they were at this very moment preparing for a series of ceremonies of unprecedented scale to ensure the well-being (*kesejahteraan*) not only of Ubud but of all Bali and even the whole world.[1]

What my friends were telling me clearly contradicted information I had received from other sources. There had in fact been (albeit relatively minor) demonstrations in Denpasar. Megawati Sukarnoputri, daughter of Sukarno and President of Indonesia at the time of writing but in mid-1998 the leader of a major opposition party (the PDI-P), and her entourage had been in Bali and had even passed through Ubud a few days previously with much fanfare. Within a few days of my arrival the entire Provincial Parliament of Bali (DPRD) had stepped down in the face of mounting public pressure.

Despite this dominant discourse of denial, there were a few people who admitted that it had been pretty scary. One man, who had lost family and friends in the 1965 massacres, said privately that the events and particularly the whole 'feeling' of it had taken him back to the atmosphere of those days.

Months later, as the 1999 elections loomed, I received a message from a foreign expatriate resident in Ubud, expressing the sentiment that

> I only wish the Balinese were more politically savvy and more socially active. Their vision is so myopic. The ceremonies must go on.

I arrived again in late 1999, this time a few days after an unprecedented afternoon of rioting in which roads were blocked and government buildings destroyed simultaneously in several district centres in Bali in protest against the election of Abdurrahman Wahid rather than Megawati as President at the time. By now I was no longer surprised that, once again, the main concern was less with the political issues themselves than with the fact that Ubud and indeed all of the Gianyar had remained immune to the disorder. The reason for this extraordinary immunity? The regency (*kabupaten*) government of Gianyar, of which a member of Puri (the royal household of) Ubud was the head, had recently performed an elaborate public ceremony of blood sacrifice (*pacaruan*) to purify the region of malign influences. When questioned about the election, most people expressed satisfaction with the ultimate outcome but hastened to add that their concerns were not with politics but with religion (*agama*) and that tourism and economic growth not be disrupted.

In the weeks that followed, the majority of people I met in the streets of Ubud, in other parts of Bali and as far afield as Lombok, were concerned less with the national political situation as such (and even less with East Timor) than with the effects upon tourism. Of the two sentiments most commonly expressed, one was summarized eloquently by the well-fed and gold-bedecked young proprietor of a car-hire establishment in Ubud: 'This president, that president – it is all the same to me as long as tourists keep coming and we can make a living', and the other, more succinctly by various persons of less worldly persuasion: 'We are interested in religion not politics'.

In previous years (especially 1993–1996) when I had attempted to warn people of what I perceived as the long-term economic risks associated with an over-dependence on tourism, the message had fallen on deaf ears. People listened politely and thanked me for my advice, but the glazed look in their eyes told me that they pitied my inability to comprehend the ritual causation of the inexorable economic cycle through which prosperity was brought by tourism.[2] Now there was no longer any need for my sanctimonious warnings. Despite the public *pacaruan*, and no doubt plenty of private ceremonies, everybody understood the process in only too material terms: 'If there are no tourists, how will we be able to eat?'

What was striking though, was that most people were expressing the causal relationship between tourism and ritual in a more direct form than I had heard it before. While they saw tourism in particular and business in general as compatible with religion, they saw both in implacable opposition to 'politics'. While they had no illusions about the effects of the political turmoil on their own livelihoods, and were prepared to make ritual investments to minimize these effects, the implicit feeling was that Ubud and Gianyar as a whole had remained free of such turmoil and were being unfairly penalized for the activities of a politicized minority located elsewhere – somewhere – anywhere, except in Ubud.

Why, during these times when things were clearly the furthest from *aman* than they had been in the living memory of most people, were they so busy trying to create the impression that everything was safe and secure? At one level this concern to suppress any hint of violence or disorder makes sense in relation to keeping tourism on track. Tourist numbers were clearly down in mid-1998 (especially the seasonal and high-spending Americans and Japanese), and inflation was running at nearly 35 per cent. So everyone was understandably concerned to maintain the contrary impression that everything was fine; business almost as usual, and ritual even better than usual. In 1999, the Rupiah had recovered considerable ground but tourist numbers were down again (especially Australians in the wake of anti-Australian sentiment following the UN-sponsored occupation of East Timor). Local investment and development, however, were continuing regardless, although ordinary people seemed more aware of their dependence on tourism and their vulnerability to political and economic instability.[3]

But I suspect there is more to it than this. The way locals were trying to suppress the bad news, any hint of violence or disorder, any hint of the political, rang a few bells for me. Throughout my 1993–1996 fieldwork in Ubud I found most people very happy to talk about all sorts of things until it came to the dark side; violence, disorder or anything to do with politics. There are two obvious explanations for such an attitude. One is the often cited pan-Southeast Asian interpersonal style in which polite circumlocution is raised to the level of art to avoid overt conflict or confrontation of less than comfortable realities. Unni Wikan has described in some detail the distinctively Balinese version of this mode of communication (1990: 82–106; see also Geertz 1994: 12). The other is the obvious fact that Indonesia is, or certainly was until 1988, a country where careless talk about politics could get you into a lot of trouble. State ideology throughout the New Order period sought to sanitize local culture of any traces of the political (Acciaioli 1985; Hooker and Dick 1995: 5) and barely concealed behind the ideology lay a willingness of the state to enforce such policies by terror and violence. Consequently, a certain reticence about the political has been noted by researchers in other parts of Indonesia. As John Pemberton puts it 'the word *politik* is marked by a sinister tonality acquired after the political killings of the mid-1960s' (1994: 4) and Indonesia during the late New Order period was home to 'an uncanny stillness [...] when it comes to political matters' (1994: 2), maintained by 'an ambiguous, internalized form of repression that makes the apparent normality of everyday life conceivable, desirable' (1994: 7; see also Steedly 1993: 225).[4]

Both of these explanations are to a degree linked to Benedict Anderson's (1990) argument regarding traditional Javanese conceptions of worldly power as an inherent property, of supernatural origin, which some people are able to accumulate in greater quantity than others. When combined with a view of historical process as cyclical and divinely ordained, political power and social inequality are thus seen as aspects of the natural order to which neither moral critique nor political resistance are appropriate or realistic responses.

There is, in the political thinking of Ubud's people, evidence of all of these factors but not sufficiently enough to explain the elevation of an understandable reticence into a positive cultural value. People I knew well, who would talk to me about all matter of things, would (with a few notable exceptions) simply clam up, even in private, when it came to the events of 1965 or to contemporary politics, local, provincial or national. More politically aware friends from other parts of Bali concurred in this judgement of Ubud to the point of questioning my choice to work in such an artificially depoliticized and culturally conservative environment.

The primary task of this chapter is neither to pass judgement on this attitude nor to suggest that it is unique to Ubud, Bali or even Indonesia.[5] My aim is to explain, or at least understand this 'culture of apoliticism' by placing it in a historical context. A secondary task is to consider the effects on this culture of the recent crisis and repoliticization of public life throughout Indonesia. Finally, linking the two is an examination of the role of the arts in maintaining and perhaps ultimately changing this culture.

KAMIS KELABU: THE PUBLIC RESPONSE

In late 1999, as the proprietors of the empty shops and restaurants of Ubud reflected dolefully on their own imminent starvation as a result of the lack of tourists, while in the coastal resorts the lively self-help cottage industries of petty crime, drug-dealing and prostitution expanded to fill the economic vacuum left by the receding tide of tourism,[6] the shocked silence following the riots of 'Ash Thursday' (Kamis Kelabu) of 21 October was gradually replaced by a chorus of public lamentation and recrimination tempered eventually with a modicum of analysis. The pages of the main local newspaper, the *Bali Post* (BP), served as a focal point of this discussion and provide a record of it. The following summary of the main themes of this discussion is based on an analysis of more than 50 articles published over the period from 2 November to 13 December 1999.[7]

The initial reaction was shock and disbelief that such a thing could occur in Bali which, as everyone knows, is 'the safest place in the world' (BP, 8 November 1999), followed by a profound sense of 'shame' or 'embarrassment' (*malu*) (BP, 8 November 1999). All but one writer accepted the rather demeaning, and less than enlightening media stereotype of the incident as 'mass madness' (*amuk massa*) (BP, 23 November 1999).[8] While nobody questioned that the catalyst for the riots had been the failure of the national assembly (MPR) to elect Megawati (the preferred candidate by many Balinese) as President at the time, explanations of underlying causes quickly bifurcated into two main directions.

On one hand was the hypothesis of a knee-jerk reaction, neither new nor surprising in itself, but articulated unashamedly by such public figures as the head of *Parisada Hindu Dharma Indonesia* (PHDI), the umbrella organization of Indonesian Hinduism, and a well-known psychiatrist; seeking to pin the blame onto 'newcomers' bringing 'new values' which seek to 'destroy the solidarity' of the religious faithful in Bali (*'ada pendatang yang membawa "nilai baru" yang berusaha merusak kerukunan umat beragama di Bali'*, BP, 4 November 1999). Even an eminent historian, reminding Balinese that their society had a long tradition of trusted residents of non-Balinese origin and that it was as much in the interests of such contemporary residents as it was of indigenous Balinese to maintain public order, did not question that what they were defending against was 'intervention by outsiders' (BP, 10 November 1999b). This assumption continued in the form of ongoing references to presumed 'provocateurs' repeated without supporting evidence by cultural commentators and local politicians and even a lawyer (BP, 8 November 1999, 9 November 1999b). While not everybody joined this chorus of xenophobia, the only dissenting voices were two local anthropologists who, while not referring directly to this discourse, independently referred to the need for Balinese to develop a more 'tolerant', 'flexible' and 'pluralistic' political culture (BP, 23 November 1999a, 1 December 1999).

On the other hand, many Balinese saw the riots as cause for self-reflection and sober reassessment of their relationship with such fundamental traditional values as 'respect' and 'trust' (BP, 23 November 1999b). Some saw the problem simply as evidence of the domination of politics over religion (BP, 1 December 1999) or the 'weakness of the spiritual contribution in political activity' (BP, 2 November 1999). The local government of Badung, the district most severely affected by both the riots themselves and the subsequent drop in tourism, implicitly accepting a *niskala* (invisible, spiritual) cause-and-effect chain to be behind the events, performed two large public rituals of purification (BP, 7 December 1999).[9] However, when a foreign resident and 'teacher of yoga and meditation from India' suggested (BP, 19 November 1999) that this may be a sign of a coming cultural-religious 'calamity', accused the Balinese of 'extraordinary hypocrisy' in their worship of material prosperity under the guise of Hinduism, and claimed that the gods had already deserted several major temples in Bali, there was an outcry of protest, expressed in the form of letters to the editor, drowning out a more muted recognition that he may have had a point (BP, 29 November 1999).[10]

As the economic consequences of the global perception of Bali's fall from grace became apparent, in the form of a rush of cancellations of tour and hotel bookings and a significant drop in overall tourist numbers, rendered all the more galling by the gains made by Thailand and Singapore at Bali's expense (BP, 4 and 10 November 1999; Jakarta Post [JP], 25 November 1999), the tourist industry went into a frenzy of damage-control public relations activity (BP, 23 November 1999; JP, 25 November 1999, Santikarma 1999), punctuated by calls for assistance from central government in their hour of need (BP, 4 November 1999a) and for speedy repair of the material damage (BP, 2 December 1999b). It also reminded others of Bali's need for development of the non-tourism sectors of its economy (BP, 25 November 1999).

By the time I left Bali in mid-December 1999, there appeared to be an emergent consensus among more reflective observers to the effect that the riots were a symptom neither of 'outside provocateurs' nor a fall from religious grace on the part of Balinese, but a spontaneous popular out-pouring of resentment against such things as 'unjust behaviour which the people have received and internalized for too long' (BP, 2 December 1999a, see also 4 November 1999b), 'public disillusionment' in general (11 November 1999, 3 December 1999) or specifically with economics, politics and the maintenance of the rule of law (28 November 1999), or feelings of 'marginalization' on the part of sectors of the community (4 November 1999b, 23 November 1999). More than one observer raised the possibility of a repeat of the disturbances if the underlying causes were not addressed (BP, 15 November 1999, 1 and 3 December 1999).

These views, from a relatively wide cross-section of Balinese society (at least the literate, newspaper-subscribing segment of it), appear at first more complex and diverse than the Ubud ones discussed above. On closer inspection, however, they seem to me to repeat, in various guises, essentially the same themes. First, the shocked reaction to the realization that contemporary Balinese reality simply did not conform to its tourism image indicated the extent to which the Balinese had come to believe that image, and the depth of collective amnesia with regard to the dark and violent aspects of their own history (as documented by Robinson 1995) and of earlier images of Bali (Vickers 1989: 11–36). Second, the assumption that anything violent, disorderly or even 'political' must ori-ginate elsewhere and outside Bali restates an Ubud orthodoxy on a larger scale. Third, the call for a return to cultural, religious or spiritual values repeats, in modified form, the implicit opposition between the religious and the political, in other words, an apolitical conception of Balinese culture. Finally, the concern over the damage to the tourism economy reflects the extent to which economics and politics are separated in main-stream Balinese thinking, with the former compatible and the latter incompatible with traditional values.

This leaves only the theme of political-economic critique, the implicit thrust of which runs counter to the other themes clearly emergent in the Bali Post debate but not yet evident in Ubud, except among a small minority who tend not to express their views publicly. We will return to this later, but for the moment let us concentrate on the themes common to Ubud and Bali Post. What I want to do in the remainder of this chapter is to explore what might be described as a 'culture of apoliticism' in Ubud, with a view to casting some light on the position of Bali as a whole in the apparently repoliticized public culture of Indonesia. My argument is that while aspects of such an ethos may be found elsewhere in Indonesia and especially in Bali, their peculiar and systematic development in Ubud becomes intelligible in the context of a specific history of relationships between the local community and wider political and economic processes. To demonstrate this involves trawling through some familiar material, rereading with an eye for the (a)political.[11]

PARADISE WITHOUT POLITICS

While recent scholarship has made a large shift from the cultural–aesthetic toward the political–economic aspects of Bali, there are two other places where this radically apolitical approach to Balinese culture and history may be found other than among its participants. The first is in the images of Bali created by foreigners from the 1920s until very recently and which is immortalized in the rhetoric of the tourist industry. The second is in the images contained in Balinese art, or at least the more public and popular forms of art.

The creation of the 'paradise' image began with the Dutch public relations campaign to cover the blood-stained traces of their own acquisition of the island, by advertising Bali as a cultural relic of ancient Hindu civilization and a nice place to go for an exotic holiday into the bargain (Vickers 1989: 91).

Gregor Krause, a German doctor whose photographs brought the first images of Balinese village life to Europe, set off the first Trans-Atlantic Bali-craze. Walter Spies, the cosmopolitan, Covarrubias and all the other Euro-American glitterati of the 1920s and 1930s saw the natural beauty, the gentle grace of the people, the cooperative organization of *banjar*, *desa*, *subak* and other traditional organizations, the religious ideas and practices, the arts, in short, all the beautiful and harmonious aspects of Balinese social life. What they were themselves hiding from was not the darker side of Balinese history but of their own history: In the wake of WW1 and political violence in Europe, the image they were creating of Bali was a mirror-image of everything they wanted to get away from (Fussell 1980: 3–8; MacRae 1992; Pollman 1990: 7; Vickers 1989: 98). Their determination to do so led to some wonderful, if somewhat romantic popular ethnography and photography. But it also created a kind of blinkered vision which enabled them to simply filter out the subtle violence inherent in maintaining colonial order and the devastating eco- nomic and social effects of the Depression on the newly monetarized

economy of Bali (Pollman 1990: 12–20; Robinson 1995). Even the professional anthropologists who worked during this era and on its social
fringes seemed oblivious to the *political* realities which conditioned what
they interpreted as manifestations of Balinese *culture* (e.g. Mead and
Bateson, see Pollman 1990: 20–21).

This was also the time when tourism began to play a part in the local
economy and culture. This tourism involved a collaboration between the
expatriate glitterati and the Ubud royal family and it emphasized two
things; religion, and especially, the arts:

> the Balinese are the greatest artists of this age [...] every Balinese
> [...] is an artist. [...] life centres around [...] religion, a beau-
> tiful mixture of animism and Hinduism [...]. Whether sculpture,
> painting, music or dancing, they simply had to [...] they could not
> help themselves.
>
> (Roosevelt 1985: x–xii)

The image on which tourism was based portrayed the Balinese as
a people living in elegant material simplicity – a kind of exotic voluntary
poverty – because their real concerns were with the finer things of life,
the arts and the gods, rather than grubbing for money. The implication
was that they were not concerned with politics either; they were content
with any stable political order whether provided by the aristocracy or by
the Dutch.

THE ART OF THE APOLITICAL

Sixty years on, a new set of expatriate-glitterati hold court in Ubud.
Amid the tropic-cosmopolitan cool of the opening of an exhibition of
paintings by a mixed (middle-class Balinese and expatriate) group of
artists in 1996, an expatriate non-artist turned to me and whispered 'If
I have to look at another painting of rice fields, sunsets, beautiful women
or happy families (*keluarga bahagia*) I think I'll vomit.' This person
subscribes to the view that the proper function of art is to address the
real political, social, and economic issues and believes that Indonesian art
in general and Balinese art in particular conspicuously fail to do so. This
observation inspired me to make a brief survey of the contents of the
three great galleries in Ubud.[12]

The oldest, Puri Lukisan is located in the centre of town, in spacious
gardens between the main road and rice fields on land donated by
a branch of the Puri Ubud. It consists of several pavilions housing the
definitive collection of the works of the 'Pita Maha' group. It is the legacy
of the glitterati-*puri* collaboration of the 1930s, especially that between
the Dutch expatriate artist Rudolf Bonnet, Cokorda Agung (the great

ruler of) Sukawati, and the artists themselves. After some years of neglect its buildings have recently been restored and new standards of curatorship and management established.

Museum Neka was established in 1982 by a local schoolteacher turned shopkeeper turned art dealer turned art collector and promoter. Its collection is broader, consisting primarily of more recent paintings of Balinese themes by both local and foreign artists, as well as a general collection of contemporary Indonesian art.

The *Agung Rai Museum of Art* (ARMA) was opened with national-level fanfare in 1996. It is the *opus magnum* of one of the most successful schoolboy-entrepreneurs of the 1970s and combines an art collection with teaching and performing facilities, hotel and restaurant. Its collection is smaller but similar in scope to that of Neka.[13]

Each museum contains several hundred works and my brief survey tends to confirm my friend's jaundiced assessment of the state of Balinese art. A cluster of three adjacent and recent paintings in the Neka Museum give some idea of the flavour and are by no means atypical. *Life in Bali* by Nyoman Lusug (painted in 1988) is a classically panoramic scene of idyllic village life incorporating women weaving, fighting cocks in cages, market trade in agricultural products, people collecting water and fishing in the river, and a fairly grand cremation complete with elaborate ritual paraphernalia – all against a background of farming activities. *Villagers* by N. Tulus (painted in 1994) depicts a very similar range of activities, minus the cremation. Ida B. Taman's *Bustling Village* (1979) is almost identical in subject matter. There is nothing in their content to distinguish them from Gregor Krause's photographs from 1912. Works by non-Balinese artists in all three galleries are distinguishable only by style rather than content from the works of locals.

The realities of economic survival appear only in the form of romanticized images of traditional agricultural production and village markets. Poverty and social inequality are obscured by images of communal labour and ritual solidarity. Political conflict appears only in the mythologized form of episodes from the Hindu epics in which the practitioners and/or victims of violence are mostly supernatural beings.

The very few images in these museums which bear any relation to contemporary reality are of a deceptively light-hearted genre introduced during the colonial era, with temple carvings incorporating overweight Dutch policemen driving motor vehicles or violating local maidens (Covarrubias 1994: 186). The most celebrated contemporary practitioner of this mode is W. Bendi whose paintings incorporate the paraphernalia of tourism: foreign visitors, cameras, cars, surfers, airplanes. The forms, composition and overall effects, however, are almost identical to those of the village scenes described above; only some of the ingredients are changed. Even with his *The War of Independence* (1986) the artist follows this same format but incorporates a few Dutch soldiers and a surprisingly cosmopolitan array of photographers, including one of brown skin but long nose and another who appears Indonesian. The effect is, like the tourist scenes, of simply another busy day in the village with the villagers dressed in uniforms and carrying guns instead of hoes.[14]

Discussion of the arts of Bali is a productive enterprise almost as rich and varied as the arts themselves.[15] I am competent to add little to this discussion beyond the observation that, with a very few striking exceptions (notably Vickers 1989: 143–46 and his forthcoming publications), it neither mentions any evidence of art containing overtly political, economic and social commentary nor does it comment upon this striking absence in a society subject to extraordinary change and elements of considerable conflict.

In a recent publication subtitled *Images of Bali in the Arts*, Garret Kam mentions without comment that the colourful 'New Artist' style in Penestanan, characterized by bright child-like colours and a quality of 'fresh innocence', flourished in the immediate aftermath of the 1965 massacres, but does not reflect them in any way (1993: 57). The same publication contains reproductions of 40, implicitly representative, paintings selected not purely for their artistic merit but to provide an overview of Balinese culture and history (1993: 20). They represent, as the main title *Perceptions of Paradise* hints, images of rural landscapes and the idyllic timeless village life, the performance of ritual, scenes from Hindu epic literature. Not one of these paintings contain any reference whatsoever to contemporary, or even historical economic or political reality. The only references to conflict or violence are framed unambiguously within mythological settings. The same general comments apply to both the sentiments and the selections illustrated in other works on Balinese painting such as Forge (1980), Darling and Rhodius (1980), and Djelantik (1990).

Ubud artists with whom I have discussed this matter recognize and do not deny the pattern. They explain it in two ways. One is that it is not the business of art to meddle in the affairs of everyday life, but to create a world of beauty and harmony apart from everyday problems. Art is to induce people to feel and behave more peacefully rather than fuelling conflict and ill-will. As one painter (who happens to hold views strongly critical of the cultural and environmental effects of tourism) put it, the last thing he wanted to do with his anger and other negative emotions was to immortalize them in the form of paintings, especially if they were good ones, in which case he, as the artist would be responsible for their negative effects upon other people.

The other category of explanations are along the lines that not only painting but all traditional Balinese art does in fact address all the problems of the *sekala* world. But it does so metaphorically through representation and interpretation of the *niskala* conflicts of the gods and mythological heroes, especially those contained in the great Hindu epics

Ramayana and Mahabharata, which are held to contain the solutions to all human problems.

One of the few exceptions to the academic tradition of ignoring this curious aspect of Balinese art is Adrian Vickers, who tends toward the latter of the two Balinese explanations. In his discussion of some of the works of the great artists of the 1930s he reads Lempad's graphic depictions of homosexuality, Deblog's images of violence between supernatural beings, and indeed the popularity of the Rangda–Barong conflict itself as metaphorical commentaries upon a 'moral order [...] undergoing rapid change' and 'an era of instability [...] in need of exorcism on all levels' (Vickers 1989: 144, 146).

A third, more prosaic explanation, alluded to by some painters themselves and consistent with the predominant political climate of the nation is simply that they are afraid to paint overtly controversial material. They repeat the Ubud orthodoxy that they are not interested in politics and want to get on with their lives in peace.

I have not made parallel inquiries with regard to the performing arts, but they appear to be similarly restricted to classical forms, genres and content: endless repetitions of the same dances in both temple ceremonies and tourist performances. There are two partial exceptions among the performing arts; *topeng* and *wayang* (see Kellar, this volume, for a discussion of *arja*). The former are masked dances in which elements of dynastic chronicles (*babad*) are enacted and recited. Although usually performed in ritual contexts, the stories are rich with (mytho-historical) political intrigue and conflict and they are often told in ways which comment obliquely upon contemporary affairs. The same is true, to a greater degree, of *wayang kulit*, the shadow-plays in which puppeteer and narrator routinely intersperse the epic sagas they relate with commentaries, usually comical, often bawdy and sometimes disguised, upon contemporary issues, including political ones.[16] In these cases the political critique, trenchant as it may be, is subtly phrased and thoroughly embedded, almost hidden in the classical form. I am not aware of any parallel tradition of hidden critique in the graphic arts.

My suspicion that this dominant pattern of cultural apoliticism is no accident is reinforced by the only case I know of an artist who has attempted to challenge it. Made Kertonegoro, an expatriate Javanese artist and performer has lived in Ubud since the mid-1980s. When I first met him in 1988, he was presenting a performance entitled *Release from World Disaster*. It utilized the style and format of traditional Balinese dance drama and was staged by local performers in the village of Petulu Gunung. Its subject matter, however, was the saving of the world from impending destruction through nuclear or environmental holocaust by divine intervention.

He had, he told me, attempted to stage it in a central Ubud venue as part of the regular nightly programme of traditional dances and dramatic genres. He was not able to find a venue willing to accommodate his show, however, nor were Ubud performers willing to take part in it. Instead he used performers and a venue in a nearby village, Petulu Gunung. He has also published a series of books which are in various ways critical of the prevailing alliance between apolitical cultural conservatism and the economic interests of tourism (Kertonegoro 1987). His books, he claims, were 'banned' from sale in main-street outlets, although they remain to this day available at a minority of 'alternative' outlets. When I last spoke to him he had retired from overt political activism – to concentrate on the spiritual dimensions of his art.

Such is the appearance of an idea, or what some of our predecessors in Bali (Bateson and Mead 1942: xi) might have called an *ethos*; of a radical apoliticism which is not merely an absence but a positive value in the local culture of Ubud. While it is supported by historical and cultural precedent and is compatible with the ethos of cultural tourism, it nevertheless seems remarkable that it should have survived so unscathed through an era in which the economic and cultural orders have in other respects been so radically altered. To understand how this has come to pass, it may be helpful to consider in more detail the history of political thought and action in Ubud for, as Judith Williamson (1978) reminds us,

> ...ideology embedded in form is the hardest of all to see. This is why it is important to emphasize process [...] it undoes the fait accompli.

A SHORT HISTORY OF POLITICAL CONSCIOUSNESS IN UBUD

In the years immediately prior to 1900, Ubud was arguably the most effective politico-military formation in South Bali. Its royal leadership entered the colonial era with vast landholdings and political influence as well as a rather privileged relationship with the Dutch – the result of Ck. Gede Sukawati's role as a facilitator of the voluntary handover of control of the kingdom of Gianyar to the Dutch (MacRae 1997: 340). After this transition he proved as able a statesman in peace as he had been in war.

By the time the 'paradise' image was in full production in the 1920s he was no longer alive, and the most powerful individual in Ubud was his eldest son, Ck. Raka Sukawati. The latter had been to the Dutch school in Probolinggo, trained as a colonial civil servant, and was generally very Dutch-influenced in his thinking and pro-Dutch in his politics. His power relative to that of the artists themselves, based upon traditional respect for (or fear of) the *puri* (royal household), was such that he could, at a whim, take from the most famous artist of all, Gusti Nyoman Lempad, his rice fields or his daughter (Vickers 1989: 142). Within his own family he was able to out-manoeuvre the combined influence of all his siblings to monopolize the vast majority of his father's considerable inheritance. Contemporary oral sources (which shall remain anonymous) both within and outside the *puri* agree that his control over *niskala* forces through black magic played a considerable part in his ability to manipulate *sekala* (worldly) affairs to his own advantage.

As Pollman (1990: 16) shows, the Dutch cultural policy of the time was one of Balinization; of keeping the overt behaviour of the Balinese as traditional as possible – or preferably making them even more Balinese than before – along neo-traditional lines defined not by themselves but by Dutch experts on Balinese culture. This approach was consistent with the cultural politics Ck. Raka practised in Ubud. There is no evidence from Ubud of any resistance to the Dutch such as occurred occasionally elsewhere in Bali (Robinson 1995: 64–69; Wiener 1999: 58).

To summarize, there were three major influences operating at the time: First, that of the Spies-glitterati toward encouraging Balinese to value and commodify traditional art and religion rather than reflecting upon the sources of their grinding poverty. Second, the influence of the Sukawati aristocracy to accept and respect the Dutch regime. And third, the fact that the two most powerful forces in Ubud life, the *sekala* economic and cultural power of the Spies-glitterati and the *niskala* and political power of the Sukawati aristocracy, were closely linked and worked together by giving much the same messages.

These influences together, I think, provide the first layer of understanding of a way of thinking in which art and religion are both separated from politics and given radically opposite valuations. Art and religion were approved by the powers as being appropriate for ordinary people to be involved in, while politics was taken care of by the *puri* and the Dutch. Furthermore, and perhaps most importantly, economics are separated from politics and begin to be attached instead to art/religion.

After leading a tour of the Ubud–Peliatan dance group to Europe in 1931 (collecting a French wife en route), and having already stripped his family of much of their wealth, Ck. Raka moved on to national level politics in Batavia, leaving his younger brother Ck. Agung in charge of the *puri*. Ck. Agung was a different personality to Ck. Raka. He was perhaps a product of the cultural and political environment in which he grew up; devoting himself to religion, the arts and his glitterati friends and apparently innocent of political ambition.

The coming of 'politics': 1935–1950

The whole established structure began to fall apart in the late-1930s when the glitterati were driven out by the Dutch on the pretext of a moral clean-up (Vickers 1989: 124–25). The last straw was the Japanese occupation, when everything was turned on its head. Local people who had previously been involved in various ways with the cultural economy of art and expatriates were suddenly suspect, and they returned to the rice fields and metamorphosed into illiterate farmers. Everything was in short supply and life was reduced to survival. Politics had come from somewhere else, had got out of hand and was making life difficult.

Ck. Agung had neither taste nor talent for dealing with this. He found himself persecuted by the Japanese who he had naively thought of as his friends because of their interest in art. After the Japanese left, the Dutch returned, but for the first time in their lives, the young men who had grown up in the apoliticized environment of Ubud, became politicized. Indeed, some of them, became involved in the struggle for independence (*kemerdekaan*).

Ck. Raka chose to ally himself with his brother-in-law A. A. Gede Agung of Puri Gianyar on the side of the federalist N.I.T. and against the republican nationalism to which his younger brother, Ck. Agung, subscribed. Once again Ck. Agung found himself in a difficult situation. The relatives to whom he felt closest were hunted, imprisoned, tortured and in some cases killed by the more politically ambitious of his own relatives (Hilberry 1979: 36–39).

After the Republic was formed, there were only more economic problems and political unrest. By this time Ck. Agung was thoroughly disillusioned with politics: 'there were so many political parties I was not interested any longer' (Ck. Agung Sukawati, cited in Hilberry 1979: 39). Although he was but one man, his experience is, I think, both a metaphor for and representative of the common Ubud experience of politics at this time. His perception of politics was as something, originating elsewhere, which inevitably ended in local suffering. What originated in Ubud by contrast, was art and religion and mutually beneficial relationships with foreigners who were attracted to exactly the same things as their Balinese hosts.

While he avoided formal political office himself, Ck. Agung was the head of the *puri* and was thus seen by most people as the *raja* of Ubud by virtue of inheriting the divine mandate and ritual responsibilities of his father. He was, unlike his brother, something of a man of the people. The gates of his *puri* were open to the people, both of Ubud and beyond, fostering a relationship between *puri* and commoners unparalleled in modern Bali. He is, again unlike his brother, fondly remembered in Ubud as a man embodying the very qualities of apolitical, religious-artistic sentiment that the Ubud people like to think of themselves as having. It was during the period of his influence that the present culture of the apolitical was instated as unwritten *puri* policy.

The politicization of civil society: 1950–1965

One of the effects of the decade of invasion, war and the struggle for independence was to take politics out of the control of the local or national elite and to involve ordinary people in political debate and action. Throughout Indonesia, the 1950s were marked by irregular localized violence and the emergence of a plethora of popular political movements and parties (Robinson 1995).

The effects of this crisis were perhaps less marked in Ubud than in many other places, as the community remained relatively united under the moral authority of the *puri* and isolated from outside influence. It was, however, not isolated from nationwide economic problems, manifest in shortages and inflation of the prices of basic commodities.

Most people in Ubud who remember this era prefer not to think or, at least, not to talk about it. According to the few people whom I could persuade to discuss it, there was little spontaneous political activity of local origin, but there was a pervasive penetration of the national political turmoil into the area. Small groups of *grombolan* or *logis* (former freedom fighters dissatisfied with the post-independence regime) were active in nearby villages and made nocturnal raids into Ubud, creating an atmosphere of apprehension and mistrust. Local farmers became aware of the nationwide agitation for land reform, which was spearheaded by the Communist Party (PKI) and especially its agrarian arm BTI (*Barisan Tani Indonesia*).

Later there were active PKI cells in nearby villages. Members visited Ubud regularly, easily recognizable by the long trousers they wore (a sign of advanced political sensibilities) in contrast to the traditional waist cloth (*kamben*) worn by village men. They would swagger around the village, boasting about the imminent downfall of traditional institutions such as the *puri* and traditional religion, saying 'there is no god – only the machines which produce food' and promising land to those who joined the party. On occasions they organized public rallies, in which local people participated, as much it is said for the entertainment than out of any real understanding of the party's manifesto. Many farmers, however, (according to a man of reputed PKI sympathies) joined BTI and most others secretly supported PKI's objectives of agrarian reform.

The land reform process began in 1963–1964, with the local *perbekel* (village head) merely acting as point of contact for officials from elsewhere who collected information. According to his recollection, the process proceeded smoothly with the owners of excess land, all *puri* members or close dependants, cooperating with officials. Subsequent investigations by the Land Reform Office tends to confirm the opinion of a minority, however, who claim that the *puri* were able to avoid detection of substantial amounts of excess land through a combination of coercion, deception and the trusting compliance of their tenants and clients (MacRae 1997: 383–93).

By 1965, the local levels of national administration were increasingly dominated by PKI members, including the local Bupati and Camat (regency and district heads). The *perbekel* in Ubud remained loyal to the *puri*. He attempted (so he told me in 1996) to maintain an even-handed relationship with all parties. But when his son, recently graduated from secondary school, was offered a job at the newly established Bali Beach Hotel, on the condition that he joined PKI, he refused to allow it.

When the killings began, later in 1965, Ubud did not suffer the wholesale slaughter recorded in some other places (Robinson 1995). The former *perbekel* believes that this was, at least in part, the result of his policy of prohibiting the entry of outsiders into the village and maintaining strict control over the behaviour of locals. No summary executions were allowed and he insisted that any suspects be dealt with via proper process by the police. When the official lists arrived he had the unenviable duty of calling friends and neighbours, offering them coffee and asking them to report to the police, knowing full well what their fate would be. Other accounts suggest a less orderly process:

> I was about four years old at the time. Lots of people came to our house. I was not used to people. I was frightened and hid behind the big water jar in the kitchen. They went to the house north of ours. There was a young man from [...] who was very outspoken about politics. He was feeding the pigs when they came. They took him away and beat him in the rice fields. Then they took him to Lebih where he was shot with the others.

According to a man who was employed at the Camat's Office, and is regarded by some as having been himself a PKI supporter (and who admits to having been pressured to join the party but skilfully avoided either denying or confirming this in conversation with me in 1996), but survived through the protection of friends; there were 'hundreds' of PKI supporters in Ubud, effectively most of the land-poor farmers.

There is, however, a version authorized by unwritten public consensus; that the number killed was between 10 and 15, of which only about four or five were PKI members, while a few more may have been genuine sympathizers and supporters. The others killed were either unfortunates caught up in something they did not understand and who found themselves in the wrong place at the wrong time or, in a couple of cases, victims of vengeful slander. Recitations of this consensus invariably conclude with the reassuring incantation that even this was an aberration resulting from 'outside influences'; for Ubud people are not really interested in politics, only in art and religion.

Paradise reinstated

Since the 1960s, and especially since the mid 1980s, the centre of economic and cultural gravity in Ubud has shifted progressively from the *puri* and even from the formal political administration, to tourism. It has been the

specifically Ubud-brand of cultural tourism oriented, like that of the
1930s, to increasingly affluent Europeans and Americans, and based
systematically on the commodification of such aspects of culture as the
wet-rice landscape, music, dance, and drama, painting, the Spies golden-age
myth, the expatriate-*Puri*-arts axis, and more recently the splendour of
temples and the supposed incorporation of the essence of these qualities
into tourist facilities such as hotels and restaurants themselves.

The tourism era has been, for those who had lived through the previous
half-century, a period of unprecedented prosperity, but more importantly, of freedom from political upheaval and the threat of either starvation or violence. For this generation, as for Ck. Agung, politics is
something originating from outside Ubud and it always brings trouble.
As one of the few people from whom I could elicit a detailed account of
the events of 1965 told me that Ubud's people 'have had their fingers
burnt by politics' (*kapok terhadap politik*).[17]

The generations born since 1960 have grown up in the tourism era and
have no direct experience and in most cases little knowledge of the
events of 1965. What they do have is a rather abstract notion, learnt
from school-books, of colonialism and the *merdeka*-struggle. In many
cases, they also have little or no experience of the agrarian economy.
Their priorities in life are defined by an unlikely hybrid of materialist
modernity and cultural traditionalism. Politics is (or was prior to 1998),
as for their parents, something that happens in Jakarta, or at closest in
Denpasar, is peripheral, and, at worst, vaguely threatening to the things
they hold dearest.[18]

It is small wonder then, that people, especially the older ones, are
confused by this new turn of events, which threaten once again, to invert
the definitions of right and wrong. Little wonder too, that, while the rest
of Indonesia began by celebrating its new-found freedom of speech
and thought, they responded by reverting to the safe formula which
emerged as the result of decades of suffering. The subsequent descent of
'democracy' into regional secession struggles and politically manipulated
'inter-religious' violence serves only to confirm, in Balinese thinking,
the wisdom of their conservatism.

THE POLITICS OF ART

> Art in the New Order supposedly represented 'individual freedom
> of expression' as opposed to ... art dictated by politics
>
> (Maklai 1995: 70)

Since Acciaioli's (1985) discussion of the absorption of local art forms into
depoliticized, sanitized and uniform cultural programs managed by the
state, several other scholars have noted similar patterns elsewhere in

Indonesia (Bowen 1986; Kipp 1993; Reuter, Chapter 8, this volume). Cultural policy has been matched by parallel programs of state intervention in matters of *adat* (tradition) and *agama* (religion). While the aims of these programs are national ones, 'to neutralize the destabilizing potential of ethnic identity and also to use traditional cultures for economic and integrative ends' (Kipp 1993: 105), at the local level they tend to be subsumed to the ends of local political players.

In Ubud, local power is strung along an axis between an entrepreneurial sector which has arisen through strategic exploitation of the new opportunities presented by tourism and the *puri*, manoeuvring to retain its dwindling but still substantial fund of both symbolic and material capital. Played out against a rapidly changing background defined by the trans-local powers of central government and the international tourism industry, this is less a direct struggle than a delicate dynamic balance of opposed and common interests.

The commonality of interest between the two poles clusters around a mutual dependence upon tourism, of a specific local brand closely linked to an image of traditional cultural and ritual excellence, local control over outside economic influence, and a minimum of outside political interference. Most of the rest of the community are in one way or another employees, tenants or clients of these two groups, dependent economically and in some cases by ties of material and/or ritual patronage, to either the *puri* or the new entrepreneurial sector. The majority, therefore, see their own interests less in terms of the inequality between themselves and the wealthy than through the lens of this dependence, as more or less congruent with the interests of *puri* and tourism.

Consequently they tend to see their well-being, first, in predominantly local rather than regional or national terms and, second, in terms of a hierarchy of mutual dependence rather than a class system of exploitation. My attempts to discuss what I saw as the exploitative aspects of *puri* dominance were usually circumvented with patient explanations of the self-evident cosmic necessity of hierarchical order and stress upon the mutuality of the relationship. As one person put it: 'the puri are more afraid of us than we are of them', implying that the bottom line of the interdependency was that the power of the *puri* was ultimately dependent upon the consent of the people. Even the strongest critics of the *puri* were at pains to point out that their criticism was of the actions of particular *cokorda* rather than of the institution itself, let alone the need for hierarchical order.

Within this constellation of local power relations, art has emerged as an area of common ground, where the inherent conflicts of interest – between foreigners and locals, between the state and the local community, between new entrepreneurs and the old aristocracy, between the emergent classes – are reassuringly blurred. Art, suitably 'traditional' in form and content, and sanitized of social, economic and political content, consisting largely of images equating beauty, tradition and order, has served as the perfect language for maintaining a culture of apoliticism. But could it be that, as the residual political structures of the New Order crumble, there are signs of change in the order of Balinese art, and its relationship with politics?

ART AND PEACE: CLOSING THE SUKAWATI CENTURY

As I embarked upon the preceding analysis of the history of apoliticism in Ubud, I asked you to forget for the moment what I described as an emergent political-economic critique of the alliance between government and development interests during the late New Order period. Recent events in Bali provide little opportunity for such practices of forgetting, time-honoured though they have become in Ubud culture over the past century. For the first time in the lives of most Balinese, they are being reminded daily by events beyond their control of the inexorably political dimension of their engagement in wider spheres of cultural and economic exchange. There are signs that these reminders are beginning to make themselves felt even in the apolitical world of Balinese art.

In the final weeks of the nineteenth century, Ck. Sukawati was engaged in negotiations with a foreign power which brought to an end a half-century of local political violence in South Bali, ushering in the more subtle violence of the *Pax Neerlandica* and the ensuing separation of culture from politics in Ubud. Precisely 100 years later, while the descendants of Ck. Sukawati rule over their kingdom of cultural tourism and as the twentieth century drew to its media-mediated close, another Balinese hero was likewise engaged in negotiations to bring together various parties, local and global in the interests of peace. Made Wianta, an artist of trans-Bali reputation, organized a massive public performance event to celebrate World Peace Day on December 10, at Padanggalak beach, about midway between the downstream end of Ck. Sukawati's domain and the place where the Dutch invasion force landed in 1906. His aim was to use the power of art, in the form of a giant white flag drawn by helicopters, to publicize the cause of peace.

This public event was preceded by a two-day seminar at the Arts Centre in Denpasar on the theme 'Art and Peace'. Although neither Nelson Mandela nor the Dalai Lama was able to attend as hoped, the speakers included a cosmopolitan array of semi-celebrity status. One made the explicit link between the policies of the New Order government and the 'destruction' of local cultures, the 'heart or spirit (*roh*)' of which is none other than art (BP, 9 December 1999b). Another speaker made the link in more general terms: that 'art cannot be separated from political priorities, because art is often used as a tool to achieve [political] ends' (BP, 10 December 1999). Yet another drew an analogy between the 'last' (at least until the next) great royal cremation, of A. A. G. Agung of Puri Gianyar,[19] in which 'tens of thousands' of people engaged in a massive public ritual of annihilation by fire, and the riots: 'Perhaps the amuk massa is a form of prayer? Can this form of violence [...] transform into peace? [...] it can happen only once [...] and Bali can hope for peace and safety as before' (BP, 11 December 1999).[20]

NOTES

1 Ceremonies of broadly similar *krisis*-averting intent were also organized by local government and PHDI at various major temples around Bali at this time. (Bali Post, 10, 11 and 27 June 1998).

2 This conception of economic causation is explained in my thesis (MacRae 1997: 144–45).

3 Figures for 1998 (obtained from Kantor Kepolisian Sektor Ubud) were down by about 16 per cent and had continued to fall each month until November 1999. The streets, shops and restaurants were obviously much quieter than normal, traders were unanimous in their belief that this was so and the operators of small tourist-dependent businesses were showing signs of distress.

4 This interiorization of repression began in the state education system, where students were left with a profound sense of social unease and embarrassment at the public discussion of religious or ethnic differences within the nation (Kadek Newson, personal communication).

5 As an anonymous reviewer pointed out, a hypothetical Indonesian ethnographer in Australia might reasonably draw parallel conclusions about the role of irreligious hedonistic materialism in Australian culture.

6 I am aware that this reference may be offensive to some readers, the more so for its lack of substantiation. It is based upon my own impressions of one night as a single male in Kuta in November 1999 which confirmed anecdotal evidence from a number of expatriate residents, an article in Jakarta Post (November 1999) on the incidence of disguised prostitution among young Balinese women running *warung* in Denpasar, and subsequent reading of press reports from various sources.

7 All newspaper articles cited herein are listed in the references under 'Bali Post' or 'Jakarta Post'.

8 It has been suggested to me (Tim Behrend, personal communication, 2000) that I should be wary of dismissing the concept of 'amuk' as an explanatory category, deeply ingrained as it is in Javanese and Balinese thought. In this context, however, a publication in Bahasa Indonesia, catering primarily to the literate middle-class, whose overt cultural traditionalism is mixed with rational-modernist attitudes to such primal excesses of village religion as trance possession, the reference seems clearly to be a label serving a categorizing and sensationalizing rather than an explanatory function.

9 The 'haunting sense of incompleteness so pervasive of New Order cultural discourse has the effect [...] of motivating an almost endless production of offerings, a constant reiteration of things cultural, in an attempt to make-up for what may have been left out in the process of recovering tradition' (Pemberton 1994: 11).

10 In Ubud, the teacher runs an ashram and a restaurant, the partners in which told me that they had been greatly embarrassed by his statements from which they were at considerable pains to disassociate themselves. They hinted also that he would be well-advised not to show his face in Ubud for some time.

11 This chapter is based primarily upon fieldwork in Ubud, in 1993–1994 and 1996, which is reported in detail in my PhD Thesis (MacRae 1997). This research was conducted under the auspices of L.I.P.I. with the local sponsorship of Dr I Ny. Erewan of U.N.U.D. and financial assistance from the University of Auckland and an APEC Research Scholarship. Some of the matters discussed here were developed in the context of conversations with many people including I W. Darta of Ubud, A. A. Ardi and Diana Darling of Tegalsuci, Melody Kemp of Sayan and the late I G. M. Sumung and his sons. I am grateful also to Hildred Geertz and Adrian Vickers for comments on the relevant parts of my thesis and to three anonymous reviewers for the publisher.

12 I record here my debt to this person while leaving him or her anonymous.

13 There are in fact other significant collections around Ubud, most notably that of the Rudana Gallery in Peliatan, but these three are generally acknowledged to be the main ones and their owners are all major players in the political-economy of Ubud. The story of the wonderfully Balinese blend of competition and cooperation between them remains to be told.

14 A partial exception to this pattern is M. Budi's *President Suharto and his wife visit Bali* (1987). At first glance the form is essentially the same but the effect is less harmonious, more subtly sinister. The President is standing, dressed in an ill-tailored western suit of lurid pinkish hue, on a podium addressing an audience neither visible nor implied in picture. The only local people visible are a two farmers trying to get on with the business of supporting themselves while a reporter tries to interview them. Dancers and gamelan perform and the first lady, in traditional costume, is amused by the frog dancers. Po-faced dignitaries sit in a pavilion behind the president. Security guards in full commando gear swarm everywhere. A telecommunications tower is erected on top of a semi-Balinese looking building. The background is mountain landscape. This painting, the only one of which I am aware which addresses contemporary political issues in a way which leaves room for critical interpretation, would appear to offer a point of departure for a student in search of such a hidden tradition in modern Balinese painting.

15 There were, according to an authoritative bibliography (Stuart-Fox 1992) 1151 books and articles on the arts in Bali published between 1920 and 1990.

16 Hildred Geertz in a recent analysis of a series of paintings from Batuan, although not addressing matters of political economy directly, appears to suggest that they refer problems of the ordinary world back to the deeper conflicts of *niskala* forces (1995: 2). This would appear to be a fruitful point of departure for further research on the arts.

17 This phrase translates literally as something like 'cured of politics' or 'learnt their lesson about politics'. I was not familiar with it at the time, so he illustrated it with the metaphor of a child's experience with fire or hot water, which suggests the English phrase 'getting ones fingers burnt'.

18 This rather generalized collective portrait is the result of many unsuccessful attempts to cajole young people into discussion of political matters. It is in stark contrast with the attitude of young people in Java and to a lesser extent in Denpasar. The few exceptions in Ubud were people who were, or had been students in Denpasar or further afield.

19 The speaker was presumably aware that this cremation was heavily subsidized by the sale of the TV rights, but as a non-Balinese he may not have been aware of the widespread belief in Bali that the ritual workers (*pengayah*) for this cremation were paid for their services.

20 This is not an isolated example of an emerging repoliticization of art. As Brita Maklai (1995) argues, there has been a minor but growing counter-current of political commentary in Indonesian art throughout the New Order period. Not surprisingly this has swelled considerably since 1998. Early in 1999, Rucina Ballinger (personal communication, 30 April 1999) reported explicit messages about the national political situation in a performance by the state-sponsored STSI academy. Later in the year, the *Far Eastern Economic Review* (see under Cohen 1999a,b) reported on the new political themes being embraced by artists in Yogyakarta, arguably the epicentre of Indonesian painting. Meanwhile, at one of the art museums of Ubud, another famous artist from Sukawati itself, Nyoman Erewan, was staging a performance of ritual-like quality which at least one critic interpreted as an indirect commentary upon the recent political violence (BP, 11 December 1999b).

REFERENCES

Acciaioli, G. (1985) 'Culture as Art: From Practice to Spectacle in Indonesia'. *Canberra Anthropology*, 8(1&2): 148–72.
Anderson, B. (1990) 'The Idea of Power in Javanese Culture'. In *Language and Power: Exploring Political Cultures in Indonesia*, Ithaca and London: Cornell University Press.

Bali Post Articles

2.6.98 Ribuan Turis Batal Kunjungi Kintamani.
10.6.98 Inflasi di Bali 34,84 Persen.
11.6.98 Sembahyang agar Krisis Berakhir.
27.6.98 Besok, Umat Hindu Adakan Upacara 'Peneduh Jagat'.
22.10.99 Bali Lumpuh Total: Akibat Amuk Massa.
25.10.98 (a) Soal Bali Rusuh, tak perlu cari kambing hitam (Warung Global Interaktif); (b) Jangan salahkan rakyat.
2.11.99 (a) Pariwisata Bali. Hikmah di Balik 'Musibah'; (b) Lemahnya Kontribusi Agama Dalam Kehidupan Berpolitik. (Mimbar Hindu, Drs. I Ketut Wiana).
4.11.99 (a) Tujuh Persen Wisman alihkan Tujuan ke Thailand; (b) Kerusuhan dan Rasa Termarginalisasi (Telewisata, Pitana); (c) Ada 'Nilai Baru' Rusak Kerukunan di Bali.
8.11.99 (a) Muspida – Adat Sepakat Provokator Diusut Tuntas; (b) Kamis Kelabu, Umat Hindu mestinya Malu (Bias Bali, Wayan Supartha).
9.11.99 (a) Gubernur: Itu Trik Negara Pesaing; (b) KUD di Bali Rugi Rp 8 Milyar Lebih; (c) Desa Adat masih ampuh Cegah Gangguan Luar; (d) Idealnya Tim Pencari Fakta Dibentuk Pemerintah.
10.11.99 (a) Keampuhan Desa Adat, tergantung para 'Manggala'? (Warung Global Interaktif – 'Bali Post'; (b) Semua Pihak harus Terlibat Amankan Bali (Fenomena); (c) Keamanan, bukan Tanggung Jawab Desa adat; (d) Mengapa orang Bali selalu Disalahkan?
11.11.99 Amuk Massa, Akumulasi Kekecewaan Rakyat Bali (Dari Warung Interaktif – 'Bali Post').
13.11.99 Amuk Massa bukan Tanggungjawab Pelaku Pariwisata.
15.11.99 Amuk Massa II mungkin Muncul lagi di Bali.
19.11.99 Saya Melihat Wajah Kemunafikan Orang Bali.

23.11.99 (a) Pasar Australia Diharapkan Normal Tahun Depan; (b) Mengapa Kita Kehilangan Wibawa dan Kepercayaan (Mimbar Hindu, Drs. I Ketut Wiana); (c) Adat, Kegelisahan Desa dan Cepaknya Negara (oleh Degung Santikarma).

25.11.99 Bali Perlu Desain Investasi untuk Tarik Investor 'Non-Tourism'.

28.11.99 (a) Amuk Massa, Akumulasi Kekecewaan terhadap Hukum; (b) Semua Pihak perlu Mawas Diri.

29.11.99 Mohan Datang Meramal, Umat Hindu Wajib Introspeksi.

1.12.99 (a) Mencegah Amuk Massa (oleh Ir. Jero Wacik, S. E.); (b) Cenderung Kedepankan Konflik (Figur).

2.12.99 (a) Amuk Massa Bali bukan Lantaran Mega tak Jadi Presiden; (b) Segera Rehab Korban Amuk Massa; (c) Upaya Preventif Kasus Rusuh Masal (oleh Yani Nur Syamsu).

3.12.99 Amuk Massa Babak Ke-2, Mungkinlah?

7.12.99 'Tawur Agung' di Badung.

9.12.99 Citra Bali yang Damai (Telewisata, Pitana).

10.12.99 Seni tak bisa Lepas dari Kepentingan Politik.

11.12.99 (a) Kesenian, Pengikat Nilai-nilai di Masyarakat (Kultur); (b) Erewan Pentaskan 'Kremasi Waktu'.

13.12.99 Pelaku amuk Massa 21 Oktober segera Diadili.

Bateson, G. and Mead, M. (1942) *Balinese Character: A photographic Analysis*, New York: N.Y. Academy of Sciences.

Bowen, J. (1986) 'On the Political Construction of *Gotong-Royong* in Indonesia'. *Journal of Asian Studies*, XLV(3): 545–61.

Cohen, M. (1999a) 'Artistic Freedom: The Art of the Possible'. *Far Eastern Economic Review*, 16 December 1999.

Cohen, M. (1999b) 'Artistic Freedom: Art against the machine'. *Far Eastern Economic Review*, 16 December 1999.

Covarrubias, M. (1994) *Island of Bali*, New York: Knopf.

Darling, J. and Rhodius H. (1980) *Walter Spies and Balinese Art*, Zurphen: Terra.

Djelantik, A. A. M. (1990) *Balinese Paintings*, Singapore: Oxford University Press. Second Edition.

Forge, A. (1980) 'Balinese Religion and Indonesian Identity'. In J. J. Fox *et al.* (eds), *Indonesia: Australian Perspectives*, Canberra: ANU Press, pp. 221–34.

Fussell, P. (1980) *Abroad: British Literary Travelling between the Wars*, New York: Oxford University Press.

Geertz, H. (1994) *Images of Power: Balinese Paintings made for Gregory Bateson and Margaret Mead*, Honolulu: University of Hawaii Press.

Hilberry, R. (1979) *Reminiscences of a Balinese Prince*, Honolulu: University of Hawaii. Southeast Asia Paper No. 14.

Hooker, V. M. and Dick, H. (1995) 'Introduction'. In V. M. Hooker (ed.), *Culture and Society in New Order Indonesia*, Kuala Lumpur: Oxford University Press.

Jakarta Post Articles

25.11.99. Travel agents look to calm after the storm (Travel Agent, by I Wayan Juniarta).

Kam, G. (1993) *Perceptions of Paradise: Images of Bali in the Arts*, Ubud: Yayasan Dharma Seni.

Kertonegoro, M. (1987) *The Guard of Ubud Corner*, Ubud: Harkat Foundation.

Kipp, R. (1993) *Dissociated Identities: Ethnicity, Religion and Class in an Indonesian Society*, Ann Arbor: University of Michigan Press.

MacRae, G. S. (1992) *Tourism and Balinese Culture*, University of Auckland: Unpublished M. Phil. Thesis.

MacRae, G. S. (1997) *Economy, Ritual and History in a Balinese Tourist Town*. University of Auckland: Unpublished Ph.D. Thesis.

Maklai, B. (1995) 'New Streams, New Visions: Contemporary art since 1966'. In M. Hooker (ed.), *Culture and Society in New Order Indonesia*, Kuala Lumpur: Oxford University Press.

Pemberton, J. (1994) *On the Subject of 'Java'*, Ithaca and London: Cornell University Press.

Pollman, T. (1990) 'Margaret Mead's Balinese: The fitting symbols of the American Dream'. *Indonesia*, 49: 1–35.

Robinson, G. (1995) *The Dark Side of Paradise: Political Violence in Bali*, Ithaca and London: Cornell University Press.

Roosevelt, A. (1985) 'Introduction'. In H. Powell (ed.), *The Last Paradise*, Oxford: Oxford University Press.

Steedly, M. M. (1993) *Hanging Without a Rope: Narrative Experience in Postcolonial Karoland*, Princeton: Princeton University Press.

Santikarma, D. (1999) 'Bali's peaceful reputation suffers a blow ahead of 2000'. *Jakarta Post*, 28 October 1999.

Stuart-Fox, D. (1992) *Bibliography of Bali: Publications from 1920 to 1990*, Leiden: KITLV Press.

Vickers, A. (1989) *Bali: A Paradise Created*, Harmondsworth (U.K.): Penguin Books.

Wiener, M. (1999) 'Making Local History in New Order Bali: Public culture and the politics of the past'. In R. Rubinstein and L. Connor (eds), *Staying Local in the Global Village: Bali in the Twentieth Century*, Honolulu: University of Hawaii Press.

Williamson, J. (1978) *Decoding Advertisements*, publisher unknown.

4   Reflections on literature and politics in Bali

The development of Lekra, 1950–1966

I Nyoman Darma Putra

The arts and literature in Bali have not always constituted a sphere of life divorced from politics (see MacRae, Chapter 3, this volume). One of the untold tales of modern Bali which can illustrate this fact, is the fate of the leftist artists and writers of the period between 1950 and 1966. Nor is Balinese art likely to remain as politically silent as it has been during Suharto's New Order period. As Bali experiences the dramatic changes that have been sweeping the whole of Indonesia since 1998, the role artists can play in shaping public and state discourses has become a matter of public interest and discussion. In view of this change, it is important now to re-examine areas of history and art history that have been hidden by the repressive measures of the New Order or obscured by its particular politics of representation.

In this chapter, I attempt to sketch the development of Lekra in Bali, a subject which is crucial to our understanding of the development of Balinese Indonesian literature, but has received no critical attention in the past. Lekra (*Lembaga Kebudayaan Rakyat*), 'The Institute of People's Culture', was a cultural organization affiliated to the Indonesian Communist Party (PKI). I begin my analysis of Lekra by describing its development in Bali from the early 1950s, Bali's national contribution, and the key figures of the movement. This is followed by a discussion of the clash between Lekra Bali and its local rivals. I will also discuss how 'left' and 'right' wing writers both articulated ideas about Balinese society in an idiom of political ideology and used their literary works as a vehicle of propaganda.

Many discussions of the rise and the fall of Lekra (Teeuw 1967, 1996; Aveling 1970; Ismail 1972; Maier 1974; Foulcher 1969, 1986; Mohamad 1988) focus only on the activities of the organization in Jakarta, the centre of authority, and therefore have overlooked its development at a regional level. A partial exception is a study by Sutedja-Liem on Nyoman Rastha Sindhu, a 1960s Balinese writer, which discusses the development of Indonesian literature in Bali at that time, but deals only very briefly with the issue of Lekra and its opponents.[1] Apart from trying to sketch

the development of Lekra in Bali, the present study also hopes to contribute to the study of the history of modern Indonesian literature. The
broader aim is to show how local Balinese intellectuals dealt with the
national political crisis of the 1950s and 1960s, and how this history is
becoming relevant again in the context of the current crisis.

A lack of source materials is a common problem for studies on the
political and cultural conflicts of this period. Following the failed Communist
coup and violent counter coup of 1965, materials or publications that
were considered to contain elements of Marxist or Communist propaganda
were withdrawn from circulation. Some were collected and burnt, and
the remainder were made inaccessible. The present study is based on
materials published in local periodicals such as *Bhakti* and *Damai* from
the early 1950s, *Suara Indonesia* or *Suluh Marhaen* (which later became *Bali
Post*), and *Angkatan Bersendjata* (which became *Nusa Tenggara* or *Nusa*).[2]
I also draw on a number of literary works by Balinese writers in national
leftist publications, such as *Harian Rakjat* and *Zaman Baru*. The local
left-wing newspaper, *Bali Dwipa*, and the magazine *Lontar*, published in
Denpasar before the coup, are not available for analysis.[3] Interviews with
writers and political activists, however, were conducted to fill these gaps
in the written record.

THE DEVELOPMENT OF LEKRA IN BALI

Lekra Bali was formally established in January 1961, when the organization held its first regional conference (*konferensi daerah*) in Denpasar.[4]
Preparation for the formation of the organization may have taken place
several months before the actual conference, but it seems that a local
Lekra branch did not exist before 1960. An account by former Lekra
writer, Putu Oka Sukanta (born in North Bali in 1939), stating that
Lekra did not yet exist in 1959 supports this hypothesis.[5] Compared to
the national establishment of Lekra on 17 August 1950 in Jakarta and of
other regional branches, Lekra Bali was far behind.

Although the formal establishment of Lekra Bali took place more than
a decade later than that of Lekra groups elsewhere, this does not mean
that Bali was free of the influences of left-wing cultural and political
movements. Since the 1920s, when the ideas of Communism first became
known in Indonesia, there had always been an intimate connection
between the development of left-wing ideas in Java and Bali. Communist
ideas were first introduced to Bali in the early 1920s by Javanese teachers
through a social organization called Soerapati. Lead by Atmodjo Koesoemo,
himself a school teacher, Soerapati began its movement from southern
Bali, where it established branches in Denpasar and Tabanan. It later
expanded to North Bali to some small villages such as Munduk, Gesing
and Gobleg.[6]

Initially Soerapati was successful in attracting followers because it re-interpreted the philosophical values of the classical epics Ramayana, Sutasoma and Bharathayudha, popular among Balinese, for use in its campaigns. Followers of the organization were school teachers, ordinary people, as well as members of the upper castes. The early activities of these leftist groups ran smoothly and were more or less out of sight of the Dutch and mainstream Balinese society. When the Dutch did become aware of the potential threat posed by Soerapati, in the mid-1920s, they banned the organization and sent Atmodjo Koesoemo back to Java.

The early spread of the Communist movement in Buleleng is also noted by Takashi Shiraishi (1990: 283). His brief note is based on an account of the Muslim-Marxist Haji Misbach, leader of the struggle in Java, who called in Buleleng (on his way to an exile in Irian Jaya) in 1924. Misbach is quoted as saying that there were 'Communists already there' (see also Vickers 1996: 18).

The way Balinese intellectuals responded to Marxist ideas, socialism and communism can be traced in debates published in periodicals such as *Surya Kanta* and *Bali Adnyana* in the 1920s, *Djatajoe* in the 1930s, and *Bhakti*, *Damai* and *Suara Indonesia/Suluh Marhaen* in the 1950s and 1960s. I shall briefly describe the shifting focus of these debates.

In the 1920s, debates about socialist ideas revolved around the focal issue of caste. The Surya Kanta organization and its publication of the same name (*Surya Kanta*) were predominantly supported by low caste people, and completely rejected the caste system because of its unfairness to commoners (*wong jaba*) in practical life. *Bali Adnyana*, the mouthpiece of upper caste (*triwangsa*) groups, by contrast, strongly defended the caste system, saying that the caste system had been and still was the essence of Balinese religion and culture (see Pitana 1997). Surya Kanta's ideas of enhancing the status of low caste people to the same level as upper caste people was considered by *Bali Adnyana* as a move to create a 'class-less as well as caste-less society' (*sama rata sama rasa*) in the Communist sense, but with a Balinese twist. Surya Kanta was also accused by the editors of *Bali Adnyana* of having a connection with the Communist organization Soerapati, but provided no evidence to support this claim. Such accusations probably arose because the key figures of both organizations were mostly school teachers.[7] *Bali Adnyana* encouraged Balinese to be aware of the 'Red Peril' (*bahaya merah*) that would put at risk the very foundations of Balinese culture and religion (see Robinson 1995: 34). During the 1930s and the revolutionary period, while Indonesians concentrated on the nationalist movement against colonial oppression, this issue of a 'red peril' was less frequently discussed.[8]

In newly independent Indonesia, however, the influence of Marxist ideas not only became central to intellectual discourse in published debates, but expanded into more concrete political movements. The personal and political attention President Sukarno paid to Bali (his mother was Balinese) – as shown by his frequent visits to the island either alone or accompanying guests such as heads of foreign countries – may have encouraged the PKI to establish a presence on the island as early as 1953 (Robinson 1995: 209). From then on, a number of other leftist organizations were formed in Bali, such as *Pemuda Rakjat* (People's Youth) and *Ikatan Pemuda Peladjar Indonesia* ('Indonesian Youth and Student Association' or IPPI), both as branches of national organizations. These organizations closely supported one another, as can be seen in the strong advocacy given by the Youth and Student Association to the Lekra writer, Made Serinata, when he was expelled from his school because he had published critical articles in *Harian Rakjat* and *Bhakti*.[9] Such cooperation in response to specific situations was to lead eventually to the formal establishment of regional left-wing cultural organizations in the years to come.

On 24 January 1954, a number of artists in North Bali, predominantly painters, established an organization known as the *Seniman Rakyat* (Artists of the People). The name of the organization as such was of the style promoted by Lekra, as it gave emphasis to 'The People' (*rakyat*). A declaration of Seniman Rakjat's aims was announced in *Bhakti* (15/2/1954: 12), with N. Wisade (a painter and illustrator for *Bhakti*) as chairman, P. Swendra as secretary, Ida Bagus Swela as treasurer, and Krinu, K. Gede, G. Artana and G. Putu as general assistants. Putu Shanty, who later became active in the leadership of Lekra Bali and Lekra Indonesia (see below), was not yet included in the committee of Seniman Rakyat. But given the fact that the announcement of the foundation of this organization was made in *Bhakti*, of which he was editor-in-chief, his support was implicit.

There is no documentary information available about the development and activities of the Seniman Rakyat. Putu Aswin, a contributor and distributor of *Bhakti*, in an interview in 1999, revealed that the group was established by left-wing activists, and invited young artists who did not know much about politics to become members as well as leaders of the organization.[10] The establishment of the organization was announced in *Bhakti*, a magazine accused of being aligned with Communist groups.[11]

Founded by a number of veterans of the struggle for Indonesian independence in Singaraja in the middle of 1952, *Bhakti* was initially meant to be a medium for maintaining the spirit of 'struggle' (*perjuangan*) among veteran members and supporting the needs of their families. It is important to note that although it was founded by veterans of the revolution, *Bhakti* was not an official magazine of veteran organizations like *Damai*, published formally by 'The Foundation of Veterans of the Revolution' (*Yayasan Kebhaktian Pejuang*) in Denpasar between 1953 and 1955. Putu Shanty, a young writer who at that time had already published a number of creative writings in national publications, was appointed as editor-in-chief of *Bhakti*.[12]

The accusation that *Bhakti* was aligned with left-wing groups was probably based on its contents and the orientation of its editors and contributors. The magazine published a number of articles, poems and short stories that did contain elements of Marxist ideology. It also repeatedly published a cartoon featuring a dialogue between a peasant holding a sickle and a labourer holding a hammer, both symbols of Communism. Putu Shanty, as the editor in chief of *Bhakti*, often published his own articles and creative writings (poems, short stories and plays) which were mainly concerned with poverty, class or caste conflict and atheism. Other occasional contributors, such as Suprijo, L. F. Risakota and Pramudya Ananta Tur, are generally considered to have been left-wing activists.

It seems that *Bhakti* tried hard to deny the accusation of being left-wing, let alone Communist. In one of its editorials, *Bhakti* denied the accusation, citing in support its motto 'a public magazine and not a party', which was boldly written on the front cover. This motto was revised from the initial one that read 'a popular public magazine' (*madjalah masarakat umum populer*).

The editorial also emphasized that the magazine remained open to contributors from all political groups rather than being the mouthpiece of the PKI, even though it did publish anti-capitalist and anti-feudalist articles.[13] Indeed, some former reporters of *Bhakti*, including Wedastra Suyasa, N. Malaya and the magazine director K. Widjana, later became key figures in the PNI, the Indonesian Nationalist Party, which was a direct political opponent of the PKI. Although not all of its editors and reporters were thus leftist, in 1982 the Balinese critic Made Sukada insisted that *Bhakti* was a PKI magazine.[14] In an interview in 1999, the former director of *Bhakti*, K. Widjana, himself a veteran of the revolution, confirmed that *Bhakti* had shown a tendency to 'favour' left-wing political ideology and that this tendency had caused a decline in the number of its subscribers.[15] Suffering from financial problems, *Bhakti* stopped publishing in July 1954.

When *Bhakti* ceased publication, Shanty continued working at the Bali Language Centre and remained active in the field of literature, together with some of his close relatives, such as Oka Derty and Ketut Putu. They later became local key figures for Lekra in North Bali as well as leaders of the regional branch of Lekra Bali. Through poetry reading competitions and other literary activities, they recruited young writers such as Putu Oka Sukanta, who went on to become prominent among Lekra writers in Bali.

When the capital city of Bali moved from Singaraja to Denpasar toward the end of the 1950s, the development of Lekra moved part of its operations to Denpasar as well, under key figures such as Harto Setiyadi (a lecturer), Wardjana (a student) and Nour Bhakti (a dancer). Putu Oka Sukanta also moved to Denpasar in 1959, where he set up his theatre group 'Gong Kronik', held public performances, and broadcasted a literary program on the state radio station RRI.[16] Other than members of Lekra, members of CGMI, a student association affiliated to the PKI, also dominated Gong Kronik.[17]

The establishment of Lekra Bali received significant support from the Governor of Bali at the time, Anak Agung Bagus Sutedja, who was very close to President Sukarno. It was President Sukarno who selected him for a second term as Governor of Bali in 1958 despite Sutedja gaining fewer votes than the PNI candidate Nyoman Mantik, in the regional assembly election (Cribb 1990: 245; Robinson 1995: 213).[18] This was in keeping with Sukarno's agenda to replace liberal democracy with his own brand of 'Guided Democracy' toward the end of the 1950s. This move enabled President Sukarno to accumulate power in his own hands, while simultaneously re-endorsing his old formula *Nasakom* (Nationalism, Religion and Communism), a political strategy designed to reconcile the interests of the three main political factions at that time. Every level of social and political structure and activity had to comprise elements of *Nasakom* through a political strategy known as *Nasakomisasi*. Given that Sukarno was close to the PKI and Lekra, *Nasakomisasi* often aided infiltration by the PKI (Robinson 1995: 230).

As a Sukarno-man, Governor Sutedja did not only show his sympathy to the PKI but also made every effort to guarantee any activities of left-wing organizations met with success. While Sutedja never formally became a member of the PKI (Robinson 1995: 209), there is no doubt that he was a leftist and always fully supportive of left-wing groups. At the same time, he often discouraged the activities of right-wing groups. In an article published in 1999, Ida Bagus Adnyana Manuaba, a former right-wing youth activist in the 1960s and the head of Indonesian Scholars Association of Bali (Ikatan Sarjana Indonesia Bali), discloses how Governor Suteja disrupted activities which were not held under the *Nasakom* banner (1999: 2–3). Tension between left- and right-wing groups grew due to this favouritism. As it will become clear in the rest of the discussion, the notion of 'left-' and 'right-wing' did not constitute a blanket category in the political and culture landscape of Bali, nor at the national level.

LEKRA BALI AND ITS NATIONAL CONTRIBUTION

Although it was formed about a decade later than the head office of Lekra in Jakarta, Lekra Bali played an important role in the history of the organization both at a national level and in its international network. Just one year after its establishment, Lekra Bali hosted two important national meetings on the island. The first was the 'National Lekra Conference' (*Konferensi Nasional Lekra*) held on 25–27 February 1962 at the Bali Hotel, Denpasar. Following the 1959 Solo Congress, Lekra had only held small meetings, and the Bali Conference was the first national meeting in the 1960s to be held outside Java.

The Bali Conference was attended by the PKI and Lekra national leaders, Lekra branch representatives from all over Indonesia, representatives of the PKI social organizations, foreign delegates from socialist and communist countries (Democratic Republic of Germany, the Soviet Union, China and Algeria) and foreign journalists. The meeting ended successfully and the participants were satisfied, according to its coverage in *Zaman Baru* and *Harian Rakjat*, the mouthpiece of Lekra and the PKI respectively.

There were specific reasons why Bali had been chosen as the venue for the conference. For Lekra, Bali provided an ideal model for the development of a 'people's culture', which was of great interest to Lekra. The other, more important reason was that the Balinese arts and culture, as Lekra conceived it, had been under threat of Western influence through the tourism industry or other forms of 'neo-colonialism'. Having held the conference in Bali, Lekra hoped not just to showcase an ideal model of 'people's culture' but also to express anti-Western sentiments. The organization had long been concerned with the development of Balinese arts and culture and had made use of it for anti-Western propaganda. In the early 1950s, for example, through the PKI newspaper *Harian Rakjat*, Lekra strongly criticized the exploitation of Balinese artists during their European and US tours, led by English impresario John Coast (1966).[19] During the conference, the participants were invited to visit several 'non-tourist' places and watch folk performances in villages. Surprisingly, the *kecak* dance, a collaborative Balinese and Western performance, was a favourite among the many performances watched by the conference participants. Probably deeply attracted by the *kecak* dance, Njoto, the PKI leader and one of the founders of Lekra, composed 'Variasi Tjak', a propaganda poem, the explicit message of which was to attack imperialism, right-wing groups and feudalism. The poem was published in *Harian Rakjat* (17 March 1962):

Variasi tjak	*Variations of tjak*
Tjak-tjak	Tjak-tjak
tjak-tjak- tjak-tjak	tjak-tjak- tjak-tjak
tjak-tjak	tjak-tjak
tjak-tjak- tjak-tjak	tjak-tjak- tjak-tjak
penari petani menari	dancer farmer dancing
di Blahbatuh sini	here in Blahbatuh village
mata menari perut menari	eyes dancing belly dancing
menuntut merdeka atau nasi	fight for freedom or rice
tjak-tjak	tjak-tjak
tjak-tjak- tjak-tjak	tjak-tjak- tjak-tjak
satu bedil	one gun

satu tjangkul	one hoe
satu bedil	one gun
satu tjangkul	one hoe'
tjak-tjak	tjak-tjak
tjak-tjak-tjak-tjak	tjak-tjak-tjak-tjak
imperialisme	imperialism
kanan baru	the new right[wing]
feodalisme	feudalism
si kepala batu	the thick headed
kita tindju	we smash
satu per satu	one by one
tjak-tjak	tjak-tjak
tjak-tjak-tjak-tjak	tjak-tjak-tjak-tjak
tjak-tjak	tjak-tjak
tjak-tjak-tjak-tjak	tjak-tjak-tjak-tjak

Njoto reiterated the message of the poem in the speech he delivered at the Bali Conference. The speech and the poem were published in *Harian Rakjat* on the same page, a few weeks after the conference.[20]

As the host, Lekra Bali contributed its own interpretation of the issue of anti-imperialism and feudalism in a very interesting way. They performed the dance-drama 'Jayaprana-Layonsari', the tragic story of the murder of an innocent man by the king of Kalianget. The king orders Jayaprana be killed in order to gain access to his beautiful young wife, Layonsari. In the generally accepted version, the king kills himself after failing to secure Layonsari as his future wife.[21] In Lekra's version, however, the people killed the king of Kalianget. By doing so, Lekra wanted to echo the typical left-wing propaganda of anti-feudalism, and to celebrate the victory of the people.[22] Note that this same folk story has been and still is popular among Balinese. In November 2001, for example, the story 'Jayaprana-Layonsari' was performed again in Bali and Jakarta, by Sanggar Kampung Seni Banyuning, a semi-modern theatre group based in Singaraja. This time, the 'Jayaprana-Layonsari' story was evoked as an allegory to the current political crisis and instability in Indonesia. The beautiful Layonsari was depicted as a symbol of power being grabbed by various parties.[23]

The attitude of Balinese artists and writers who fully supported left-wing ideology was reflected in Putu Shanty's paper '*Arahkan Udjung Pena ke Djantung Imperialisme Feodalisme*' (Direct the Tip of Your Pen at the Heart of Imperialism and Feudalism) which he presented at the conference. In this paper, Shanty urged writers to use literary works to attack imperialism and feudalism.[24] He encouraged writers to use social realism themes to expose more of people's daily experiences, and discouraged writers from dealing with romantic subject matters (compare MacRae, Chapter 3, this volume). He argued that literature is not for entertainment but to shape people's character. Shanty's rejection of the universal credo 'art for art's sake' is typical of the left-wing writers of his time.

The other event held in Bali in which Lekra Bali acted as the local organizing committee was the Executive Committee Meeting of African and Asian Writers (Sidang Komite Eksekutif Pengarang Asia-Afrika). This international meeting was held from 16–21 July 1963 and was attended by writers and artists from African and Asian countries as well as national Lekra leaders. Pramudya Ananta Tur and Sitor Situmorang, both left-wing writers, were chairmen of the national committee of this meeting, while Gde Puger, the leader of the PKI Bali, acted as the head of the local committee. This meeting was not exclusively for Lekra members, but the committee and participants from Indonesia and Bali were dominated by left-wing writers and activists. Local right-wing activists and writers, who understood themselves as belonging to the nationalist wing, had no chance to take part in the main event held at the Bali Hotel. To celebrate the event, however, they held a traditional Balinese performance and poetry reading on an open stage in Puputan Badung, just a few hundred meters from the Bali Hotel.[25] The exclusion of nationalist representatives from participation and from the Writers Committee Meeting meant that Surkarno's *Nasakom* principle was not applied as intended. Such exclusion contributed to a growing political polarization between left- and right-wing groups in Bali.

One aim of the international meeting was to emphasize the idea of a 'people's culture' and a 'people's struggle'. Based on Marxist theory, they divided world culture into two parts; the culture of high-class and low-class people. The former dominated and oppressed the latter, who struggled against the former. These two cultures were often identified in an Indonesian context as colonialist's culture as opposed to the colonized people's culture. The Afro-Asian Writers backed the 'people's struggle' against colonialism (Moeljanto and Ismail 1995: 302–3). Pramudya Ananta Tur, in his speech as the chairman of national committee, illustrated the clash between colonizers and the colonized with examples from Balinese history. He mentioned Surapati, a Balinese born hero who fought for the country to overthrow colonialism in the seventeenth century.[26] Gde Puger, the local committee chair, also proudly pointed to the heroism of the Balinese people when they defended the island from the Dutch colonial army in wars, from the Bandjar War (1868) to the Puputan of Klungkung (in 1908).[27] It may be that the examples of how the Balinese struggled against colonialism in the past were used more as anti-colonial propaganda than as an acknowledgement of the role the Balinese had played in the history of Indonesia's struggle for independence.

Like the National Lekra Conference a year earlier, the Afro-Asian Writers Meeting in Bali ended successfully. To extend their gratitude to the Balinese people, particularly the victims of the Gunung Agung eruption in 1963, the delegation donated 205,500 Rupiah.[28] Most importantly for the development of Lekra Bali, the National Lekra Conference and the Afro-Asian Writers Meeting provided a significant opportunity for Balinese writers and political activists to develop national and international contacts. After these two meetings, Putu Shanty and Putu Oka Sukanta, for example, began to be involved in Lekra at the national level and thus contributed to the national integration of the organization's branch in Bali.[29]

LEKRA BALI: KEY FIGURES AND THEIR WRITINGS

Putu Shanty and Putu Oka Sukanta, both from Singaraja, were prominent Lekra members from Bali who were active at local as well as national levels of the organization. In the following section, their life and works will be briefly discussed along with those of other, less popular left-wing writers such as Made Serinata, Gde Wardjana, Ketut Putu, Oka Derty and Gde Mangku.

Nothing has ever been written about Putu Shanty. In his *Bibliography of Indonesian Literature in Journals*, Kratz (1988) only lists a few of Shanty's works in national publications while omitting details of his works published in *Bhakti*. From as early as 1950, Shanty produced dozens of creative writings and many articles on topics ranging from literary criticism, culture and religion, to history and politics, for both local and national publications such as *Siasat, Indonesia, Mimbar Indonesia, Zaman Baru* and *Bhakti*.

Shanty was born in 1924 in Jombang (East Java), where his father worked as a mechanic and later as a chauffeur for Dutch officers. He went to primary school in Singaraja, but could not continue his education because his parents were poor. Most of Shanty's immediate relatives were writers and intellectuals like Wayan Bhadra (his uncle), M. Kirtya, Ketut Putu and Oka Derty (his cousins). His relationship with these relatives, with Dutch intellectuals such as Dr R. Goris and Jef Last, and with the nationally renowned Balinese writer Pandji Tisna, made it possible for Shanty to develop his knowledge and writing skill regardless. Above all, he was self-educated.

While working as editor in chief for *Bhakti* between 1952 and 1954, Shanty often went to Jakarta for conferences. He took this opportunity to visit several key national writers in the capital, many of whom became well-known left-wing writers later on, including Sitor Situmorang and Utuy Tatang Sontani. His contacts in Jakarta, particularly to left-wing groups, became a general influence on literary life in North Bali. When the leader of the PKI, Sobron Aidit, celebrated the death of the most famous and yet controversial Indonesian poet Chairil Anwar in Jakarta in 1953, Shanty held a parallel celebration in Bali.[30] This celebration, among other things, was marked by the staging of the play 'Awal dan

Mira' (Awal and Mira) written by Utuy T. Sontani, a Sundanese writer whose works centred on class conflict (Aveling 1970: 4). Later Shanty became deeply involved in Lekra at the local and national level, which granted him, Oka Derty and others the chance of a trip to China and other communist countries in the early 1960s.[31]

Unfortunately, none of Putu Shanty's creative writings are available from the time after these visits to communist and socialist countries. He was very productive during the early 1950s, however. Whilst his poems mainly dealt with personal matters, his concern for poor people and social issues dominated his short stories and dramas. In the short story 'Rentenir' [A moneylender], published in 1954 in the national and local magazines *Mimbar Indonesia* and *Bhakti*, for example, Shanty depicts a conflict between a poor peasant of low caste, I Sukra, and an arrogant money-lender of high caste, I Gusti Gede Kaler. Burdened with debt and unable to pay the high interest to I Gusti Kaler, poor Sukra runs amok and stabs the money-lender in the chest. This story might be read as a representation of both class and caste conflict in Balinese society. This had been a persistent theme in the works of radical Balinese writers since the 1920s, for example, in the play *'Kesetiaan Perempoean'* [Woman's Fidelity] published anonymously in *Surya Kanta* in 1927 (see Bagus 1996; Darma Putra 1998). The similarity between the two works is that both realistically depict the struggle of the low classes against high class people and call for social change in their favour, a typical theme of Marxist writing (Birchall 1977: 96).

Another significant theme often reflected in Shanty's work and that of other North Balinese leftist writers of the 1950s is the attitude of the poor toward religious beliefs and rituals. Shanty's short story *'Kekalahanku yang keempat'* (My fourth defeat) is set in the 1940s and 1950s and tells of a domestic conflict in a poor family who are unable to hold frequent religious rituals because of the high cost.[32] In the husband–wife quarrel, the futility of belief in God is often articulated. This attitude is also clearly expressed in Shanty's drama *'Bangkerut'* (Bankrupt) published in *Bhakti*.[33] Writers such as Putu in their poems and short stories also explored themes which express doubt in the existence of God. Atheism, however, did not fit with the religious attitude of Balinese people in general, and *Bhakti* in promoting it became associated with the promotion of communism.

An example of an explicit exercise in political propaganda is Ananta's poem 'Baji' (The Baby) published on 5 May 1952 in *Bhakti*.[34]

Baji	The baby
Berikan dia setetes susu,	Give him a drop of milk
djangan beri susu banteng	do not give cow's milk
berikan dia susu beruang.	give him bear's milk
Djangan beli dengan dollar,	Do not buy it with dollars

| djangan beli dengan uang dan benda | do not buy it with money or goods |
| belilah dengan tenaga dan kringat. | just buy with energy and sweat |

A sense of contrast is articulated in the poem through the juxtaposition of 'cow's milk' with 'bear's milk' and of 'dollars' with 'energy and sweat'. 'The cow' is the symbol of the Indonesian Nationalist Party, while 'the bear' is the symbol of The Soviet Union; 'dollars' refers to America or the bourgeoisie, while 'energy and sweat' refer to working class people. This contrast is well played out by the poet in order to create a space for political propaganda. In such propaganda, a sympathetic tribute is paid to working class people and socialist countries as opposed to capitalists and imperialist countries.

Putu Oka Sukanta, born in North Bali on 29 July 1939, is another prominent Lekra figure from Bali. His connection with Shanty began when he won a poetry reading competition in North Bali, became the district representative at the provincial level of the same competition, and won the best poetry reading award in Denpasar for the year 1958. From that time onward he was involved in the arts and cultural activities in Singaraja, which led him to join Lekra. After he moved to Denpasar in 1959 and then in early 1960 to Yogyakarta to continue his education, his involvement with left-wing groups became ever more apparent. He returned to Bali in 1962, where he set up a theatre group called 'Gong Kronik' with students and predominant young leftist artists. When he attended the National Lekra Conference in Denpasar in 1962, he met a number of Lekra writers who encouraged him to publish in leftist publications. The more he published in left-wing magazines and newspapers the more popular he became as a writer, and eventually he decided to become a full Lekra member.[35]

Many of Putu Oka's poems (and later his short stories) express his concern for low class people, peasants and labourers, or 'the proletariat' in Marxist terms. Without denying the aesthetic achievement in his poems, many of them are laden with communist political propaganda, as is evident in his poem '*Bali*' published in *Harian Rakjat* in 1964:

Bali	*Bali*
I.	I.
Seperti tangan seorang kawan bergetar	Like the trembling hand of a friend
lidah ombak meraih ujung jariku	the ripples reach for my fingertips
dan angin segar menyambut sebagai	and the cool breeze welcomes me
seorang ibu bapak mengenali anaknya	like a parent recognising a son

selat bali.	the straits of Bali.
anak rantau pulang kampung	the wandering son is coming home
di mana pun juang kan terus berlangsung	but wherever, the struggle will go on
sejenak kuarahkan mata ke bukit-bukit	I turn my eyes toward the hills
pulau jawa	of Java
terbayang perumahan yang kutinggal,	and I see the home I'm leaving behind,
kawan-kawan, rasa cinta	friends, and the love I feel for them
(kw musayid, gunoto, waseso, masih	(KW Musayid, Gunoto, Waseso and
banyak lagi yang menempa	many others who struggle
kusni sulang, afif, timbul masih banyak	Kusni Sulang, Afif, and so many more
lagi kawan sebaya)	of my own age)
ah, kupalingkan muka melepaskannya	ah, I look away and leave them behind
rasa haru memanggil-manggil cepat	emotions calling me to come back
kembali	soon
kendatipun meninggalkan rumah datang	and though I leave one home behind
ke rumah	yet I come home
di mana-mana pun itu rumahku	wherever I go I am at home
di jawa, sumatera, kalimantan, bali dan	in Java, Sumatra, Kalimantam, Bali,
di mana saja	everywhere
sebab ke mana-mana aku	because everywhere I go
pulang kepadanya	there await me
kawan tercinta, perjuangan,	beloved friends, our struggle,
hati dan tekadnya.	devoted and determined
sepanjang jalan.	all along the road.
di celah pohon-pohon randu dan	Between the kapok trees and
gubuk	the village huts
aku berjumpa perumahan baru, yang	I see new settlements where once was
dulunya tanah-tanah rengkah	only cracked and broken ground
angin laut dan gunung	breezes from the sea and the

menyuluk-nyuluk di batang jagung	mountains slip between stalks of corn
betapa ulet kawan-kawan bekerja	how tirelessly comrades are working
– menggarap kemiskinan jadi keyakinan	– turning poverty into conviction
ketakacuhan jadi ketekunan –	indifference into perseverance –
padanya terpancang papan	before them stand the signs of the
partai komunis indonesia	Communist Party of Indonesia

II.	II.
semakin remaja kampung tempatku	My village seems more youthful
pulang	than it did, now as I return
kendatipun ibu jadi nenek,	though mother is now a grandmother
abang jadi ayah	and my elder brother is a father
tapi kebencian telah lebur	but all hatreds have dissolved,
jadi kebangkitan	to become awakening
dan kegairahan berjuang	and apathy has turned into
menyemarakkan partai.	a struggle for the glory of the party
mereka bukan tenaga-tenaga dulu lagi	they are no longer the workers they once used to be
dilihatnya,	they have seen,
di hati kawan-kawan	in the hearts of the comrades
satu pikiran satu tekad	one mind and one determination
bagi kembangapi-kembangapi revolusi	like fireworks of the revolution
mereka komunis	they are communists
yang tak takut mati	who do not fear to die.[36]

Putu Oka Sukanta's concern for the poor and oppressed, particularly in his early works, was expressed in an idiom of Communist Party ideology. He was outside Bali at the time of the 1965–1966 killings, and is one of the few former Lekra writers who are still alive today. Nevertheless, he was jailed for 10 years, from 1966 to 1976. Following his release, he has been able to publish several books of creative writing, some of which have been translated into English. Like most leftist writers, Putu Oka Sukanta is not as well known in Bali and Indonesia as he is overseas, where his works have been well received among scholars and students of Indonesian literature (see Foulcher 1983, 1986; Hill 1985).

Putu Oka has just released (in August 1999) an anthology '*Perjalanan Penyair, Sajak-sajak Kegelisahan Hidup*' (Journey of the Poet, Poems on the

Restlessness of Life) and his first novel *Merajut Harkat* (Knitting Dignity).[37] The novel contains an interesting account of the 1960s events narrated by a leftist activist prior to, and during his time in prison. The poems provide a more diverse and sensitive social and political commentary. Unlike his work in the 1960s, which according to Foulcher (1986: 138) 'is standard Lekra verse of the period', his recent poems are more metaphoric commentaries on current social and political issues. In one of his new poems, Bali is portrayed as 'a slice of world's cake' being consumed by tourists from around the world, and the poet raises the question of what will be left of this cake for the Balinese people.[38] In this poem, too, his sense of anti-capitalism is still very strong.

Other prominent members of Lekra Bali included Ida Wayan Wardjana and Gde Mangku. Wardjana was the general secretary of Lekra Bali and a political figure more so than a writer or artist. In the years 1955–1958, Wardjana studied at the Taman Siswa School in Yogyakarta, where he was able to read widely on communism.[39] He continued his study at the Department of Archeology of Udayana University in Denpasar and was active in left-wing groups. Gde Mangku also studied in Yogyakarta and, after returning to Bali, had dozens of poems published, mostly in *Zaman Baru*. Like Putu Oka and Wardjana, Gde Mangku became acquainted with Lekra figures and publications while in Yogyakarta. Another Balinese writer who published his works in *Zaman Baru* is Anak Agung Ngurah, but no information on him is available.[40] The honorific title of his name 'Anak Agung' suggests he belonged to a high-caste group and, along with other leftists of higher caste status such as Ida Wayan Wardjana, this indicates that leftist activists or supporters also came from the *triwangsa*.

THE MASSACRES OF 1965–1966

Many thousands of Balinese were killed in the wake of the failed communist coup attempt and the bloody counter-coup of 1965 that brought Suharto to power (Cribb 1990: 256; Robinson 1995: 273–74). Among them were many Lekra writers including Putu Shanty, Ketut Putu, Oka Derty, Wardjana and Gde Mangku. Even their immediate family members, many of whom were unable to flee Bali and knew practically nothing about the communist movement, became victims of the mass killings from late 1965 to early 1966. Indeed, many Balinese suffered the same fate although they had no connection whatsoever to Lekra, let alone the PKI.

During the entire 32 years of Suharto's rule (1966–1998), those of *Bhakti*'s contributors who were still alive and were not or no longer imprisoned, faced continuous and systematic persecution, as did their relatives and children. Some were forced to reside outside Bali, in Surabaya or Jakarta, while others took refuge locally in communities that knew nothing about their social and political background. The victims and their families, whether or not they were indeed communists, have been socially isolated and politically disempowered, for example, by barring them from holding positions at universities and in the public service.

The Post-New Order government under Indonesia's first democratically elected President, Abdurrahman Wahid, has shown a much more relaxed approach to former left-wing political activists. The new president, shortly after coming into office, proposed the eradication of the state laws that had banned communist organization and the spreading of communist ideology (Tap XXV/MPRS/1966), prompting a protest from conservative elements even within his own government. Wahid's argument is that communist ideology should be openly available to Indonesians for critical study. Predictably, his proposal received a mixed response. Whatever the outcome may be, a positive consequence is that the issue of communism and of the 1965 massacre of communist activists (along with their innocent family members) is now a topic for open and public discussion.[41]

Following the collapse of Suharto's New Order, several former Lekra writers, including Putu Oka Sukanta, were able to publish their works. Pramudya Ananta Toer's book, which was banned under Suharto, has now become available. The flood of so-called '*buku-buku kiri*' (books with a left-wing orientation) includes the writings of Karl Marx in Indonesian language, which are now sold in many book stores. Toward the down-turn of Wahid's power in mid 2001, however, the selling and distribution of *buku-buku kiri* received negative response from a group who called themselves the 'Anti-Communist Alliance' (*Aliansi Anti Komunis*).[42] Members of this organization took books from book stores by force and burnt them, a repetition of what happened during the purge of Lekra and Communist Party literature after September 1965. Although the current action only lasted for about two weeks, and ended due to protests by intellectuals and discouragement from the government, the threat and fear of further such actions has put a damper on the more relaxed attitude toward communism or Marxism that had been initiated by the Wahid government. It is still hard to predict what will happen with regards to the issue of communism and communist literature in the future. Wahid's successor, Megawati Sukarnoputri (since August 2001) has not yet given serious thought to these matters as she has been concentrating instead on fixing the country's economic crisis and reigning in separatist movements.

Some Indonesians still consider communism as a threat, but much less so now than during the Cold War period. In any case, President Wahid's initiative has provided an opportunity to face the injustice in the persecution of those who were not personally or not at all involved with the communist movement. It is also an opportunity to examine some of the enduring social and political inequalities that allowed communist as well as right-wing political ideologies to gain such tremendous

popularity and divisiveness in Indonesia in the 1960s. For the people of
Bali, some of these issues were and still are local Balinese issues, rather
than national ones.

THE CLASH BETWEEN LEKRA AND THE CULTURAL
MANIFESTO AT THE NATIONAL LEVEL

As I have indicated earlier, the development of modern literature in Bali
was part of a national development centred in Jakarta. Clashes between
left- and right-wing artists that occurred in Jakarta and other parts of
the archipelago during the early 1960s, for example, also happened
in Bali. The underlying economic, political and cultural conflicts in
Balinese society, however, were not the same as in Jakarta or elsewhere.
Before examining the particular local issues which led to clashes
between right- and left-wing artists in Bali, the following section will
briefly outline the key issues in clashes at a national and general
ideological level.

By the early 1960s and with close support from PKI, Lekra became
one of the strongest cultural organizations in Indonesia. Lekra in turn
also lent its support to the movement of the PKI. Literature and arts
were used by these organization as a medium for political propaganda
under their credo 'politics is the commander' (*politik adalah panglima*).
Writers were urged to write in the style of socialist-realism, in accordance
with party ideology. Those who refused were labelled anti-revolutionary.
Some writers who felt uneasy with Lekra's proposition eventually
organized themselves, however, and declared their own position on the
arts and literature, known as *Manifes Kebudayaan* (acronym *Manikebu*) or
'Cultural Manifesto'.

The Cultural Manifesto was declared in October 1963 by a number of
centre- and right-wing artists. The text of the manifesto itself was written
by August 1963, and first published in October 1963 in the literary
magazine *Sastra* (9/10, III, 1963). When it was first declared, the manifesto was signed by 20 artists and writers, including Wiratmo Sukito,
H. B. Jassin, Goenawan Mohamad and Arief Budiman. In a relatively
short time, the Cultural Manifesto received overwhelming support from
writers and artists who had felt uncomfortable about identifying themselves
with the aims of Lekra. The manifesto firmly rejected Lekra's principle
of the subordination of art and culture to politics.

Lekra and the Cultural Manifesto were not entirely at odds, but each
entertained its own views on the role of culture and intellectuals in society.
Lekra imposed a single and monolithic cultural ideal, while the Cultural
Manifesto acknowledged a need for a cultural diversity of ideals (Teeuw
1996: 36). Where Lekra advocated a style of socialist-realism based on
Marxist ideology, the Cultural Manifesto first declared that the Indonesian

state philosophy *Pancasila* would be its ideological inspiration and then ultimately adopted a universal humanist approach (Ismail 1972; Teeuw
1996; Foulcher 1986, 1994; Goenawan Mohamad 1988; Moeljanto and
Ismail 1995). The Cultural Manifesto provoked a stunning response
from many artists throughout Indonesia, particularly those who had
refused to become involved in Lekra, including some writers from Bali
(see below). The Indonesian Army under General A. H. Nasution also
supported the Cultural Manifesto because they were aware of the importance of this group in mobilizing a popular anti-PKI movement (Ismail
1972: 92; Foulcher 1986: 126; Teeuw 1996: 36).

In its ideological battle with the Cultural Manifesto, Lekra received
support from some revolutionary cultural organizations such as LKN
(*Lembaga Kebudayaan Rakyat* or 'Institute of National Culture'), a cultural
organization established in 1959 and affiliated to the nationalist party,
PNI. Personal support also was given by PNI leader and President
Sukarno, who explicitly distanced himself from the Cultural Manifesto.
When the Cultural Manifesto group held the 'Indonesian Writers'
Worker Conference' (*Konferensi Karyawan Pengarang se-Indonesia*, or
KKPI) in Jakarta on 1–7 March 1964, President Sukarno, who had been
invited to the opening ceremony, did not attend. Lekra and the LKN
boycotted the meeting as well, and accused the conference of sparking
an anti-revolutionary spirit (Foulcher 1986: 126). If it had not been for
the support of the Indonesian army, the conference would have failed.
Even so, the participants and supporters of the Cultural Manifesto felt
uneasy because Lekra, LKN and other revolutionary cultural organizations continued their agitation. Finally, on 8 May 1964, President
Sukarno agreed to ban the Cultural Manifesto altogether for political
reasons. He stated:

> The reasons for the ban are that the Political Manifesto [Manipol] of
> the Indonesian Republic as a product of the *Pancasila* has already
> become the broad lines of national direction and cannot possibly be
> accompanied by any other Manifesto, particularly if that other Mani-
> festo shows a hesitant attitude towards the Revolution, and gives the
> impression of standing aloof from it, whereas in the interests of the
> success of the Revolution, all our efforts, also in the field of culture,
> must be on the rails of the Revolution in accordance with the guid-
> ance of Manipol and other materials on indoctrination
> (cited in Foulcher 1969: 445, fn. 47)

The ban on the Cultural Manifesto had a serious impact on its signator-
ies and supporters and was a victory for Lekra and LKN, who used this
opportunity to keep building their domination over organizations in the
arts and literature. From 27 August to 2 September 1964 Lekra held
a 'Conference on Revolutionary Literature and Arts' (*Konferensi Sastra*

(*Warta Bhakti,* 27 Februari 1964)

Figure 4.1 Caricature on the ban of the independent artists of the Manikebu
(*Warta Bhakti,* cover illustration, 27 February 1964).

dan Seni Revolusioner) in Jakarta. The conference was opened by President
Sukarno at the State Palace. The presence of Sukarno and the venue of
the ceremony at the State Palace indicated unreserved presidential support for both Lekra and the PKI (see Figure 4.1).

In short, the battle of left- and right-wing cultural groups at a national
level clearly occurred between Lekra–LKN on one side and the Cultural
Manifesto group on the other. This clash extended to many Indonesian
provinces, where representatives of Lekra and LKN also attacked those
of the Cultural Manifesto group.

CULTURAL CONFLICT IN BALI: LEKRA BALI
AND ITS LOCAL RIVAL

In so far as the clash between Lekra and LKN on the one hand and Cultural Manifesto on the other can be defined as a clash between left-wing and right-wing groups, the supporters of LKN should also be categorized as leftists similar to those of Lekra. In Bali, however, conflict did not occur between Lekra and LKN in one camp and the Cultural Manifesto in the other, but between Lekra and LKN themselves. How could it be that Lekra and the LKN, the national allies which were together supported by Sukarno and shared much of the same revolutionary spirit, became enemies in Bali?

Competition for supremacy among cultural institutions in Bali has had its own history, form and contenders. It began at an institutional level in the early 1960s when some right-wing Balinese and non-Balinese writers and painters such as Raka Santeri (1966), Judha Paniek, IGB Arthanegara, Apip Mustofa Muchamad Lucky Besar, Bambang Sugeng and Theja first established a group of 'literature lovers' called HPS (*Himpunan Peminat Sastra*).[43] It is worth noting that these writers and artists were ethnically plural.

HPS began as an independent group without political affiliation, but later it became an organization whose members supported the right-wing movement and its Cultural Manifesto and stood against Lekra (Darma Putra 1994: 387). In order to gain political support and sponsorship for its members, however, HPS eventually joined the PNI's cultural institution, LKN. There was almost no difference between HPS and LKN-Bali because most of the members of the latter had been members of the earlier group.

Tension with Lekra grew in Bali when some 'right-wing' writers in the HPS/LKN showed open support to the new Cultural Manifesto in Jakarta. Although the Cultural Manifesto was widely published, it was Kirdjomuljo who brought it to the Balinese artists' attention. Kirdjomuljo was a poet and dramatist from Yogyakarta who had spent a period of time in North Bali during the 1950s. In Singaraja, Kirdjomuljo produced a collaborative theatre with local dramatists such as I Gde Dharna and Made Kirtya. Occasionally, he also published his creative writing in *Bhakti*. Young Balinese writers and literary activists such as Raka Santeri and Judha Paniek became interested in the Cultural Manifesto group because they could see that this group would support them in their opposition to Lekra Bali.[44]

Raka Santeri and Judha Paniek (probably also Gde Mangku) received a mandate to promote and popularize the principles of the Cultural Manifesto in Bali.[45] They were also appointed as Bali regional coordinators for the Indonesian Writers' Worker Conference (KKPI) which was going to be held in March 1964 by the Cultural Manifesto and right-wing political groups. As soon as Raka Santeri, Judha Paniek and Gde Mangku showed their support for the Cultural Manifesto they came under serious attack from Lekra. In a meeting in February 1964 in Denpasar, they were forced to sign a petition to repudiate the Cultural Manifesto. The meeting, as they conceived it, was going to be a forum to support the Cultural Manifesto, but in fact, it had been set up by Lekra to attack it.[46] A call to withdraw support from the Cultural Manifesto was also extended by LKN–Jakarta. Such oppression eventually forced Raka Santeri and Judha Paniek to withdraw their support for the Cultural Manifesto. They did not do this just to distance themselves, but also to criticize the anti-revolutionary aspect of the Cultural Manifesto.[47] In short, left-wing groups managed to silence supporters of the Cultural Manifesto in Bali as they had done in other regions.

The suppression of open support for the Cultural Manifesto in Bali, however, did not alleviate the underlying conflict between left- and right-wing cultural institutions. In fact, it contributed to a growing resentment and conflict between Lekra and LKN. The conflict arose as a local dispute between members of the two organizations and, secondly, as an extension of escalating political polarization between the PKI and PNI – the two main political factions which had emerged in Bali since the middle of the 1950s. The tension between the PKI and PNI arose due to the poor implementation of the *Nasakom* principle by President Sukarno and the Governor of Bali, Anak Agung Bagus Sutedja. Both leaders gave more support to the communists than to the nationalists, thus upsetting an already precarious political balance. Evidence of this, in relation to cultural activities, is that the government supported members of left-wing groups to be on the central committee, rather than simply being participants in the Executive Meeting of Afro-Asian Writers held in Bali in 1963. The Nationalist wing, supposedly one element of *Nasakom*, was excluded from this international meeting. Tension between the two groups of artists developed when in return right-wing groups excluded left-wing writers from the activities they organized and dominated.

The political conflict between PKI and PNI was felt throughout Bali, but cultural conflict between Lekra and LKN only occurred in Singaraja and Denpasar, the two biggest cities in Bali.[48] Public speeches and per-formances, such as choirs, *janger* dances, poetry readings (declamation) and modern drama, became the sites of a battle between Lekra and LKN. Both institutions tried to show themselves at their best and to mock the opponent in order to gain public sympathy. The leader of LKN Singaraja of 1963–1965, Gde Dharna, in an interview in 1998, commented that Lekra generally had a talented group of orators who could attract people's attention in public gatherings or debates, while LKN had better choir groups and better drama performers. Choirs of both organizations attacked each other through the medium of their songs and performances. If Lekra's song expressed their admiration for communism, LKN mocked it and promoted the spirit of *Pancasila* and the unity of Indonesia. In the field of modern drama, still according to Gde Dharna, Lekra performances were often full of slogans and ignored plot structure, and hence were less attractive from an aesthetic perspective, while LKN drama was more artistic and entertaining.[49] Gde Dharna was one of the best composers for choir or *jangger* in the LKN. His songs were not only popular in Singaraja, but also in Denpasar.[50]

Party-colours also became an important political symbol in the course of the Lekra–LKN conflict. Lekra always used 'red' while LKN identified themselves with 'black' (Setia 1986: 128). The song '*Buah Buni*' (The Buni Fruits) by Gde Dharna expresses the contrast between red (unripe) buni fruit which is sour in taste, while black buni (ripe) is sweet. Created by an LKN figure, the song certainly gave preference to black as the colour that symbolized the 'sweetness' of the LKN.[51]

The reaction to the Communist coup attempt in 1965 spelled the end of the PKI and Lekra. The New Order Government banned this and all other left-wing organizations, and their key figures and followers were killed or imprisoned. The banning of Lekra brought victory to former Cultural Manifesto artists and supporters in Jakarta, but in Bali, it also brought a victory for right wing LKN members. In subsequent months, LKN continued to attack Lekraism, Marxism and Manikebuism ('Cultural Manifesto-ism'). They wanted to warn people of the dangers of what they saw as an anti-*Pancasila* movement. Raka Santeri, in his 1966 article '*Watak kiri tari-tarian Bali*' ('Balinese dances with a leftist character'), attacked both Manikebu and Lekra's principles. Artists and writers from both groups were accused of being 'hypocrites' (*munafik*) and anti-revolutionaries. His criticism is interesting, given that he once had been a supporter of Manikebu.

In 1966, a new military-sponsored newspaper *Angkatan Bersendjata* first appeared in Denpasar, which was to provide more space for artists to promote anti-Communist sentiments. This has to be considered as another form of support given by the army to 'artists against communism'. A short story entitled *Matinja seorang merah* ('The death of a red person [communist]') by Sunartoprajitno tells of a left-wing political activist who was optimistic about becoming a district head (*bupati*) but died after a public attack.[52] In this short story, images of how left-wing activists or followers were attacked and killed are conveyed and celebrated. While Lekra had been banned, LKN continued to be active in supporting various arts and cultural activities such as *gamelan* music and dance festivals, performances and discussion in order to proliferate what they consistently described as the 'People's Culture'. The way this concept was used was often similar to how it had been promoted by Lekra.

CULTURE AND IDEOLOGY AFTER THE CLASH

While the cultural clash between 'right-' and 'left-wing' activists in Bali appeared to have been settled by the 1965–1966 anti-Communist purge, cultural activities remained dynamic and dominated by the LKN. LKN activities were always related to those of the PNI. On 26–27 July 1966, for example, LKN Badung held a seminar to commemorate the thirty-eighth anniversary of the PNI or 'Front Marhaenist'. The seminar discussed ways of implementing the Marhaenist Declaration in cultural practice. Marhaen(-ism) is a term which refers to Indonesian peasants and had been invented by Sukarno in the 1920s to replace the Marxist term *proletariat* which, he felt, did not suit the situation of Indonesia as a non-industrial country (Penders 1974: 46–48). This seminar was an important one, because it was held just after the conflict between Lekra and LKN was over (see Figure 4.2).

In his paper, *Menudju Sastera Marhenis* (Toward a Marhaenist Literature), Wajan Warna defines the principles of Marhaenist ideology and the implementation of that ideology in literature.[53] Marhaenist literature, for Wayan Warna, must express a rejection of capitalism, imperialism and colonialism. Not unlike Lekra's Marxist literature, which was used to support the people's struggle and served as the goal of the Communist political party, LKN's Marhaenist literature was used to back up peasants in their struggle against landlords. To make the concept of Marhaenist literature clear, Wayan Warna gives an illustration by quoting a poem written by Sitor Situmorang, the LKN national leader, as follows:

Hidup, hiduplah	*Be alive, be alive!*
Kaum melarat, kaum penggarap	The poor, the farmers of
tanah tercinta	this lovely land
Karena cinta pada hidup	Because of love of life
Tak pernah menunggu perintah	They do not await orders
Apalagi dari tuan tanah	Let alone from the landlord

Sitor Situmorang had been a popular national poet and an idol to Balinese writers, particularly to members of LKN–Bali. In the early 1960s, he visited Bali several times and was usually met by young Balinese writers in art or literary discussions. As a poet, Sitor Situmorang had been very much obsessed with Balinese cultural life and had written a number of poems about Bali, both before and after his release from jail toward the end of the 1970s. His poem, quoted above, contains strong elements of socialist-realism, the stylistic approach disseminated by Lekra.

Situmorang's poems and the way Marhaenist literature was defined in general suggest that the LKN shared aesthetic conceptions and cultural

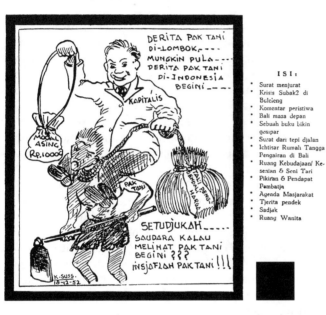

Figure 4.2 Caricature of an Indonesian peasant oppressed by international capitalism (*Bhakti*, cover illustration, 20 January 1953).

principles with Lekra, in Bali as it had been nationally. Moreover, the slogan that LKN adopted looked much like a Lekra slogan in its politic-ization of culture. While Lekra had claimed that 'politics is the com-mander', LKN adopted a modified version with 'Marhaenism is the commander' ('*Marhaenisme sebagai panglima*').[54] Like Lekra, LKN rejected the concept of 'art for art's sake' and 'universal humanism' which had been promoted by the Cultural Manifesto group.

Although there were various similarities between LKN and Lekra, this did not automatically mean that they shared the same ideology. LKN members explicitly acknowledged *Pancasila* as the philosophical basis for their struggle for a fairer society (Warna 1966). Lekra, by contrast, only focused on Communist ideology and did not show any commitment to *Pancasila*. It is hard to agree, therefore, with Geertz's argument when he says that conflict between PKI and PNI was not essentially ideological, but rather political (cited in Warren 1993: 275). Instead, Lekra and LKN-Bali shared many of the same practical political aims and their differences were precisely ideological. Polarization on ideological grounds was indeed paradigmatic of the politics of this period, and this cut across as often as it 'reflected' socio-economic divisions in Balinese society along the lines of caste or class.

Themes in the literature, dance, drama and song produced by LKN artists tended to be revolutionary and to promote 'the people's struggle'. Folk dances such as *tari tenun* (weaving dance), *tari nelayan* (fishermen's dance), *tari gotong royong* (community cooperation dance) were among those created by LKN's choreographers. Writers like Putu Widjaja, Raka Santeri, IGB Arthanegara, AA Aju Sulastri, Nyoman Bawa, Ngurah Parsua, and Ida Bagus Pudja published poems or short stories which used revolution as their social background or main theme. A number of poets even dedicated their poems to President Sukarno, as the leader of the Indonesian revolution.

Suluh Indonesia (which later became the *Bali Post*) was the medium through which they published their works. This newspaper was affiliated to the PNI; therefore, it was not simply a mediator but rather an active supporter of the revolution and the Marhaenist ideology (Sutedja-Liem 2000: 162). This was evident in the works of Balinese artists sympathetic toward President Sukarno's Marhaenism, which remained strong in Bali until 1966. The other local newspaper where writers published their works was *Angkatan Bersendjata* (which became *Nusa Tenggara*), owned by the Kodam Udayana regional military commando, whose leaders at that time had a political interest in diminishing the popularity of left-wing ideas.

The fall of the Sukarno's Old Order and the rise of the New Order in 1966 brought about a significantly different political, social and cultural setting in Indonesia. As soon as Suharto took power, affiliation of cultural institutions with political parties was no longer allowed. In addition, cultural institutions had to be formed under government sponsorship and control. This, however, did not spell 'art for art's sake'.

The establishment of Listibiya (*Majelis Pertimbangan dan Pembinaan Kebudayaan*), the 'Council for Cultural Consideration and Development' in Bali on 21 August 1966 was a good example of how the government and Suharto's all-dominant Golkar party became fully involved with the arts, and tightly controlled the development and activities of arts and culture organizations on the island. Most of Listibiya's members were former members of LKN. Note that Listibiya is still in existence and under government control, and with its authority, is still the main cultural organization in Bali. Listibiya focuses on traditional arts and culture but has left behind the field of modern literature, which had previously dominated cultural movements.

At the national level as well, the Suharto government cautiously regulated the influence of literature and other modern art forms. Literary publications, although not directly censored, were subject to close surveillance. To a point, this censorship was not just a political tool but also a psychological reaction to the chaos of the 1950s to 1960s, to which literature was seen to have contributed, more so than any other form of art.

CONCLUDING REMARKS

The history of Lekra and its opposition to the LKN in Bali suggests a need to reconsider several assumptions about Indonesian cultural history. Indeed, Bali looks quite different when viewed through the lens of Lekra, and Lekra too appears in a new light when seen from a Balinese perspective. Focusing on Lekra draws attention to the cultural role of the modernizing sector of Balinese society, of people like Shanty, who remained well outside the 're-traditionalization of art' program espoused by the New Order government.

I have described the development of Lekra in Bali, its contribution to left-wing cultural institutions at the national level, and its clash with 'the right' in Bali. As a left-wing cultural institution, Lekra had a strong presence in Bali between the 1950s and 1960s. More importantly, Bali played a significant role in the development of Lekra Indonesia. This is not only because Lekra Bali successfully hosted national and international meetings, but also because Bali provided an important example of an ideal 'People's culture' amidst, according to Lekra, a strong and continuing threat of destruction by Western interference through the tourist industry and other forms of neo-colonialism. This idealized and romanticized 'People's culture' (compare MacRae, Chapter 3, this volume) was used by Lekra as a showcase and to raise anti-colonialist and anti-imperialist sentiment during the Lekra National Congress in Bali. Even more importantly, a number of Balinese writers played an important personal role in the development of Lekra.

Attention to local-level issues involving Lekra Bali leads to a reconsideration of two aspects of Indonesian cultural and political history. First, the development of modern literature in Bali has never been isolated from the national development of Indonesian literature. This also means that the dichotomy between 'centre' and 'regional periphery' in Indonesian literature is quite artificial, and should not be applied to the 1950s and early 1960s. Second, there has been a clear-cut relationship between literature and politics in Bali. Cultural conflict between Lekra and LKN in Bali, however, was not an extension of the conflict between Lekra and the Cultural Manifesto group in Jakarta, but rather a more complicated extension of the political contention between the PKI and PNI. Thus, there was a significant difference between the form of, and the parties to, cultural conflicts in Jakarta and Bali.

Art and culture in Bali has had its own social dynamics and unique characteristics and therefore this should not be sidelined as peripheral to the conflict at the centre. Robinson (1995; also Vickers 1989, 1997), for example, has argued that, in terms of politics, Bali depended heavily on its relationship to the central government in the decades after independence, a trend which continued throughout the New Order period. This may be true enough, but the same has not been the case in relation to literary and cultural affairs at that time, let alone now. The cultural conflict that occurred in Bali between the 1950s to 1960s was never completely controlled by outsiders, nor could it be resolved entirely by political means. At the same time, Bali has had considerable influence on national cultural development and debate, as a small, dynamic centre with its own unique identity and its own local struggles.[55]

NOTES

1 Sutedja-Liem's study focuses on Nyoman Rastha Sindhu (1943–1972) and his works. Her discussion on the 1950s and 1960s deals with the social setting in which Rasta Sindhu's works were written (Sutedja-Liem 2000: 155–82).
2 Names of persons, organizations or literary works from this period are given in the original (rather than the modern) Indonesian spelling.
3 According to Sukada (1982: 12), *Lontar* was first published in November 1958 and appeared just once.
4 See 'Laporan Lekra Bali', *Harian Rakjat* (7 April 1962: 3). This report was presented by the general secretary of Lekra Bali, Wardjana, at the Lekra National Conference held in Bali in 1962. The report, however, does not say much about the 'regional conference' (*konferensi daerah*), but in such conferences there were usually three important agenda items; a formal declaration of the organization's aims, inauguration of its elected leaders, and proposals for the adoption of specific programs.
5 Interview with Putu Oka Sukanta in Denpasar (16 December 1998).
6 See 'Agama dan Adat Bali terantjam Bahaja Merah', *Bali Adnyana*, 10 February 1929, pp. 2–5.
7 K'toet Nasa, the editor in chief of *Surya Kanta*, was a school teacher, and so was Nengah Metra. Both were key figures of Surya Kanta. For an interesting discussion of Metra, see Vickers (2000), 'I Nengah Metra, 1902–1946: Thoughts on the Biography of a Modern Balinese'.
8 Articles on socialism appeared only occasionally, for example, K. Maroeta's 'Socialisme' (*Djatajoe*, 7, February 1937: 183–85). *Djatajoe* (Messenger) was the cultural journal *Bali Dharma Laksana* (by a Balinese study group first established in Malang, East Java), published between 1935–1941.
9 Serinata was a student at SGA (College for Teacher Training) Singaraja. Under the pseudonym Durma, he published 'Surat Seorang Peladjar, Nasib Peladjar

S. G. A. di Singaradja' in *Bhakti* (1 April 1954: 12–13, 15) and 'Mengapa Saja Menjadi Siswa SGA' in *Harian Rakjat* (6 June 1953). Both articles criticized the school he was in and caused the headmaster to expel him. Serinata received support from the Indonesian Youth and Student Association, who pushed the school rector to withdraw his decision to expel Serinata, yet this attempt failed. Serinata's article published in *Harian Rakjat* is included in Foulcher (1986: 89–91).

10 Interview with Putu Aswin in Singaraja, 28 June 1999. Putu Aswin is the son of Wajan Bhadra and a cousin of Putu Shanty, who occasionally published poems in *Bhakti*. While Bhadra and Shanty worked as editors, Aswin concentrated more on distribution.

11 Such accusation was expressed by *Bhakti* in its editorial 15 June 1954. See also Darma Putra (2000: 135–53).

12 He was supported by members of the editorial board comprising N. Malaya, A. Tenriadji, Nyoman S. Pendit, K. Surawan, Wisade (illustrator), along with several corespondents in the main cities of Java, Kalimantan and Lombok.

13 See the editorial of *Bhakti*, 15 June 1954.

14 See Sukada, 'Perkembangan Sastra Nasional di Bali' in *Catatan Kebudayaan dari Bali* (1982: 12).

15 Interview with K. Widjana in Singaraja, 26 June 1999.

16 When he was in Singaraja, Putu Oka aired a similar program on the state radio station in Singaraja.

17 Interview with L. K. Suryani in Denpasar, 16 December 1998. Suryani was an activist for the Nationalist Students' Movement of Indonesia (GMNI), an organization affiliated to the PNI and opponent of CGMI.

18 Sutedja's first appointment was in 1950 as Regional Head of Bali which at that time was still part of the provincial government of the Lesser Sunda Islands (see Robinson 1995: 193).

19 See 'Lekra Gugat J. Coast' (*Harian Rakjat*, 29 October 1952, p. 1); 'Protes terhadap John Coast' (*Harian Rakjat*, 23 October 1952: 1), 'John Coast memeras penari2 Bali' (*Harian Rakjat*, 15 October 1952, p. 1), and 'Sebuah kesan tentang rombongan penari2 kita jang baru tiba' (*Bhakti*, 10 April 1953: 5–6). For an indirect response to this criticism, see John Coast's article 'Bali Revisited', in *Dance Magazine*, November 1966, pp. 46–49, 72.

20 See *Harian Rakjat*, 17 March 1962, p. 3. Beside Njoto's speech 'Ideology adalah badja' and his poem 'Variasi Cak', *Harian Rakjat* also published Pinoraga Gangga's 'Bali', a poem dedicated to a Balinese dancer Gusti Ayu Wardani.

21 For an interesting study of this folk story, see H. J. Franken (1984 [1960]: 235–65).

22 I am indebted to Prof I Gusti Ngurah Bagus who brought this issue to my attention. Ngurah Bagus himself watched the performance 'Jayaprana-Layonsari' when it was staged for the Lekra National Conference at the Bali Hotel (interview with Ngurah Bagus in Denpasar, 15 December 1998).

23 See 'Layonsari Itu Menjelma Kursi', in *Kompas*, 27 November 2001.

24 Shanty's paper was published in *Zaman Baru*, 8(9), 1965: 7–8.

25 Interview with IGB Arthanegara in Denpasar, 29 June 1999.

26 See 'Pidato Pramudya Ananta Tur' in *Harian Rakjat* (21 July 1963: 1, 4). In an interview in his house in Jakarta in January 2000, I asked Pramudya Ananta Tur about his involvement in the meeting he convened in Bali, but he declined to answer. His response was 'I do not remember, I forgot'.

27 See 'Menjambut teman seperdjuangan' in *Harian Rakjat*, 21 July 1963, pp. 1, 4.

28 See Delegasi KE-KPAA Sumbang 'Gunung Agung' in *Harian Rakjat*, 23 July 1963. Rate exchange in 1960 was Rupiah 45.28 per US$ (Warren 1993: 328).

29 See 'Pleno P. P. Lembaga Sastra Indonesia' in *Harian Rakjat* (11 August 1963: 1) and 'PPH dan SPP Lestra' in *Harian Rakjat* (8 September 1963).

30 Shanty 'Chairil Anwar dan Binatang Djalang' in *Bhakti*, 1 May 1953, pp. 12–13.

31 Although I found no written evidence of Shanty's trip to China, a number of persons I interviewed between 1998 and 1999, including Ngurah Bagus, Gede Dharna, K. Widjana and Putu Aswin, confirmed his trip to China and Eastern European countries.

32 See *Bhakti*, 10 March 1953, pp. 8–10. This short story had already been published in *Mimbar Indonesia*.

33 I found only the first part (8 scenes) of the supposed three parts of the drama in *Bhakti* (1 September 1953, pp. 25–32). The futility of belief in God already dominates as a theme in this first part of the drama.

34 See *Bhakti*, 10 November 1952. It is not clear whether Ananta was a Balinese or not.

35 In an interview with Putu Oka Sukanta in Denpasar, 16 December 1998, he pointed out that he was not aware of this public image until some right-wing publications in Yogyakarta refused to publish his works.

36 This poem was published in *Harian Rakjat*, 29 March 1964. The translation is taken from Foulcher (1983: 147–48).

37 Both of Putu Oka's books were published by Pustaka Pelajar, a well-known publisher in Yogyakarta, in cooperation with Jendela Budaya.

38 See the poem 'Sepotong Kueh Dunia, Bali' (Sukanta 1999: 64–66).

39 Interview with AA Putra Agung in Denpasar, 21 June 1999. Putra Agung was Wardjana's school friend at Taman Siswa.

40 His short story entitled 'Bendera' appeared in *Zaman Baru*, December 1964, pp. 18–19. This story is about the revolutionary spirit felt by a young boy who had long been refused to carry a flag in his school rally.

41 See as an example, two articles with a modest approach to the issue of communism in Indonesia, published in *Kompas* in the same edition; 'Komunisme dan Pancasila' by G. Moedjanto and 'Tap XXV/MPRS/1966' by Sulastomo (*Kompas*, 12 April 1999).

42 The action of the 'book-sweeping' (*sweeping buku*) and the protest against it gained wide coverage in Indonesian magazines and newspapers. See for example *Tempo Interaktif* (on line) 'Ikapi Tolak Pelarangan Buku' (11 May 2001), 'Buku Kiri Lenyap di Pasaran Semarang' (10 May 2001), 'Soal Sweeping Buku Kiri: PKI Betul-betul Sudah Habis' (12 May 2001).

43 HPS deserves to be known as the first and the most important artists' organization in Bali in the 1960s because it served as a model to right-wing writers groups established subsequently, such as Himpi Bali (The Balinese Indonesian Writer's Group) established in 1969, and Lesiba (The Balinese Indonesian Artis's Institution) established in 1971, which still exist today. Members of both organizations were predominantly, though not exclusively, former members of HPS. For a brief account of Lesiba and Himpi activities, see Nyoman Tusthi Eddy (1997: 27–29) and Sutdeja-Liem (2000: 155–82).

44 See 'Seniman 15 Kota Menyokong Manifes Kebudayaan' in *Sastra* (No. 9/10, Th. III-1963) (quoted in Moeljanto and Ismail 1995: 436–37). Raka Santeri in an interview in Denpasar (18 December 1988 and 4 January 1999) also confirmed his support for the Cultural Manifesto, although he cast doubt on whether he really signed the actual document of the manifesto.

45 IGB Arthanegara recounted that Raka Santeri and Judha Paniek were writers who received a mandate from the Cultural Manifesto. Another was Gde Mangku, a poet and a school teacher. Interview with IGB Arthanegara in Denpasar, 29 June 1999.

46 Interview with IGB Arthanegara in Denpasar, 19 June 1999.
47 See 'Tiga Pengarang Menolak jadi Koordinator KKPSI' (Three writers rejected as coordinators for the Indonesian Writers' Worker Conference), *Bintang Timur*, 2 March 1964 (in Moeljanto and Ismail 1995: 309).
48 Made Sanggra, a modern Balinese writer from Gianyar recalls that although Gianyar was only 30 km from Denpasar the conflict between Lekra and LKN was not felt. Interview with Made Sanggra in Sukawati, 14 December 1998.
49 Interview with Gde Dharna in Singaraja, 6 January 1999.
50 See Arthanegara 'In Memoriam Dangin Harnama, Kecil Orangnya, Hebat Otaknya' in *Bali Post* (3 January 1996, p. 2). This article is about Dangin Harnama, but some activities and figures of LKN Bali are also mentioned, including Gde Dharna.
51 There are many political songs from the time Lekra and LKN were in conflict. Gde Dharna himself composed more than 50 *janger* songs. Both LKN songs and Lekra songs have not been studied yet.
52 This story was published in *Angkatan Bersendjata*, 10 April 1966, p. 2.
53 See Warna's paper published in *Suluh Indonesia* (8 May 1966: 2–4 and 15 May 1966: 2–4).
54 See Wajan Warna 1966: 2.
55 I would like to thank Thomas Reuter, Helen Creese, Adrian Vickers and Thomas Hunter for their helpful comments on various drafts of this chapter. Research for this chapter was carried out in conjunction with ARC Large Grant project, entitled 'A Literary History of Bali: New Perspectives on Regional Literature in Indonesia' and administered by Dr Helen Creese, University of Queensland.

REFERENCES

Aveling, H. (1970) 'Indonesian writers and the Left Before 1965'. *Review of Indonesian and Malaysian Affairs*, 4(1–2): 1–7.
Bagus, I Gusti Ngurah (1996) 'The Play "Woman's Fidelity": Literature and Caste Conflict in Bali'. In A. Vickers (ed.), *Being Modern in Bali, Image and Change*, Yale Southeast Asia Studies Monographs, No. 43.
Birchall, Ian H. (1977) 'Marxism and Literature'. In J. Routh and J. Wolff (eds), *The Sociology of Literature: Theoretical Approaches*, Sociology Review Monographs, No. 25.
Coast, John (1966) 'Bali Revisited'. *Dance Magazine*, November 1966, pp. 46–49, 72.
Cribb, Robert (1990) *The Indonesian Killings 1965–1966*, Clayton: Centre for Southeast Asian Studies, Monash University.
Darma Putra, I Nyoman (1994) 'Kebangkitan Puisi Indonesia Modern di Bali'. *Basis*, October 1994, pp. 384–96.
Darma Putra, I Nyoman (1998) 'Jejak Postkolonial Teks Sastrawan Bali'. *Dinamika Kebudayaan*, September 1998, 1: 18–30.
Darma Putra, I Nyoman (2000) 'Bali and Modern Indonesian Literature: The 1950s'. In A. Vickers, I Ny. Darma Putra and M. Ford (eds), *To Change Bali*, Wollongong and Denpasar: Institute of Social Change and Critical Inquiry, University of Wollongong/Bali Post.
Eddy, Nyoman Tusthi (1997) 'Puisi Bali, Selintas-Pintas'. *Horison*, XXXI (3/1997): 27–29.

Foulcher, Keith (1969) 'A Survey of Events Surrounding "Manikebu": The Struggle for Cultural and Intellectual Freedom in Indonesian Literature'. *Bijdragen tot de Taal- Land- en Volkenkunde*, 125(4): 429–65.

Foulcher, Keith (1983) 'Another side of Bali. The Poems of Putu Oka Sukanta'. *Inside Indonesia*, November 1983, pp. 32–35.

Foulcher, Keith (1986) *Social Commitment in Literature and the Arts: The Indonesian 'Institute of People's Culture 1950–1965'*, Clayton: Centre for Southeast Asian Studies, Monash University.

Foulcher, Keith (1994) *The Manifesto is not dead: Indonesian Literary Politics Thirty Years On*. Clayton: Centre for Southeast Asian Studies, Monash University, Working Paper No. 87.

Franken, H. J. (1984) 'The Festival of Jayaprana at Kalianget'. In J. van Baal *et al.* (eds), *Bali Studies in Life, Thought, and Ritual*, Dordrecht: Foris Publications. First published in 1960, pp. 235–65.

Hill, David T. (1985) *Who's Left? Indonesian Literature in the Early 1980s*, Clayton: Centre for Southeast Asian Studies, Monash University, Working Paper No. 33.

Ismail, Yahaya (1972) *Pertumbuhan, Perkembangan dan Kejatuhan Lekra di Indonesia*, Kuala Lumpur: Dewan Bahasa dan Pustaka.

Kratz, E. U. (1988) *A Bibliography of Indonesian Literature in Journals. Drama, Prose, Poetry*, London and Yogyakarta: School of Oriental and African Studies – Gajah Mada University Press.

Maier, H. M. J. (1974) *Ideologievorming van de Lekra 1950–1959: Een aanzet tot bewustmaking*, Leiden University, unpublished Doctorandus Thesis.

Moeljanto, D. S. and Ismail, T. (1995) *Prahara Budaya Kilas-Balik Ofensif Lekra/PKI*, Jakarta: Mizan Republika.

Mohamad, Goenawan (1988) *The Cultural Manifesto Affair: Literature and Politics in Indonesia in the 1960s, a Signatory's View*, Clayton: Centre for Southeast Asian Studies, Monash University, Working Paper No. 45.

Penders, C. L. M. (1974) *The Life and Times of Soekarno*, London: Sidgwick & Jackson.

Pitana, I Gede (1997) *In search of difference. Origin groups, status and identity in Contemporary Bali*, Australian National University, unpublished Ph.D. Thesis.

Robinson, Geoffrey (1995) *The Dark Side of Paradise: Political Violence in Bali*, Ithaca: Cornell University Press.

Santeri, Raka (1966) 'Watak kiri tari-tarian Bali'. *Angkatan Bersendjata*, 6 March 1966, p. 2.

Setia, Putu (1986) *Menggugat Bali*, Jakarta: Grafiti.

Shanty, Putu (1965) 'Arahkan Udjung Pena ke Djantung Imperialisme Feodalisme'. *Zaman Baru*, 8(9): 7–8.

Shiraishi, Takashi (1990) *An Age in Motion: popular radicalism in Java, 1912–1926*, Ithaca: Cornell University Press.

Sukada, I Made (1982) *Catatan Kebudayaan dari Bali*, Denpasar: Lembaga Seniman Indonesia Bali.

Sukanta, Putu Oka (1999) *Merajut Harkat*, Yogyakarta: Pustaka Pelajar.

Sukanta, Putu Oka (1999) *Perjalanan Penyair/Sajak kegelisahan Hidup*. Yogyakartakarta: Pustaka Pelajar.

Sutedja-Liem, Maya (2000) 'Nyoman Rastha Sindhu: Humanity in Balineseness'. In A. Vickers, I Ny. Darma Putra and M. Ford (eds), *To Change Bali*, Wollongong and Denpasar: Institute of Social Change and Critical Inquiry, University of Wollongong/Bali Post.

Teeuw, A. (1967) *Modern Indonesian Literature*, Leiden: The Hague.

Teeuw, A. (1996) *Modern Indonesian Literature II*, Leiden: The Hague. First published in 1979.

Vickers, Adrian (1989) *Bali A Paradise Created*, Harmondsworth: Penguin.

Vickers, Adrian (1996) *Being Modern in Bali, Image and Change*. Yale Southeast Asia Studies Monographs, No. 43.

Vickers, Adrian (1997) *Selling the Experience of Bali, 1950–1971*. Paper presented at the 'Commodification Seminar Series', 20 August 1997, University of Wollongong.

Vickers, Adrian (2000) 'I Nengah Metra, 1902–1946: Thoughts on the Biography of a Modern Balinese'. In A. Vickers, I Ny. Darma Putra and M. Ford (eds), *To Change Bali*, Wollongong and Denpasar: Institute of Social Change and Critical Inquiry, University of Wollongong/Bali Post.

Warna, I Wayan (1966) 'Menudju Sastra Marhenis'. *Suluh Indonesia*, 8 and 15 May 1966, pp. 2–4.

Warren, C. (1993) *Adat and Dinas: Balinese Communities in the Indonesian State*, Kuala Lumpur: Oxford University Press.

5 Transformations of a genre of Balinese dance drama

Arja Muani as the modern-day agent of classical Arja's liberal gender agenda

Natalie Kellar

My earlier research on the classical Balinese dance-drama Arja (Kellar 2000) confirmed that the performing arts have an important and enduring role in Balinese society and lend expression to the specific socio-political issues and currents of each particular historical period. In this chapter, I show how the performing arts reflect changes occurring in Balinese society during the current period of national crisis and cultural transition. More specifically, I aim to substantiate the observations of other scholars of Balinese and Indonesian performance that the theatre is an important repository of the gender values of a particular period. In its engagement with contemporary gender concepts, the theatre is a key site of reproduction and confirmation for Indonesian society's cultural values and ideals. The theatre is also a site for the contesting of such values, however, and within it one may find innovative deviations from mainstream gender ideology – particularly so at a time of political crisis and cultural change.

James R. Brandon, a prominent scholar of the wayang shadow theatre, once argued in reference to Asian societies generally that we are to 'expect theatre to be related to local social processes in more subtle – perhaps more intimate and important – ways than a medium that is a government mouthpiece' (cited in Peacock 1968: 4). And similarly, in relation to Bali, John Emigh has contended that the theatre realm provides the Balinese with the means to 'subvert and playfully reconstruct traditional notions and behavioural patterns concerning sexuality and gender within the confines of aesthetic play' (1992: 216). My own research supports this general view of the theatre as both a mirror and instrument of social change, while also revealing the theatre's role in reproducing the dominant values of a given historical period or *jaman*. This connection between the theatre and the *jaman* was stressed by renowned Balinese dancer, I Wayan Rawit, of the Arja Keramas dance-drama troupe, who asserted that developments in theatre closely mirror the social developments of the time.[1]

In this chapter, I will extend and build upon these ideas, by applying them as a model for an investigation of Balinese theatre in the context of the new *jaman* that Bali is now experiencing, that is, the 'Post-New Order' or '*Reformsi*' period. Given the argument by Balinese feminist scholars that the generally repressive New Order regime under former President Suharto also had a very restrictive impact on gender, its passing should be expected to have important consequences in this regard. The inevitable shift in this era of *Reformasi* to new forms of public discourse is likely to bring about some new and intriguing possibilities for change in gender conceptions. In light of the theatre sector's role in both representing and engendering new directions in social thinking, it is illuminating to look at Balinese performance as a site where shifts in the 'gender-agenda' of Balinese society may be occurring, as they are in Indonesian society as a whole. Is there indeed a new liberalism in the arts in response to the democratic aspirations of Indonesians in the post-Suharto era or are we to witness a renewed traditionalization?

As my focal example, I concentrate on a popular Balinese theatre form of New Order origin – the all-male dance-drama *Arja Muani* which is a modern offshoot of the classical Balinese dance-drama *Arja*. Keeping in mind the limitations inherent in its New Order genesis, I consider this modern-day Arja troupe in terms of its potential as a contemporary medium of classical Arja's rather liberal position on gender identity, and thus as a modern dramatic form containing the potential to reinterpret, contest and dismantle lingering New Order discourses on gender.

THE NEW ORDER AND '*KODRAT WANITA*': REINFORCING TRADITIONAL NOTIONS OF FEMALE IDENTITY AND WOMEN'S PLACE

A substantial literature by feminist scholars points to a marked shift in gender ideology that occurred upon the establishment of the New Order government, beginning with Suharto's coming to power in 1966. Documentation of the New Order state's policies points to a systematic reinforcement of women's subordinate status under the auspices of a 'National development' campaign. Traditional values were promoted to offset the demoralizing impact of the forces of modernization, and to this effect women were exhorted as mothers of the nation, responsible for ensuring that the familial realm remained harmonious and strong. Most importantly, for the purposes of this chapter, the New Order period was characterized by a strict gender code operating to reinforce traditional notions of male and female identity and of appropriate gender roles. As a result, the essentially male-dominant social structure of Indonesian society was newly secured, particularly by the state's restrictive female stereotyping, exemplified by the notion of *kodrat wanita* or women's inherently refined nature.

Bali shows a similar picture of restrictive gender ideology from the 1950s onwards. Vickers, Darmaputra and Wijaya (1998) reveal features of late-Old Order Indonesia that provided fertile ground for the subsequent New Order regime's rigid gender policies. Their study of Balinese cultural debates from the 1950s onwards reveals a backlash against expanding female roles at the time of Indonesia's struggle for independence. A shift away from the progressive gender thinking of the 1930s and 1940s with its calls for women's liberation, involved contrary moves toward the revision and ultimately curtailment of the legitimate roles available to 'modern' Balinese women. The debates about women's roles in public forums such as magazines, focused in particular on the problematic issue of women entering the workplace.[2]

As documented by a number of feminist scholars, the transition to the New Order government saw a more extensive penetration of the state's restrictive gender ideology into Balinese society. Lyn Parker's work on the education sector has revealed the gendering process at work in schools, where young girls were inculcated with the ethics of femininity or *kodrat wanita*, and encouraged to prepare for their future primary social role as mothers (Parker 1993). Megan Jennaway's study of polygyny in Bali points to the increasingly stigmatized status of divorced women or aging widows in New Order Balinese society, which afforded few options to women beyond matrimony and motherhood (Jennaway 1995). Similarly, Linda Connor has highlighted the cultural dominance of men in the public domain, by describing the constraints imposed on Balinese women's careers as healing practitioners or *balians* due to social expectations that they pursue their primary reproductive function as mothers (Connor Asch and Asch 1996). These studies reveal that, like their Javanese counterparts, Balinese women have been subjected to the highly gender-specific behavioural codes and social roles promoted by the New Order state. Through political directives as well as social institutions and media images, women have been systematically constructed as the dependents of men, cementing the male-hierarchical ethic which reigns over an alternate, grass-roots ethos of 'complementarity between the sexes' (*rua bineda*).

THE INDONESIAN PERFORMING ARTS IN THE NEW ORDER PERIOD

Studies by F. Hughes-Freeland (1993), Amrih Widodo (1995) and Barbara Hatley (1995) have shown that these New Order values had a significant impact upon the Indonesian theatre sector. The research reveals an ongoing process of control or 'development' of the performing arts since

the establishment of the New Order government, with particularly negative consequences for the status of female performers. Hughes-Freeland
underlines how the government's assumption of the role of 'preserver of
the traditional performing arts' has seen a re-invention of traditional
genres as new state-endorsed art forms designed to support a New
Order vision of modern Indonesian nationhood. As she contends, 'To
speak of "the arts" is to enter a modern discourse with a political
programmatic character' (Hughes-Freeland 1993: 92). In particular, one
discerns from feminist scholars' studies an overall pattern of male control
reasserting itself in the domain of Indonesian performing arts, and cementing the historically ambiguous status of female performers in forms such
as Tayuban, Kethoprak and Golek.

Both Hughes-Freeland, in her paper *Golek Menak and Tayuban: Patronage
and professionalism in two spheres of Javanese culture* (1993), and Widodo, in
his article *The Stages of the State: Arts of the people and rites of hegemonization*
(1995), maintain that in the wake of a state monopoly on Tayuban
performances, the empowerment that female performers (*ledhek*) formerly
possessed as the central players, has been greatly jeopardized. The
ledhek's role as temptresses, once bringing them a status as empowering as
it was demeaning, has been played down by the State's domesticization of
the genre. According to Widodo, the once 'sensual', 'dynamic', 'crude'
and 'free' Tayuban became 'formal', 'sterile' and 'ritualistic'.

Hatley's study of the modern theatre sector also attests to the narrow-
ing of female roles in the late-New Order period, attesting to the
'reduced power and autonomy of women in modern as compared with
traditional regional performance' (1995: 1). Significantly, her study also
points to the containment of the modern '*branyak*' female character type
of the popular theatre form, Kethoprak, in the late New Order era.
A strong female character renowned for their confident assertiveness
and direct, unself-conscious speech, the *branyak* female type has been central to Kethoprak theatre's promotion of female advancement and a
shared sense of female identity.

THE BALINESE PERFORMING ARTS IN THE NEW ORDER PERIOD: A DEPARTURE FROM INDIGENOUS BALINESE THEATRE TRADITION

A similar picture emerges when one reviews the impact of New Order
gender ideology on the performing arts in Bali. My earlier research on
Arja, as a case study of female identity and experience in the performance realm, revealed that classical Arja, as a traditional genre predating
the New Order period, differs significantly from its neo-traditional or
modern counterparts from the New Order period onward (Kellar
2000). In the New Order era, characterized by a rigid gender ideology,

only Arja and some other classical Balinese dance forms like Gambuh were able to retain a high degree of flexibility in conceiving gender identity. This is manifest in their variable role allocation method and the ensuing cross-sexed performances on stage. Classical Arja, a drama form unique in the prominence of its female actors playing refined and coarse, male and female roles, reflects a play with the current gender code, a subversion which is uniquely appealing in its rich range of gender identities.

In view of the paucity of studies on the gender imagery of the Balinese theatre, it is significant to note that in the work on Balinese performance prior to the New Order period, what observation is made of gender at all centres on the Balinese theatre convention of gender-switching on stage. Early writers make mention of this phenomenon with evident fascination at such divergence from gender norms. In his memoirs on Bali, Colin McPhee makes reference to Arja, one of the most popular theatre genres in the 1930s–1940s period, illuminating its intriguing practice of 'gender-bending':

> In this theatre of the imagination, free of scenery or properties, the actual sex of the performer was forgotten... The young girl, it had been discovered, could give the final touch of delicate grace to the portrayal of a prince of the alus, the "gentle-serene" type, while a man no longer young, but widely known for his finished and classical style, could give a far more feminine performance than any girl.
>
> (McPhee 1979: 66–67)

Later studies by John Emigh and Jamer Hunt similarly point to the casting-inversions deployed in Balinese secular theatre, asserting that these dance forms 'mischievously juggle perceptions of appropriate behaviour and, perhaps in the process serve to encourage a re-evaluation of traditional conceptions of gender' (Emigh and Hunt 1992: 218).

That Arja is reflective of a Balinese theatre tradition of gender fluidity in dance was further revealed in my recent study of dance training both at the official site of the Performing Arts Academy, STSI, the realm of *seniman akademik* ('educated artists'), and in Balinese villages, the realm of *seniman alam* ('grass-roots artists') (Kellar 2000). The traditional dance training process affirms a free blending of masculine and feminine traits in each individual. In niches of dance training, the conventional gender ideology of the New Order State that assigns men and women gender-specific traits, *keras* ('coarse') and *alus* ('refined') respectively in the Balinese case, was found to be blurred. At STSI and in the more tradition-oriented dance training in Balinese villages, there is an acceptance of in-between dance styles – referred to as *tari laki bebancihan* and *tari wanita bebancihan* or dance styles which are based on the ability of the dancer 'to assume the other gender's traits in dance'.[3]

Most significantly, for the present discussion, this study noted a tension between traditional gender-fluid artistic practices in dance circles and modern Balinese society's bipolar notion of gender identity. For example, problems were caused by STSI's cross-gender training of young male dance students for the performance of the female dance form Legong. Male Legong students experienced embarrassment at the time of their exam performance, and were laughed at rather than admired by their peers.[4] The evident shift in gender thinking in performing arts circles from the period of classical genres like Arja and Gambuh to that subscribed to in the New Order period was illuminated by the comments of female dance students, one of whom claimed that 'Men can't perform Legong in society. In society, men perform only male dance.'[5]

SENDRATARI AND DRAMA GONG – NEW ORDER INDONESIAN *GENDER* IDENTITY ON THE MODERN BALINESE STAGE

The contemporary Balinese theatre forms that first emerged in the New Order era, most notably Drama Gong and Sendratari, have in a sense betrayed traditional Balinese theatre practice in relation to gender. They adhere instead to the dominant gender stereotypes of the political era in which they were conceived. These modern drama forms see men relinquishing their traditional freedom to assume the roles of 'refined' (*halus*) or female characters such as princesses. Likewise, women have lost their once socially acceptable stage role as the 'coarse' (*kasar*) and male king. The absence of cross-sexed performance in the Balinese theatre of the New Order suggests the theatre sector's gravitation towards state-promoted ideas about gender, and signals its departure from the fluid gender attitudes embraced by original forms like Arja. In order to illustrate this process of change, I shall briefly describe the development of Sendratari and Drama Gong in Bali.

Former Chairman of STSI, Professor Dr I Made Bandem, states that Bali's Sendratari is a version of the Javanese Sendratari genre which he first brought to Bali because of its perceived appeal to foreign tourists: 'The idea was coming from Java, because Java, 1960–1961, already had Sendratari there. The performance of it was designed for tourist attraction – like a classical ballet in the West' (Interview, 19 October 1997). Sendratari rapidly acquired its current status as the most prestigious art form in Bali. This status as the premier event of the Balinese performing arts annual calendar is signalled both by Sendratari's staging on the giant Ardha Candra stage of the Arts Centre and by its marking both the opening and the finale of the June–July Bali Arts Festival since 1979. Such performances consecrate the academic sector's superior standing in the development of Bali's modern performing arts.[6]

Sendratari's gender representation reflects its alignment with the gender ideology of the Indonesian state. There is very little cross-gender play to confuse gender distinctions in Sendratari performances, with its fixed roles for both male and female performers. Female dancers work within a stereotypical and narrow framework of gender roles in this modern-day dance-drama form. Gender representation in a Sendratari performance is based chiefly upon traditional epic narratives, centring on the actions of a male figure (usually a prince or hero) and various female subordinates. Roles for women include the *putri* or princess, her maidservants, and *bidadari* ('angels' or 'fairies'). The only reminder of the once common practice of cross-gender play is that of young women playing the refined prince. The overriding justification for this role allocation, however, is a modern-day disassociation of men from the *alus* qualities of the good prince of the classic narratives. As DeBoer claims, 'As state art, Sendratari can not help but reflect the self-concept of the nation sponsoring it' (cited in Hough, 1992: 8).

Drama Gong, a much less grandiose form of theatre than Sendratari, first appeared in Bali in 1966. After its initial creation in the academic environment by KOKAR graduate student Anak Agung Gede Raka Payadnya, Drama Gong went on to develop almost wholly in a grass-roots, community setting. Like Arja, troupes were initially formed in local neighbourhoods (*banjars*). Later, 'all-star' troupes developed which transformed artists from amateur to semi-professional status. Drama Gong was officially named by Dr Panji, an influential figure at KOKAR, with the intention of indicating the nature of Drama Gong as 'a syncretistic fusion of "classical" Balinese theatre (as denominated by the continuous accompaniment of the gamelan gong) with modern "drama", or Western-style realistic theatre' (DeBoer 1996: 165).

In the case of Drama Gong one finds a total absence of cross-gender play. While this can be partly accounted for by the fact that it was a theatre form that attempted to mirror the Western theatre model in some respects, Drama Gong is also regarded as a form of theatre derivative of Arja, minus the song and dance. The loss of these aspects of Arja does not sufficiently account for Drama Gong's complete shift from Arja's gender fluid, cross-gender performances to its gender-specific role allocation and gender representation.

Studies by Picard (1996), Hough (1992) and DeBoer (1996) suggest that the development of Drama Gong and Sendratari has been tainted, if not wholly determined, by the political interests of the New Order state. Picard draws a critical distinction between artistic practice in the time of court patronage of the arts and the contemporary institutional monitoring of the performing arts realm by institutions such as SMKI, the 'Conservatory of Music' and STSI, the 'Academy of Indonesian Dance', set up by the New Order government in the 1960s. Picard argues that while the courts took care to maintain their own distinctive styles true to an indigenous Balinese theatre tradition, the arts created by these modern institutions are politically engineered: 'The Indonesian government, through its regional apparatus, is deliberately centralizing, normalizing and decontextualizing the Balinese performing arts' (1996: 140). Moreover, he speaks of the cultural authority of these institutions as compromised by their expected allegiance to Jakarta, questioning how 'estranged' they might be from their Balinese roots. Brett Hough likewise documents the state's appropriation and redefinition of ethnic cultural forms within a national framework. Hough argues that this 'process of appropriation and recontextualization of cultural forms within the rituals of state' constitutes 'one means of maintaining and reinforcing ideological control' (1992: 2). Likewise, DeBoer describes Sendratari as 'a very conscious invention of the state' (cited in Hough 1992: 2). Moreover, he relates how Drama Gong and Sendratari were both used as instruments for the inculcation of 'official' values to youth: 'the two forms can be paired. Both came to popularity in the 1960s, both were encouraged by the "New Order" regime. Both strive for continuity with Indonesian cultural traditions, both reaffirm "official" values' (DeBoer 1996: 176).

ARJA MUANI: THE RE-EMERGENCE OF ARJA'S LIBERAL PLAY ON GENDER IN MODERN BALINESE PERFORMANCE

The Balinese dance-drama Arja in its classical form has suffered a marked decline in popularity since the emergence of Drama Gong and Sendratari in the 1960s. As a grass-roots theatre tradition, Arja has been marginalized by these modern forms, which have received more support and sponsorship from the political elite in Bali. As DeBoer argues, in New Order period

> many of the traditionally important 'classic' theatrical forms [...] even the once wildly popular *arja*, have fallen into comparative neglect [while modern drama forms like Drama Gong and Sendratari] closely associated with Indonesia's New Order, received strong encouragement and support from the central Indonesian government in Jakarta.
>
> (DeBoer 1996: 158–59)

In effect, Arja, renowned for the predominance of its female players, has been eclipsed by the New Order phenomenon in Bali of a male cultural elite controlling of the arts (see also Hughes-Freeland 1993), in combination with an increasing appropriation of the arts world by the patriarchal Suharto state. This ongoing social and political transformation of the performing arts has characterized artistic developments in Bali generally throughout the New Order period.

Given the evident shift in the Balinese performing arts in the New Order era, from 'gender-bending' in art performance to a 'gender-agenda' performed for the state, it seems timely in this *'Reformasi'* era to expect challenges to state-sanctioned gender ideology, particularly given the historically liberal and innovative attitudes within Balinese theatre circles. With the modern theatre sector mirroring the New Order period's strict regulation of sex and gender, Arja's broad conceptions of female identity and its affirmation of gender ambiguity in its cross-gender performance, presumably lost its previous social resonance. The *'Reformasi'* era represents an opportune period for the reassertion of traditional Balinese theatre conventions and, by extension, the reassertion of liberal ideas of gender in Balinese theatre.

It is in this light that Arja can be seen as having been provided with a contemporary medium from which New Order discourses on gender may, perhaps be reworked and contested. This new medium is a modern form of Arja, the all-male troupe Arja Muani (from *muani*, 'male'). Arja Muani is a genre in which all female roles are played by men, unlike Arja as traditionally known, in which women play most of the roles, male and female alike.

Arja Muani acts as a counter-discourse to mainstream gender notions chiefly by its return to the Arja convention of cross-sexed performance. Beyond its fluid gender imagery, Arja Muani also advances the liberal gender notions that are the legacy of its predecessor. Drawing from old Arja conventions, Arja Muani overtly takes up themes of gender, specifically those of feminism and transvestitism. I therefore argue that Arja Muani performances can be seen to embody a call for social change in favour of women and transvestites as culturally marginalized groups. At the same time, however, I will show that Arja Muani engages in contemporary gender ideology on its own terms. Arja Muani did indeed emerge in the late-New Order era, inevitably saddling this contemporary male troupe with some of the political conservatism characteristic of that era. In addition, while Arja Muani draws from old Arja conventions, and so overtly takes up themes of gender, the implications of an all-male troupe portraying women on stage are necessarily problematic, as has been contended by feminist theorists on the theatre.

ARJA'S CROSS-GENDER PLAY IN ITS MODERN CONTEXT

In Peliatan, Ubud, villagers are gathered around the great temple celebrating the *Upacara Odalan*[7] of Peliatan's *Pura Dalem*[8]. Most sit transfixed around a small stage located in the temple square, watching a performance by the latest dance-drama sensation, the new all-male Arja Muani.[9] In contrast to the mixed gender composition of conventional Arja – the formula with which Balinese audiences have long been accustomed – here men perform all characters of Arja with astounding dexterity. Backstage, I Kadek Widnyana, performer of *Mantri Manis* ('the noble prince or minister'), stands in the wings about to go on stage, monitoring the response of the audience to the clowns who are preceding him. Immediately behind him stands his colleague, I Wayan Sugama, the *Liku* of this troupe, wearing the dress and the long braids that are the hallmark of Arja's 'crazy princess'. Behind them the rest of the troupe are casually chatting, comparatively unconcerned about the performance's proceedings. With padded breasts thrust forward and backside out in the standard pose of a female dancer, the 'maidservant' player, I Made Jelada, stands chatting to a fellow troupe member while smoking a cigarette. Meanwhile, Ida Bagus Made Wiantika, player of the *Galuh* or 'good princess', is preoccupied doing his face, a task to which he gives immeasurable care. As his colleagues sitting around him tell jokes that inspire intermittent bouts of husky laughter, Wiantika invites them to admire his looks, fluttering his eyelids in a coy yet flirtatious manner. He strikes a peculiar appearance as a princess with a man's made-up face, as he rises and parades around in search of his headdress – the beautiful long tresses embellished with flowers – which completes the costume of the Galuh. He then joins his on-stage partner, I Made Jelada, and they pose together in a corner for a photo. An obvious pride in their new image is indicated as the pair show-off to best advantage their 'feminine' beauty. Meanwhile, laughter signals the scene between the Liku and the *Desak Rai* ('maidservant') on stage. As the Liku loses his headdress exposing a slightly bald and indisputably male head, the audience goes into hysterics. The audience's titillation is indicative of a conscious play on gender identity that pervades both the backstage environment and the on stage drama.

On the surface, Arja Muani's immediate appeal is its new and different style of theatrical 'gender-bending'. Arja Muani has the character of a spectacle, manipulating conventional ideas of femininity and, by extension, male identity with its all-male set of performers. It is arguably this transgression of conventional gender boundaries which satisfies its modern audiences' thirst for sensational entertainment. Arja Muani is also intriguing, however, in terms of the other levels of significance on which it operates. In the following, an attempt will be made to explore Arja Muani's multiple dimensions, focusing in particular on its mode of cross-gender play and its approach to gender issues. This examination will take into consideration the performers' accounts of the objectives of this contemporary all-male Arja genre, as well as theories about transvestitism in theatre. Feminist theories of theatrical representation will assist in assessing Arja Muani's gendered meanings. One feminist theorist of the theatre in particular, Jennifer Robertson (1992), hints at the awareness raising potential of Arja Muani performance in her general comments on transvestite theatre: 'Parody itself is ambivalent and ambiguous: it can be intended and read as merely comical and playful, and as demystifying and subversive' (1998: 40).

THE EMERGENCE OF THE ARJA MUANI PHENOMENON

Arja Muani or Men's Arja, was formed as a new dance troupe in 1993 by a group of male dance graduates of Bali's most important Arts College, STSI. The members of this group maintain that their activities had been primarily a spontaneous means of filling in some spare time. The troupe, which mimicked the essential conventions of Arja, was unique in its all-male composition. Their training in Arja chiefly consisted of viewing prominent classical Arja troupes, and committing their respective parts to memory by practicing at home. Initially, the troupe would appear at local temple ceremonies where they were received warmly. The young actors obtained a wider sponsorship with the establishment of Printing Mas Sanggar, a dance studio in Denpasar under the chairmanship of I Nyoman Suarsa, and were transformed from a fledgling troupe into a new Balinese dance-drama phenomenon. Defying its critics in the arts world, many of whom labelled it an amateurish Arja troupe of inferior artistic quality, this troupe has enjoyed soaring popularity.[10] This popularity reached a peak at the Balinese Arts Festival of 1997 and continues to rise until today. At the time of writing, the Arja Muani players were accepting invitations to perform for ceremonial occasions almost every night, travelling all over Bali. The troupe has attained an almost legendary status in Bali, with many saying that '*Arja Muani muncul lagi*', that is; 'An all-male troupe of Arja has emerged again.'[11]

Scholars and observers of the arts in Bali as well as artists of prominent classical Arja troupes are generally dismissive of the new troupe, regarding it as a group of amateurs who fail to do justice to the Arja tradition. While former Deputy Director, now Chairman of STSI, I Wayan Dibia (1992), appreciates what he sees as the ingenuity of this troupe in their obvious ability to meet the tastes of modern Balinese audiences, he is critical of their heavy reliance on humour at the expense of artistic skill:

> I wish they could perform better. It is not just [our task] to present something amusing but something artistically entertaining. So they have to be able to create serious drama to make a more contemplative kind of theme.
>
> (From an interview with I Wayan Dibia, 9 September 1997)

According to the Arja Muani artists themselves, the humorous flavour of their performances is part of a specific strategy, with aims far nobler than the troupe is given credit for. I Kadek Widnyana and I Wayan Sugama are two prominent actors of Arja Muani who insist this is the case, and are quick to combat negative reviews of their troupe's performances.

A graduate of STSI in 1992 and currently a lecturer in *pedalangan* or 'puppeteering' at STSI, I Kadek Widnyana has a respected standing in Denpasar. He also has a prominent position as the player of the noble prince in Arja Muani, the Mantri Manis. Fellow actor I Wayan Sugama, also a graduate of STSI in 1992, had been famous for his comic performances long before the Arja Muani sensation hit Bali. Sugama formerly performed in a highly popular Drama Gong troupe playing one of the clowns. The clowns are the draw card of Drama Gong theatre, as by far the most popular characters, and also the most highly paid actors. Sugama's theatre profile has remained high in Bali following his decision to leave Drama Gong and form the Arja Muani troupe. As the actor of the Liku or crazy princess character of Arja, now deemed the most popular of all Arja's figures, Sugama has confirmed his position in the Balinese theatre world as a leading comic performer. Both actors were centrally involved in the formation of Arja Muani and in the creation of its new and original repertoire of plays.

In defense of his troupe, I Kadek Widnyana insists that Arja Muani's primary objective is to revive Arja's dying popularity and thereby to ensure the preservation of the genre. Highly aware of public perceptions of traditional Arja dance-drama as archaic and boring, Kadek maintains that classic Arja's demise in popularity over the last few decades has been caused by its failure to adapt to modern audience tastes. Young people in particular are quick to label Arja as a dramatic form for 'old men', particularly in its employment of a language loosely termed by younger viewers as '*bahasa kuno*' (old-fashioned or outdated language).[12] Moreover, as Kadek's colleague, I Wayan Sugama puts it, people are no longer tolerant of the philosophical and educational functions of a performance.[13] Rather, in an era of Television and other entertainment media, people are 'thirsty' (*haus*) for 'easy entertainment' (*hiburan*).[14]

This young troupe's perception of a need to forsake Arja's 'high culture' conventions has seen them introduce a number of new tactical elements to their Arja performances. The high-caste characters' songs have been diluted to become more readily consumable. Kadek suggests they now occupy 30–40 per cent of the performance time rather than 60–70 per cent as before, with the use of 'old-fashioned' language reduced in favour of everyday Balinese. Indonesian as well as tourist languages such as English and Japanese are used intermittently in Arja Muani, while the troupe has also introduced elements foreign to Arja conventions, including pop songs, Chinese songs, and elements of other kinds of dance such as ballet. As for Arja's philosophical and moral content, Kadek relates that the troupe has reversed the customary practice of only occasionally interspersing philosophy-laden dialogue with humour. Instead, Arja Muani places a primary emphasis on humour as a means to attract the attention of the viewers to ensure their easy 'digestion' (*menelan*) of the intended philosophical message:

> In the past there was philosophy first, then came the jokes. We of Arja Cowok don't avoid philosophy. High philosophical content is still the primary aim, its just in the way it is expressed that we are different. [...] Arja Muani has only modernized Arja in accordance with the times [..., while] the laws of Arja are still employed.
> (Interview with I Kadek Widnyana, 22 September 1997)[15]

While Widnyana makes clear the rationale behind his troupe's comic artifice, he does not elaborate further on the themes of Arja Muani-style humour. Even a cursory glance reveals, however, that one of these themes is gender. Arja Muani's play upon taboo gender categories is obvious. In a political climate in which a restrictive official code of sexuality and gender prevails, or still lingers as a product of the New Order period, the Arja Muani phenomenon spells sensationalism. By far the greatest advantage of Arja Muani over other, less popular Arja troupes of the classic mould in Bali has been the thrill of seeing men cross-dress. The Balinese crowds love Arja Muani precisely for this reason and often line up back stage as the actors dress to witness these men transform into female characters. Actors play on this in performance, with transvestite jokes and emphasis on female form by the male princess and maidservant.

GENDER AMBIGUITY IN THE INDONESIAN THEATRE CONTEXT

Play on gender in performance is a long-standing characteristic of Indonesian theatre forms. Peacock's study of the East Javanese 1960s theatre form Ludruk, composed chiefly of male transvestite singers and male clowns, provides a good example of this. Peacock (1968: 206–207) noted the allure of cross-sexed performance for 1960s audiences of this theatre form. Ludruk theatre, he argues, represented an entertainment form of the masses in a political era of burgeoning aspirations toward building a modern and progressive Indonesian state. Included in this modernizing ideology was propaganda aimed at reinforcing a more restricted idea of female identity, and the gender code in general.

This had a restrictive effect on Ludruk's previously liberal attitude toward transvestite or homosexual expression. Male performers were urged by troupe leaders to be *maju* ('progressive') by cleaning up the homosexual reference of Ludruk and behaving strictly as men do beyond the theatre site; a practice alien to many actors traditionally effeminate offstage as well as onstage. It was in this climate of a tightening of gender politics in society that the Ludruk theatre represented sheer titillation nevertheless, in its overt flaunting of the modernizing society's rigid gender stereotypes. Peacock observed that this gender ambiguity served to heighten the appeal of the characters:

> Emphasis of the fact that the singers facade covers a male body (the hybrid "culture over nature" aspect) almost seems to enhance the spectators attraction to the character.
>
> (Peacock 1968: 198)

Claire Hanson's (1995) study of modern Indonesian society's attitudes to gender ambiguities enables one, similarly, to situate Arja Muani's special sensationalism within its specific gender-political context. Hanson outlines how the strict regulation of matters of sex and gender prefigured in Peacock's study grew more regimented in the New Order period in the name of a return to supposedly 'traditional' values. Potentially deviant sexual activities and gender categories were vehemently suppressed in the name of a re-invented tradition. Although they were accepted as legitimate within a traditional societal context, transvestites in modern urban Indonesia have become increasingly marginalized over the course of the New Order period, and have been associated with social deviance. In reaction, contemporary attitudes to sex and gender incorporate a fascination for the taboo. It is arguably in the context of this environment that Arja Muani successfully plays its gender-bending draw card.

ARJA MUANI AND FEMALE ADVANCEMENT: MODERN IDEAS OF WOMANHOOD IN PERFORMANCE

The contemporary origins of Arja Muani are suggested by its more markedly female-centric agenda. It is ironic that Arja Muani evidently voices more progressive views on gender issues, particularly female interests, than the conventional female-dominated Arja troupes that are their precursors. Discussions with the troupe reveal, however, that these men, as educated artists, have been more exposed to Western notions of feminism than their predominantly village-based counterparts, making them better positioned and, arguably, more likely to raise challenges to traditional notions of gender. An examination of the way in which Arja Muani conveys its views on female roles and identity in modern-day Bali reveals that this troupe's revision of key elements of traditional Arja performance have been central.

Arja Muani's narrative content, dramatic structure, and method of female characterization may be distinguished from that of the traditional troupes in terms of this troupe's more politicized agenda. However, one still does need to keep in mind the pivotal factor that all of the roles in Arja Muani are played by men. Again, it is this problematic feature of Arja Muani that places its credibility as a genre purported to hold women's interests at heart in some doubt, particularly in the light of a debate amongst feminist theorists as to whether any portrayal of women by men can ultimately be free of negative implications.

I Wayan Sugama, player of the crazy princess, maintains that his Arja troupe seeks to promote women's interests. Another cornerstone in these STSI graduates' remodelling of Arja has been their refusal to rely upon the old traditional scripts derived from the Panji (warrior) stories which other Arja troupes constantly recycle. Instead, Arja Muani have created three of their own new genres of dramatized stories.[16] Described by Sugama as Balinese folktales (cerita rakyat), the two most popular and frequently used of these stories comment on the issue of women's emancipation. This is an issue prominent in Bali today, Sugama argues, due to the permeation of Western gender ideology.

The stories take place in a palace world identical to that of the Panji tales of traditional Arja, but the specific settings are the kingdoms of Madura and Minangkabau. Sugama relates that, respectively, the story of Siti Makonah depicts the dilemma of the modern woman while Ayu Bangsing critiques polygamy. The less popular Dagang Daluman story is more conservative by comparison, with its main themes being 'loyalty' (kesetiaan) and 'service' (pengabdian) to one's king and family. Nevertheless, all of the stories share as a key theme women's right to choose a marriage partner of their own liking, as well as the standard Arja theme of marriage for romantic love, rather than marriage by parental arrangement.

With these innovative narrative contents as outlined by Sugama, Arja Muani arguably has at least the potential to generate more social change than the older Arja troupes which rely on recycling traditional Balinese legends that do not usually offer liberating female role models. Arja Muani is directed strongly (though not exclusively) to a female audience and evidently aims to overturn discriminative practices and the double standards women have borne in relation to men in the past. This can be illustrated by looking more closely at some of the new plays performed by the Arja Muani troupe.

SITI MAKONAH

Siti Makonah is the most popular of Arja Muani's new repertoire of plays. The version of this story frequently used by Arja Muani in their village performances and documented in the written media's coverage of Arja Muani shows, sees Siti Makonah overturn traditional beliefs about women's appropriate submissiveness in the courting game. In her quest for a husband, Siti Makonah humiliates her desired male suitor, the Datuk Raja of Bumi, by pursuing him by deceptive means. As in the TVRI (Indonesian national television) scenario of this play, the good prince and Siti Makonah's sister, Siti Aisyah, had formerly met and fallen in love. But Siti Makonah desires her sister's suitor, so she sends a 'photo of her sister', in fact a picture of herself, to Datuk Raja di Bumi in order to trick him into coming to the palace and marrying her. Siti Makonah is flatly refused by the Datuk Raja who, upon coming to the palace to propose to her, finds that she is not the beautiful princess he had expected. He is afraid, however, to inform the Queen of his rejection of her younger daughter. So humbled, the Prince flees the palace, seething with anger over the guile of Siti Makonah.

This popular play (*lakon*) stands as evidence for the way in which Arja Muani seeks to manipulate traditional folklore in order to advance modern-day, Western notions of female advancement. Siti Makonah alias Arja's crazy princess, the Liku, represents a female figure whose treachery toward the good Prince is conceived by Sugama as overturning the traditional passivity of women in the courting game. Siti Makonah actively pursues the man she desires. While this is not new to Arja and is in fact standard Liku behaviour in the older troupes, Arja Muani's attempt to equate it with the modern context does represent an innovation. Arja Muani exalts Siti Makonah as the embodiment of 'the modern woman' and endorses her choice to exercise self-determination in selecting a marriage partner, by elevating drastically the status of this eccentric female character within its scripts.

AYU BANGSING

In the play Ayu Bangsing, the plot centres around the Liku alias Ayu Bangsing's attempt to steal her sister's husband by using the powers of *guna-guna* or 'magic'. The Liku herself is already attached but attempts nevertheless to attain for herself a second and more desirable spouse. The Liku's use of *guna-guna* to deceive the prince and make him fall for her is construed in Arja Muani as a female backlash against the more customary use of this same art of magical manipulation by male perpetrators. According to Sugama, Arja Muani shows men how it feels to become the victim of love-magic, accenting the injustice of this male tactic by demonizing the Liku. This mythical practice wherein a man would use magic to trick a girl into falling madly in love with him still continues in contemporary Bali.[17]

Ayu Bangsing's Liku also subverts the gender hierarchy of Bali's traditional polygamous unions in which it was almost always women who held the subordinate position as the co-wives of a shared husband. Sugama's account of the story emphasizes that Ayu Bangsing 'gender-bends' the traditional Balinese practices of *guna-guna* and polygamy (*maduan*) specifically to highlight the way these strategies generally were used to oppress women. He speaks passionately about the sufferings born by women in polygamous unions in the past, citing the fact that a woman's failure to have a child was often cause enough for her husband to take another wife. Conceiving himself as a wife in those times, Sugama underlines women's subordinate position:

> Although I really loved my husband, nevertheless in that happiness I suffered. I was even willing to return to my parents home. But I was sacrificed, rather than his children or my former husband himself.
> (Interview with I Wayan Sugama, 7 October 1997)[18]

Sugama outlines that through the medium of entertainment, Arja Muani hopes to stamp out customs unjust toward women:

> We want to determine that [these practices] never return, using media like TVRI [a station which often televises Arja Muani performances].
> (Interview with I Wayan Sugama, 7 October 1997)[19]

Thus, in the role of Ayu Bangsing, the Liku's use of magic is said to have metaphorical purpose in Arja Muani. Sugama underlines that what on the surface appears to be the Liku's indulgence in the black arts to steal the Galuh's husband, in fact represents a princess' attempt to determine her own fate albeit from within the confines of her subordinate position in a traditional feudal state. As Sugama puts it,

> ...her magic is symbolic of determining one's fate, just as a flower is a metaphor for a woman's suffering.
> (Interview with I Wayan Sugama, 7 October 1997)[20]

In addition to this reference to women's self-determination, Sugama relates that the Liku's magic also works on another, apparently contradictory level in Ayu Bangsing, as a metaphor for the suppression of the Balinese people as a whole under colonialism. At this level, the Liku's use of magic has a negative association, representing the *kelicinan penjajah* or 'the cunning and artifice of the colonizers'. Speaking of the way that the

Indonesian people were blinded by the white people's grandeur, and stripped of their national integrity, Sugama declares:

> We were stupid to allow ourselves to be deceived like that. Because in my opinion, that black magic [*sihir*] was not only a magic formula. We gave our money too.
>
> (Interview with I Wayan Sugama, 7 October 1997)[21]

Sugama's representation of the Liku's use of magic in Ayu Bangsing represents a peculiar inversion of the contrary and equally widespread view of the destructive potential of women in the use of black magic. Both Megan Jennaway's (1995) study of polygyny and Lynette Parker's (1993) study of women's sexuality and fecundity in Bali highlight the negative attitudes toward women accused of practicing witchcraft.[22] Both cite the petty witchcraft accusations launched by bickering co-wives in polygamous unions, symptomatic of their competition for the regard of one dominant male. Parker goes further, citing the male fear of female use of black magic, which the Balinese believe to be capable of causing failures in reproduction such as miscarriages. Thus one could equally argue that in Arja Muani's Ayu Bangsing the 'modern' woman is shown as acting in a destructive way. It seems likely that ambivalent attitudes do surround the Liku character in Arja Muani. For while Sugama portrays her as a champion of modern women's cause, the Liku is still often seen in an unfavourable light by audiences because of her unchanged role in upsetting the affairs of the virtuous Galuh through her tampering with black magic.

EXPRESSION OF FEMALE GENDER ATTITUDES IN ARJA MUANI

That expression of female interests reaches new heights in Arja Muani is inextricably connected to the male actors' engagement in a much coarser mode of dialogue than their traditional counterparts. Arja Muani does take up contemporary women's interests, albeit enmeshed in sexual innuendo – a comic strategy potentially making the troupe's deeper messages on gender relations and female agency all the more penetrating. In addition to this, Arja Muani's female comic figures, the female characters who have always served as vehicles in Arja for the expression of female-centric values, are far more radical and outspoken on women's issues than those of classic Arja troupes. This unrestricted public airing of contemporary gender issues skilfully packaged in the most humorous part of the play is apparently positively received by Arja Muani audiences. The scene featuring the Liku and Desak is always the most popular one in any performance.

Early in her standard introductory scene, in both Siti Makonah and Ayu Bangsing, the Liku's maidservant, the Desak Rai, states with gusto: 'In this era, women must be able to, once in a while, stand on top of a man's erect penis.'[23] This erotic reference is used here not only as a joke but as a metaphor, a discursive device frequently used in Arja Muani's dialogue. The Desak is clearly urging women to empower themselves and, interpreted more literally, it suggests that rather than being subordinate to men, they should in fact be dominant. This feisty male Desak often mentions '*emancipasi wanita*' (women's emancipation) in Siti Makonah, and makes strong commentary upon the issue of female oppression. In her championing of female autonomy and empowerment, the Desak also expresses strong anti-male sentiment in encouraging women never to trust men: 'If you're a woman, don't just believe a man! Men nowadays, for one word, there's 1000 lies.'[24] Moreover, the Desak stresses the importance of education and a career for women in the modern era, again using the technique of metaphor to convey her stance on this women's issue. Speaking of herself as a 'lost soul', the Desak relates how she has never studied and now just 'walks around aimlessly'.

DISPLACEMENT OF A FEMININE PARADIGM IN ARJA MUANI: THE LIKU SUCCEEDS THE GALUH AS THE LEADING FEMALE CHARACTER

A unique feature of this male troupe's shows is their displacement of the Galuh, the good princess, by the Liku, the crazy princess figure, newly cast in Arja Muani as the most prominent female character. While the Galuh remains the angelic female character she had been in classical Arja, she is sidelined in Arja Muani by her more interesting female inferiors.

This is achieved by the Galuh's restriction to Kawi song and associated incapacity to hold an easy dialogue with her audience, and by the greater weight given to the actions and affairs of her vocal female antagonist. An icon of traditionalism, the Galuh is identified with Arja's reputation as an archaic tradition, and like the remodelling of the genre itself to suit modern tastes, the Galuh's role too has been played down to accommodate Arja Muani's modernizing agenda. This lends the Galuh's outspoken female counterparts greater credibility in this male troupe, with the Liku acquiring a new platform upon which to act as a model of 'modern' womanhood, and the Desak's prominence raised accordingly alongside that of her mistress to become Arja Muani's leading proponent of female advancement. In this way, the Desak and Liku pair, buffered by their eccentricity, together espouse liberal viewpoints on women's status vis-à-vis men, speaking directly to their mostly female audience.

NOTIONS OF FEMALE MODESTY IN ARJA MUANI

Audiences also receive mixed messages on matters of sexuality and gender in Arja Muani. On one level, the increase in sexual innuendo in Arja Muani compared to traditional troupes has had a liberating effect on the lower caste characters' sexual impulses. In Arja Muani one finds the increased blatancy of lower caste characters sexual licentiousness; characters whose reputations were already rather dubious in this regard in conventional Arja performances.[25] A primary example of this is the scene between the Condong (a female servant) and the clown Wijil which, like in the older troupes, ends in the Condong surrendering to the Wijil's advances, being affectionate with him at back corner stage. The dialogue used among this lower-caste pair makes explicit reference to the Condong's promiscuity, as the Condong cites her fall from grace on three occasions as a result of their intimate relations: 'I am still alone and already three times I have had a miscarriage/lost my good name.'[26]

One could also interpret this emphasis on the sexual activity of the lower caste characters as fitting in with a more conservative stance on female sexuality in Arja Muani at a pragmatic level. The example made of the Condong, for example, could ultimately be aimed at reinforcing among young women an awareness of the consequences of sexual looseness, by highlighting through the Condong's experience the male infidelity and inconstancy so bemoaned by the Desak. This is certainly in line with a rather problematic feature of this troupe's promotion of female interests via the Liku figure. For while the Liku and Desak do promote female independence and astuteness in dealing with men, they direct their moral teachings exclusively to women, and depict men's sexual licentiousness as a 'natural' inherent quality of masculinity. This puts the onus upon women to say 'no'. The Liku encourages women not to be readily available to men, and further warns that they will go to hell (*neraka*) if they become 'naughty girls' (*perempuan nakal*).

Arja Muani's residual traditionalism in regard to female sexual behaviour is also reflected in their attack on the influence of western values and the surmised escalation of promiscuity amongst the younger generation in Bali. Asia-centric values of female modesty are preached through a criticism of Western style dress, for example, with skimpy clothing cited by the Liku as inappropriate attire for Balinese women. Couching her criticism in a tenor of joviality, the Liku states:

> Even now girls wear clothes such that their belly can be seen. They don't want to spend the money buying [lots of] material.[27]

Similarly, the clown Wijil remarks in the play 'Ayu Bangsing':

> I am only warning the girls and the women to not sit so comfortably
> that their genitals can be seen [...] There's nothing wrong with eyes
> that stare because there is something stimulating to be seen![28]

This fear campaign launched at girls in response to concerns about
modernization was also noted by Peacock as being a standard feature of
Ludruk in the 1960s. As in Arja Muani, it was again the comic characters
who sought to reinforce the traditional code of modesty amongst young
women, assuming that to break with tradition causes girls to become sexu-
ally loose. Directing their ire towards young women, Ludruk's clowns
castigated them for abandoning modest dress-codes and portrayed
promiscuity as immoral behaviour leading to a bad fate; reminiscent of
Arja Muani's reference to hell.

Commentary upon the young generations' sexual activity in that era took
on similarly moralistic overtones, with the clowns conveying advice such as:

> Young men and women, if you mingle freely with one another, do
> not go past the limits. If girls are not able to guard their honour,
> finally they will be pregnant without being married.
>
> (Peacock 1968: 177)

THE LIMITATIONS OF ARJA MUANI'S LIBERAL GENDER
DIALOGUE AND FEMALE CHARACTERIZATION

Their evidently conservative stance on female sexuality aside, there are
other limitations on this male troupe's expression of female-centred
interests. Specifically, Arja Muani has preserved the Arja tradition of
voicing liberal viewpoints on gender relations and women's status via its
comic female characters. As in its forerunner, it is again by virtue of the
Liku and Desak's renowned eccentricity that they have such unrestricted
license to engage in their radical dialogue on gender; a mechanism that
both qualifies their messages and protects them from the sharp social
criticism their stance might otherwise arouse. In addition, one could
argue that the accentuation of the comic in Arja Muani performance
further tempers their alleged seriousness about women's issues. The
sharp increase in sexual innuendo lacing the characters' dialogue arguably weakens these characters validity as 'female' role models respectable
young Balinese women might feasibly emulate.

A further and perhaps more problematic feature of Arja Muani's representation of female interests is identified in feminist debates about the
implications of female impersonation by men for notions of female identity and women's status in general. While Marjorie Gerber, for example,

is of the view that 'transvestism tells the truth about gender' (1993: 250) and advances an argument for the 'subversive power of transvestitism both to undermine and to exemplify cultural constructions'(1993: 249), her study of Chinese opera and Japanese Kabuki theatre also highlights the problematic aspects of a representation of women and women's interests by men. According to Gerber's assessment, the art of female impersonation may be regarded as a 'political and cultural act'(1993: 243). She concludes that Chinese opera and Kabuki traditionally 'present "woman" as a cultural artefact of male stagecraft' (Gerber 1993: 245).

Mary Russo's (1986) study of the historical use of female masquerade by men for political purposes supports this view of male cross-dressing as an appropriation of the feminine, ultimately reinforcing men's dominant status. In Russo's view, 'to put on femininity with a vengeance suggests the power of taking it off'(1986: 224).

Arja Muani does not represent 'fetishized female images' in the manner of the older Asian traditions of Chinese Opera and Japanese Kabuki theatre examined in Gerber's study.[29] Moreover, Arja Muani is unlike Ludruk in that its constant humorous undercutting of the gender allusion works against male sexual attraction to transvestite players as embodiments of 'fantasies of sexual escape from adult responsibilities' (Peacock 1968: 204). Arja Muani is an explicitly comic form – in contrast to the 'serious parody' of other theatre forms – with its portrayal of women overwhelmingly aimed at getting laughs. But on a more serious note, the fact that these men play women in such a coarse way arguably has a [reverse] perverse effect on the female behaviour code. The bawdy reinvention of Arja's female characters in Arja Muani ultimately reinforces an idea of what a young woman should *not* be. In Arja Muani, the Galuh and Liku, the two female characters who in classic Arja traditionally served to represent bipolar extremes of femininity, are closer in Arja Muani in that both share elements of *kasar* (coarse) masculinity.

ARJA MUANI AND TRANSVESTITISM

Arja Muani can also be seen as a flamboyant parade of men flaunting their talent and aptitude at becoming women within the legitimate setting of the stage. As such, Arja Muani could be said to offer renewed authenticity to nonconforming gender identities, such as transvestitism, especially in view of their marginalized position as taboo gender categories in mainstream Indonesian society today. Arja Muani is an innovative troupe for its time, especially in terms of its exploitation of 'deviant' gender imagery. In response to the tightening of state-promoted gender categories, its contemporary theatre counterparts, by contrast, seem to have followed suit in promoting state-endorsed stereotypes, with their realist and fixedly gender-specific mode of gender representation.[30] This pattern has also been observed more broadly in the Javanese performing arts, which have witnessed a cleaning up of sexual elements in general. A primary example is the polishing of Ludruk transvestites' sexual image noted earlier. Also mentioned earlier was the example of the Tayuban dance form of Java, and Amrih Widodo's (1995) contention that the image of the *ledhek* dancer as temptress in Tayuban has been played down with the state's domestication of the genre.

Arja Muani constantly plays upon the fact of the players' 'real' male identity in their performances. Actors adjust the stuffing in their chests and lapse into a male stride upon occasion – candid illustrations that they are not really women but men in women's clothing. They also allude to transvestitism and even homosexual relations, for example in the standard scene between the princess's maidservant, the Condong, and the male clown. While the maidservant is played by a female performer in classical Arja shows, here it is a crass love scene between two men. Having surrendered to his male pursuer, the maidservant stands in a corner with him, as in old Arja shows where the pair usually gives the illusion of unbridled affection. Here however, this male maidservant drops his female persona and adopts a male stance, smoking a cigarette as the clown chats him up. That Arja Muani players can get away with the controversial nature of their shows has much to do with the fact that they employ the art of gender-switching in a fundamentally humorous way.

Arja Muani does offer affirmation of the blending of the two genders' traits in each individual in their shows – a view traditionally accepted in Arja circles and in the wider theatre community as a whole.[31] The actors make constant physical allusions to their containment of both male and female elements, and this theme also recurs in the comic characters' dialogue. In the scene between the Limbur, Liku and Desak Rai, the Liku calls upon the Hindu–Balinese philosophy of dualism to explain her divergence from the gentle behaviour expected from her as a young woman. The Liku tells her mother that she has been drinking green *jamu* (a medicinal potion) to make her soft and gentle. However, a moment later she stands up from her sitting position in a rough manner, abandoning her earlier attention to refinement. When asked why her manner changed so suddenly, the Liku refers to *rua bineda* – the idea of the 'two different' forces in all things. As she has elements of both of these forces, like every individual, the Liku states: 'because I [was] gentle, I must [now] be rough.'[32] The dialogue here has subversive overtones, drawing on a cosmological concept of spiritual balance in reference to gender and sexuality in such a way as to justify the blurring of New Order society's rigid distinction between female and male, and to imply that *alus* and *keras* are not necessarily gender-specific traits after all.

The actors' personal stories also testify to Arja Muani's inheritance of Arja theatre's traditionally liberal attitudes to gender. This is illustrated best by the case of I Made Jelada. Jelada, who plays the role of Condong in Arja Muani, is a highly revered artist in Bali, famous for his ability in male and female dance styles and his capacity to perform both male and female characters. He notes that

> when in male costume I look appropriate, [but] when dressed as a female character I look appropriate too.
>
> (Interview with I Made Jelada, 22 October 1997)[33]

Moreover, while he is obviously adept in cross-sexed performance and at ease assuming a female identity onstage, Jelada further relates that he is best suited to the refined dance style: 'I am gifted as a refined dancer' (Interview, 22 October 1997).[34] For this reason, in a trial all-male Arja troupe of the 1980s, Jelada performed the refined character roles of the Mantri Manis and later the Galuh. He is now playing the role of Condong in Arja Muani because of his mature age.[35] In arguing that his *kodrat* or 'inherent nature' makes him most suited to *alus* roles, Jelada openly identifies with an *alus* style more commonly associated with the female dance style than the male in contemporary Balinese theatre. Like its Arja counterparts and unlike most other theatre forms today (including Ludruk), Arja Muani's flexible stance on gender thus transcends purely aesthetic purposes, accepting in its dancers the embodiment of ambiguous gender traits not just on stage, but in their 'real' lives.[36]

One still needs to ask whether Arja Muani's style of cross-sexed performance is primarily a send-up of '*banci*-hood', that is, of the effeminate male homosexual.[37] Dede Oetomo's (1996) study of society's 'third gender' immediately brings to mind a parallel between *banci* identity and Arja Muani's cross-gender play. As Oetomo relates,

> embodying elements of maleness and femaleness, *banci* display gender behaviour over a range that runs from the refined, coy [*halus*] attributes of the 'proper' woman to the coarse, aggressive [*kasar*] characteristics of the typical lower-class man.
>
> (1996: 266)

The representation by Arja Muani's male actors of fluid gender identities similarly spanning refined to coarse traits in their 'male-as-female' roles, is clearly reminiscent of *banci* behaviour. For example, Oetomo's reference to the striking contrast sometimes found between the *banci's* feminine dress and his masculine behaviour may similarly be paralleled with Arja Muani performance. Oetomo's '*banci kasar*' who, while adopting a matronly image, nevertheless behaves in *kasar* ways upon occasion, such as showing his panties or punching young men, immediately conjures up the Arja Muani Condong. Actor of the Condong, I Made Jelada, uses similar means of disclosing the fact he is male, such as raising his fists to hit the Mantri Buduh in defence of the Galuh.

It is this comic dimension of Arja Muani's references to gender ambiguity that signals the ambiguity of this troupe's 'gender-bending'. While Arja Muani performances offer affirmation of the idea of the 'natural' blending of genders, there is also an element therein that clearly subverts the allusion of feminity by riotously bringing out masculinity as if to undermine the more serious implications of their radical, gender fluid performances.

CONCLUDING REMARKS

A modern offshoot of the Arja genre, Arja Muani unites the traditional theatre conventions of the original Arja troupes with its own dramatic devices so as to cater to Bali's self-consciously *moderen* ('modern') social climate. As a result, the style of Arja Muani's cross-gender performance is indicative of an inherent conflict in this new Arja troupe between its liberal roots and the opposing rigid gender code marking the conservative *jaman* or social period of the New Order in which this contemporary Arja troupe first emerged. It should be noted, however, that the Suharto regime at the time, in 1993, was already beginning to show signs of weakening, illustrated, for example, by Suharto's increasing supportiveness of and reliance on the political support of Islamic organizations.

At the same time, the use of humour as a disguise for social criticism is still typical of how the arts in Bali and elsewhere had to operate to escape censorship. The main contribution to social critique in the case of Arja Muani is its commentary on gender identities.

This all-male troupes' gender representation and gender imagery reflects a stance on gender identity which encompasses elements of radical liberalism through to extreme conservatism. Ultimately, an analysis of Arja Muani's current and future potential to rework New Order gender notions in the current *jaman* of *Reformasi*, will have to address all of the plural dimensions and potential meanings of its gender references.[38]

The findings of my earlier research underlined the significance of the performing arts of Bali as a place to explore shifts in Balinese attitudes to and consciousness of gender issues (Kellar 2000). Arguably, the complexities and contradictions inherent in this contemporary male Arja's gender representation reflect similar complexities and tensions in gender issues and ideas about the 'modern woman' in Balinese and Indonesian society as a whole.

Maila Stivens and Krishna Sen (1998), in a volume on gender relations in the more affluent circles of Asian societies, argue that stereotypes of female identity are more complex now than ever before. Stivens' observation of Asian societies' response to the break down of traditional concepts of women's place, as exemplified in the New Order 'woman-as-housewife' ideal, may help to explain some of the ambiguities of Arja Muani's gender dialogue:

> The anxieties about the threats posed to the 'Asian family' and to women's 'traditional' roles seem to have become a favoured site for expressing more general tensions and ambivalences about the costs of modernity and 'development' in both mainstream political and cultural forums.
>
> (Stivens 1998: 8)

Thus, in Arja Muani one finds both a new liberal concept of the modern woman *and* a fear of the destructive influence of global forces and modernity on Bali; a fear couched specifically in terms of the threats posed to women's virtue.

In the end, however, one has to return to the fact that this troupe attracts the masses of its followers chiefly because of its reputation for witty and sensationalist humour. It is this overwhelming image of Arja Muani which distinguishes it most from its theatrical roots – the 'high culture' label that now acts to the disadvantage of classical Arja troupes. It is also this image which has aroused the negative responses of arts critics and observers. For despite its success amongst the masses, questions of authenticity have arisen, with dancers of classic Arja and arts scholars in Bali contending that Arja Muani reinvents Arja and to some extent abuses its conventions. Arja Muani is seen by these groups as failing to do justice to Arja and as being preoccupied with exploiting the once orthodox practice of cross-sexed performance for its modern-day sensationalist appeal.

A prominent Arja performer and grass-roots artist (*seniman alam*), Ni Nyoman Candri stands for the majority of her colleagues in her belief that Arja Muani departs from original Arja's conventions.[39] She distinguishes this troupe from the all-male troupes of Arja in the 1920s, stating that

> According to my father, the Arja of the past was focussed on literature and Arja dance, indeed Arja dance, while in this contemporary troupe it is the jokes which are emphasized.
>
> (Interview with Ni Nyoman Candri, 31 August 1997)[40]

Whichever way one chooses to view Arja Muani, this troupe's huge success in Bali attests to the fact that they are attuned to the tastes and concerns of modern Balinese audiences, which leaves them better placed than their traditional counterparts in terms of achieving the common aim to preserve the Arja genre.

As a final note, the ultimate irony of the Arja Muani phenomenon lies in the fact that the success of Arja Muani has brought about the marginalization and disenfranchisement of the prominent female performers, whose rise through Arja I have documented in my earlier work (Kellar 2000). Arja Muani, as Arja's modern-day manifestation, has essentially transformed Arja from a female to a male-centric genre, reflecting the trend earlier outlined towards an overall pattern of male control reasserting itself in the performing arts domain.

Ironically, Arja Muani – a troupe espousing liberal Western notions of female empowerment – has undermined classic Arja's other 'feminist' gains, with women's troupes struggling to survive and unable to compete with the popularity of the outrageous new genre. As members of Arja Muani themselves acknowledge, the championing of female interests in their shows was largely inspired by the example of the very women whose art form they have appropriated. As previously noted, a key factor in this picture is that most of Arja Muani's performers possess a modern education. For it is a further irony that as highly schooled, sophisticated and socially aware men – indeed, as products of the New Order era – Arja Muani performers have been successful in undermining New Order discourses on female roles and identity. This practice has become particularly significant in the current *Reformasi* era. Arja Muani promotes and presumably will continue to promote ideas of women's progress in a more informed and strategic way than their *seniman alam* counterparts.

NOTES

1 *'Perkembangan kesenian itu mengikuti perkembangan jaman'* (Interview with I Wayan Rawit, 3 September 1997).
2 The Balinese magazine *Damai*'s stance on career-orientated women was expressed in the following way: 'Mother: "Child, woman and man are always different. Their progress is always different too. And why, my child? If a man is too progressive it won't ruin him, but suppose a woman is too advanced. Her stomach becomes large [...] and the village head will have difficulty with the birth registration. This is the difference".'(Cited in Vickers, Darma Putra and Wijaya, 1998 from *Damai*, II/2, 17 January 1955: 10). This excerpt also underlines the promotion of the idea of men and women's gender-specificity, a notion fundamental to the New Order regime's gender policies.
3 Both STSI and village dance trainers uphold the traditional Balinese practice of cross-gender dance training. In both sites of dance tuition in Bali, once they are sufficiently adept in the dance style of their own biological gender, male and female students are free to seek further advancement in forms of their own gender, cross-gender dance styles or dance of the opposite sex. Those who are successful commonly go on to perform in this style for unofficial ceremonial occasions and may also teach this skill to young protégés. Koming, daughter of renowned classical Arja performer Ni Nyoman Candri, is a primary example. This young woman openly prefers *'tari laki'* or male dance, and is a renowned teacher and dancer of men's dance styles such as *baris* (a warrior dance) in her village of Singapadu.

4 The Legong Lasem exam, witnessed by the author during her time as a student at STSI, was suggestive of modern society's intolerance of cross-sexed performances in Balinese dance. Three male Legong students participated in this otherwise all girl dance exam. They were dressed in the female costumes of the Legong dance, wearing makeup and jewellery as the role demanded and one student had even shaved off his moustache that morning. Their confidence waned, however, as they left their changing rooms and got up on stage – embarrassed and nervous in the face of the jeers and laughter of their male peers from the visual arts faculty. Comments like 'Who is the most beautiful?' directed towards these brave male Legong dancers was striking testimony to the rigid ideas about gender identity in New Order Balinese society – ideas that made a mockery of this 'liberal' and flexible role allocation characteristic of the Balinese theatre tradition.

5 '*Tidak bisa kalau di masyarakat, laki-laki tidak pentas Legong di masyarakat. Kalau masyarakat, laki-laki ambil tarian laki-laki saja*' (Interview with Sriyanyi, 20 May 1997).

6 The colossal Sendratari performances put on by the Denpasar dance academies SMKI and STSI for the Bali Arts Festival each year are spectacles of great extravagance. The productions often involve hundreds of dancers and costuming is elaborate, with dancers dressed in shimmering and richly coloured traditional costumes often of gold, reds and brilliant greens, and golden headdresses and jewellery adorning the dancers. The staging and lighting moreover, adds to the overall effect of a breathtakingly beautiful performance which usually draws crowds of over 4000. No expense is spared for these performances.

7 *Odalan* is the periodic celebration of a 'temple festival' (usually every 210 days), during which time the gods descend from the heavens to receive homage from the temple congregation (see Picard 1996).

8 Literally, the 'temple of the interior', the *pura dalem* is where the disruptive influences of the not-yet-purified dead are placated and the deity of death is honoured.

9 The term '*Arja Muani*' literally means 'male Arja'. The term Arja *Cowok* has the same meaning, *cowok* being the Indonesian term for male. This second term is often used for this troupe at an informal level, particularly amongst the older generation of artists and audience members.

10 See comments by prominent figures of classic Arja as well as arts academics and observers later in this paper.

11 This common remark refers back to an all-male Arja of the past, seeing this new troupe as a reincarnation of an all-male Arja troupe in the 1920s. While this original all-male Arja troupe was not literally called 'Arja Muani' at that time, the informal term for both the male Arja of the past and the contemporary Arja Muani has been *Arja Cowok*.

12 In his study of *Wayang Kulit* in Java, Ward Keeler also found that Indonesia's young generation are increasingly losing an appreciation for the refined and 'flowery' nature of the traditional performing arts due to their illiteracy in the classical languages of these oral traditions. Despite their relatively high education, the young people of modern Indonesia are not reading classical literature. They remain ignorant of their forefathers literary and artistic legacy while they become increasingly familiar with Western forms of popular culture (Keeler 1987: 186–87).

13 Comparing modern audiences' tastes with those of Arja audiences in the past, Sugama notes that: *Jaman dulu adalah jaman filsafat* or 'the past era was the era of philosophy' (Interview, I Wayan Sugama, 7 October 1997).

14 Interview with I Wayan Sugama, 7 October 1997.

15 'Arja Cowok telah memperbarui Arja sesuai dengan jaman [. . .] hukum-hukum Arja masih tetap dipakai' (Interview, I Wayan Sugama, 7 October 1997).

16 Sugama discussed his ideas for a fourth story with the author at the time of research; a story in which a career-wise Desak Rai would marry.

17 A Balinese friend of the writer insisted that the practice of guna-guna is still used today in his northern Balinese village in Singaraja. He contended that it was predominantly men who used guna-guna in order to attract the girl they desired and make her fall madly in love with them.

18 'Walaupun saya sangat mencintai suami saya, tapi dengan kebahagianya saya rela menderita . . . Saya pun rela kembali ke rumah orang tua saya. Saya ikhlas daripada anaknya atau suami bekas saya' (Interview, I Wayan Sugama, 7 October 1997).

19 'Kita mau menentukan tak kembali, lewat media seperti TVRI' (Interview, I Wayan Sugama, 7 October 1997).

20 'Sihirnya begitu untuk menasibkan seperti bunga ibarat menderitakan untuk wanita' (Interview, I Wayan Sugama, 7 October 1997).

21 'Kita bodoh kita bisa ditipu seperti itu. Sebab bayangan saya, saya bayang itu sihir itu tidak hanya mantera. Dengan duitku saya kasih' (Interview, I Wayan Sugama, 7 October 1997).

22 See also Jennaway (1995) and Parker (1993).

23 'Jaman sekarang wanita itu harus bisa sekali-sekali berdiri di ujung tombaknya laki-laki.' The Desak Rai, Arja Muani's performance of Siti Makonah, Bali Arts Festival, 27 June 1997.

24 'Jangan percaya omongan laki-laki. Laki-laki jaman sekarang, satu kata seribu dusta.' The Desak Rai, Arja Muani's performance of Siti Makonah, Bali Arts Festival, 27 June 1997.

25 Similar scenes as those in Arja Muani described above take place between the servant characters in traditional Arja performances. Arja has thus always offered such deviant images of male and female sexuality, but without the emphasis on smutty humour introduced in this contemporary troupe's dialogue.

26 'Saya masih sendiri, sudah tiga kali mengugurkan.' Transcribed script of Arja Muani's Ayu Bangsing, performed in July 1997.

27 'Sekarangpun orang gadis memakai pakaian tetapi perutnya bisa dilihat. Mereka tidak mau membayari bahannya.' The Liku, Arja Muani's performance of Siti Makonah, Bali Arts Festival, 27 June 1997.

28 'Saya hanya memberi tahu gadis-gadis dan ibu-ibu supaya jangan duduk seenaknya saja sehingga tak sampai kelihatan anunya . . . tak salah mata memandang karena ada obyek merangsang.' From transcribed script of Arja Muani's Ayu Bangsing.

29 Peggy Phelan (1988) argues that the boy-child Balinese dancer represents a gender-neutral state upon which are projected male fantasies of idealized femininity. For Phelan, his dancing in the feminine dance style represents 'a substitution for the female in the sphere of visual desire' (1988: 111). This observation links the tradition of Balinese male transvestite dance, newly categorized in academic circles as tarian berbancihan laki, to Ludruk.

30 For a more detailed discussion of the modern Balinese dance-drama forms Sendratari and Drama Gong's reflection of New Order gender ideology in their mode of role allocation and gender representation, see Kellar (2000).

31 Highly flexible attitudes to gender identity prevail in traditional Arja troupes. Gender-switching constitutes a natural and unproblematic phenomenon within the framework of traditional Balinese theatre aesthetics. Arja's role allocation method always has seen the objectives of theatre aesthetics and perfect categorization override any consideration of an actor's gender identity offstage. In Arja, an actor is allocated a part in accordance with her or his personality traits, with this process often recognizing the actor's possession of

traits later assigned more strictly to the other gender, under the New Order bipolar notion of gender identity. A similarly flexible code of gender operates in the dance training environment, both at the academic institution STSI and in Balinese villages. In both dance training settings, an essentially non-gender-specific dance training method is customary. For more details, see Kellar (2000: Chapters 2 and 4).

32 '*Sebab saya lembut, jadi saya harus keras.*' The Liku, Arja Muani's performance of Siti Makonah, Bali Arts Festival, 27 June 1997.

33 '*Kalau perias itu, perias laki – cocok, perias perempuan – cocok*' (Interview, I Made Jelada, 22 October 1997).

34 '*Karena tenaga saya sudah ditakar ukurannya segini itu – untuk penari alus itu*' (Interview, I Made Jelada, 22 October 1997).

35 This practice is similar to one seen in conventional Arja troupes, whereby dancers stop performing roles considered to demand youthful looks and beauty such as that of the Galuh, and assume more matronly roles befitting their own aging appearance.

36 This broad view of gender identity is notably one held by scholars of the performing arts, including the former Director of STSI, Professor Dr I Made Bandem. As Bandem asserts: '*Sekeras dan halus itu selalu ada pada orang*' (some coarseness and refinement are always found in every person).

37 The *banci* figure in Indonesia is regarded as a third gender and is stigmatized as such. He is usually a cross-dressed male who is often assumed to be homosexual but is also often bisexual.

38 It needs to be remembered that *Arja Muani* can be seen to be working on all of its various levels simultaneously, so that, inevitably, a degree of overlap occurs in an analysis of this troupe's performances, particularly in terms of the kind of gender imagery and gender representation that is projected.

39 The fact that Arja artists like Ni Nyoman Candri are affiliated with other Arja troupes whose popularity has plummeted as a result of Arja Muani's success needs to be born in mind. Arja artists of traditional troupes, like Candri herself, often speak of Arja Muani in a tone that is not only patronizing but also resentful, suggesting that they view Arja Muani as their competitor.

40 '*Kalau menurut bapak saya jaman dulu itu Arjanya berdoman dengan sastra dan tari Arja, memang tari Arja. Kalau sekarang ia lelucon yang ditonjolkan*' (Interview with Ni Nyoman Candri, 31 August 1997).

REFERENCES

Connor, Linda, Asch, Patsy and Asch, Timothy (1996) *Jero Tapakan, Balinese Healer: An Ethnographic Film Monograph*, Los Angeles: Ethnographics Press.

DeBoer, Fredrik E. (1996) 'Two Modern Balinese Theatre Genres: Sendratari & Drama Gong'. In Adrian Vickers (ed.), *Being Modern in Bali: Image and Change*, New Haven, (Conn.): Yale University Southeast Asia Studies.

Dibia, I Wayan (1992) *Evolusi dan Eksistensi Arja – Arja Dilihat Dari Perubahan Masyarakat Pendukungnya*. A speech for Dies Natalis Ke XXV, Denpasar, 18 April 1992.

Dibia, Wayan (1992) *Arja: A Sung Dance-Drama of Bali: A Study of Change and Transformation*, Los Angeles: University of California, unpublished Ph.D. Thesis.

Emigh, John and Hunt, Jamer (1992) 'Gender Bending in Balinese Performance'. In Laurence Senelick (ed.), *Gender in Performance: The Presentation of Difference in the Performing Arts*, Hanover (N.H.): University Press of New England.

Gerber, Marjorie (1993) 'Phantoms of the Opera: Actor, Diplomat, Transvestite, Spy'. In Marjorie Gerber (ed.), *Vested Interests: Cross-dressing and Cultural Anxiety*, New York: Harper Perennial.

Hanson, Claire (1995) *Representation of, and Attitudes Towards, Gender Ambiguity in Indonesia's Indigenous and Contemporary, Urban Societies*, Clayton: Monash University, unpublished Honours Thesis.

Hatley, Barbara (1995) 'Women in Contemporary Indonesia Theatre – Issues of Representation and Participation'. *Bijdragen, Tot de Taal-, Land- en Volkenkunde*, 151 IV, Gravenhage: M. Nijhoff.

Hough, Brett (1992) *Contemporary Balinese Dance Spectacles as National Ritual*, Clayton: Centre of Southeast Asian Studies, Monash University.

Hughes-Freeland, Felicia (1993) 'Golek Menak and Tayuban: Patronage and Professionalism in Two Spheres of Central Javanese Culture'. In Bernard Arps (ed.), *Performance in Java and Bali: Studies of Narrative, Theatre, Music and Dance*, London: School of Oriental and African Studies, University of London.

Hughes-Freeland, Felicia (1995) 'Making History? Cultural Documentation on Balinese Television'. *Review of Indonesian and Malaysian Affairs*, 29 (1&2), Sydney: Department of Indonesian and Malayan Studies, The University of Sydney.

Jennaway, Megan (1995) *Bitter Honey: Female Polygynous Destinies in North Bali*. Paper presented at the Third WIVS Workshop on 'Indonesian Women: In the Household and Beyond: Reconstructing the Boundaries'. 25–29 September 1995, Leiden Univerisity, The Netherlands.

Keeler, Ward (1987) *Javanese Shadow Plays, Javanese Selves*, Princeton (N.J.): Princeton University Press.

Kellar, Natalie (2000) *The Politics of Performance: Gender Identity in Arja and Other Contemporary Balinese Theatre Forms*, Clayton: Monash University, unpublished Ph.D. Thesis.

McPhee, Colin (1979) *A House in Bali*, Kuala Lumpur and New York: Oxford University Press.

Oetomo, Dede (1996) *The Chinese of Pasuruan: A study of Language and Identity in a Minority Community in Transition*, Ann Arbor, Mich.: University Microfilms International.

Parker, Lynette (1993) 'Flowers and Witches in Bali: Representations and Every-day Life of Balinese Women'. In Freda Freiberg and Vera Mackie (eds), *Disorientations: Embodiments of Women in Asian Cultural Forms*, Sydney: Wild Peony Press.

Peacock, James L. (1968) *Rites of Modernization: Symbolic and Social Aspects of Indonesian Proletarian Drama*, Chicago and London: University of Chicago Press.

Phelan, Peggy (1988) 'Feminist Theory, Post-structuralism, and Performance'. *The Drama Review* 32, T. 117.

Picard, Michel (1996) 'Dance and Drama in Bali'. In Adrian Vickers (ed.), *Being Modern in Bali: Image and Change*, New Haven (Conn.): Yale University Southeast Asia Studies.

Robertson, Jennifer E. (1992) 'The Politics of Androgyny in Japan: Sexuality & Subversion in the Theater & Beyond'. *American Ethonologist: The Journal of the American Ethnological Society*, No. 19.

Robertson, Jennifer E. (1998) *Takarazuka: Sexual Politics and Popular Culture in Modern Japan*, Berkeley: University of California Press.

Russo, Mary (1986) 'Female Grotesques: Carnival and Theory'. In Teresa de Lauretis (ed.), *Feminist Studies – Critical Studies*, Bloomington: Indiana University Press.

Stivens, Maila and Sen, Krishna (eds) (1998) *Gender and Power in Affluent Asia*, London and New York: Routledge.

Vickers, Adrian, Darma Putra, Nyoman and Wijaya, Nyoman (1998) *Balinese Cultural Debates 1950–1997: Modernity and Television*. Publisher unknown.

Widodo, Amrih (1995) 'The Stages of the State: Arts of the People and Rites of Hegemonization'. *Review of Indonesian and Malaysian Affairs*, 29 (1&2): 1–35, Sydney: Department of Indonesian and Malayan Studies, The University of Sydney.

6 Ritual as 'work'

The invisibility of women's socio-economic and religious roles in a changing Balinese society

Ayami Nakatani

> The Balinese, perpetually weaving intricate palm-leaf offerings, preparing elaborate ritual meals, decorating all sorts of temples, marching in massive processions, and falling into sudden trances, seem much too busy practicing their religion to think (or worry) very much about it.
>
> (Geertz 1973: 176)

One of the long-standing problems of women's work in most parts of the world is its lack of public visibility. Many of women's directly productive activities are not categorized as 'work' in official censuses or researchers' reports, especially when they are performed within or around the home. Women's work such as the preparation of food for sale, handicraft production including embroidery, weaving, and knitting, or the rearing of small livestock, is more likely to be thought of as 'non-work' or as part of their domestic responsibilities, both by researchers and the women themselves (Boserup 1970; Moir 1980; Rogers 1980; Mies 1982; Pittin 1987; Moore 1988). This issue is, of course, closely connected with a general understanding on both sides that women's daily labour for the household deserves less social recognition than male activities. A somewhat inherent lack of visibility is thus further exacerbated, broadened and institutionalized by a social act of maintaining silence on the topic of women's labour. In this chapter, I shall examine and attempt to address this problem of invisibility and silence in relation to the changing status of rural Balinese women and their work, particularly their ritual work.

At least in Marxist-feminist writing and the so-called 'women-in-development' literature, a considerable degree of scholarly attention has been given to the investigation of the spheres of reproduction and intra-household dynamics as important determinants of women's entry into paid employment (Kuhn and Wolpe 1978; Young *et al.* 1991). With regard to the societies of Indonesia, a good number of empirical studies reveal that – in their income generating activities both inside and outside the home – women face various problems such as greater instability, lower pay or less favourable working conditions compared to their male counterparts. This is largely due to the general perception that women are not supposed to be the main income providers of the household and their primary role should be that of wives and mothers (Manderson 1983; Van Bemmelen *et al.* 1992; Grijns *et al.* 1994; Saptari 1995). It is thus increasingly evident that any analysis of women's work should pay attention to its productive and reproductive aspects and their inter-relatedness.

Yet the tasks performed by women in daily life do not necessarily fall into either of the two distinct categories of production and reproduction. In my view, women's labour contribution to religious activities form a third and different domain, and this work too has remained invisible or undervalued in both official statistics and scholarly works.

It may be said of many societies that the religious sphere is primarily associated with men, and that women are not directly involved other than as admiring followers or spectators (Van Baal 1975: 72–73). But even in societies where women devote a substantial amount of time and energy to ritual and related tasks, their contributions are often glossed as an extension of their domestic tasks (see Ram 1991: 201 for South India) or are completely omitted from the overall analysis of female labour (Suratiyah *et al.* 1991 for Java and Bali). In rural areas of Bali, as I shall argue, female involvement in religious activities is truly extensive. It is thus essential to incorporate this aspect of their work in an analysis aiming to achieve a proper understanding of the daily experience and activities of local women.[1]

My own research was located in a village in Karangasem, the easternmost regency of Bali, and has been informed by a holistic approach to the study of all kinds of women's activities, without deciding in advance what constitutes 'work' and what does not. This project involved documenting the daily activities performed by women, investigating the proportional allocation of their time and labour to different types of activities, and examining how the women themselves and other villagers perceive and evaluate their labour contributions. For that purpose, careful attention was paid to changes relating to the socio-economic context in which these women's activities are placed, and to differentiation among women according to their age group, life cycle stage, and status in the traditional hierarchy of the village.

In this chapter, the religious activities of women are the primary focus of investigation, in particular the preparation and implementation of rituals. The profound importance of ritual in Hindu Bali generally has been well documented by prominent scholars on Balinese society (e.g. Belo 1953; Geertz 1973). As for women's involvement in ritual, even a short-term visitor of Bali would easily notice the remarkable degree of women's active participation in a wide range of tasks associated with ritual, foremost among them the preparation of intricate offerings. While this much of it may be obvious, a systematic analysis of women's religious roles in relation to their other, more secular obligations has been largely missing in previous studies of Balinese society.

My approach to the study of ritual has been shaped by my experiences as a researcher. Initially, I attempted some systematic research about the composition of individual offerings prepared for different types of rituals, and their names, functions or meanings in the overall religious scheme. In the course of my enquiry, however, it soon became evident that most women with whom I was socializing were not very well informed on such matters beyond certain basic principles. My persistent questions were typically met by embarrassment or the following kind of advice, 'Well, you should go and talk to so-and-so.' These so-and-so's were mostly male religious experts such as *pedanda* (Hindu priests of the *brahmana* 'caste'), *pemangku* (temple priests) or local intellectuals such as schoolteachers or village officials.

There were also female 'specialists in the making of offerings' (*tukang banten*), who would be called in to instruct and supervise the preparation of large-scale rituals, which usually require a variety of offerings in massive quantities. Their knowledge was extensive, but mainly involved practical matters such as the numbers, types and ingredients of the offerings appropriate for a given occasion. Had I seriously sought an eloquent explanation concerning the esoteric meaning of each offering or the source of its name, the most obvious thing to do was to go to male experts. Yet I resisted the idea.

As a researcher and a tentatively adopted daughter of a Balinese family, I attended numerous rituals of all sorts throughout my stay. On such occasions, the guests of honour were usually local men of importance, including some religious experts, who would spend time smoking and chatting with the male host. They would have readily welcomed my questions and provided me details on ritual proceedings and other information. However, I preferred to sit next to a group of women who still busied themselves with last-minute preparations, and listen to what they had to say. Then I started to think about the 'meaning' of their relative ignorance of religious matters despite their active, and indeed indispensable participation.

This chapter is thus an attempt at shedding new light on Balinese rituals from a female and practical perspective, both of which are often marginalized in scholarly work on religion. I shall view ritual activities as a separate category of women's (as well as men's) work, and as an one placing a great demand on female labour, thereby detracting from women's other work opportunities.

IS RITUAL 'WORK'?

The Balinese term for 'work' is *karya* (in 'High Balinese' [*basa alus*]) or *gae* (in 'Low Balinese' [*basa biasa*]). In both of its forms, this is a generic term for paid labour. At the same time, the term is used for unpaid labour specifically related to ritual undertakings and for rituals themselves, ranging from simple life passage rites to elaborate temple ceremonies. Those who host a certain ceremony, for example, are said to 'own the work' (*maduwe karya* or *ngelah gae*). The three broad meanings of the term *karya/gae* are thus productive work, ritual-related work, and ritual itself.

While remunerated activities in general can be referred to as *karya*, in a daily context such activities are more likely to be specified by reference to the type of activity, such as weaving (*nunun*) or farming (*mamacul*). Engagement in waged day-labour is normally described as *maburuh*. On the other hand, rituals of all kinds are generically referred to as *karya*, regardless of their purpose and the contexts of conversation.[2]

To explain this differentiated use of the term my conjecture is that, by and large, *karya* was used to signify activities in the religious domain during the pre-colonial and colonial periods. Men of land-owning households, mostly but not exclusively those of *triwangsa* ('the three [privileged] castes'), did not engage in physical labour as such, because they could live off the yield of their land by leasing it to sharecroppers. Under such conditions, work in religious contexts was the only significant task to perform that involved all segments of the population. In addition, there used to be far fewer specialized occupational options in the village. A general term to cover remunerated (and non-ritual) activities ('work' in a modern Western sense) was absent, perhaps, because it was unnecessary or irrelevant in the context of village life.[3]

With the gradual transformation of village economies, most notably in the era following Indonesian independence, a greater variety of job opportunities became available. These new forms of gainful employment have been accommodated within the concept of *karya*. As I have argued elsewhere (Nakatani 1999), alongside the increase in male access to various jobs outside the home and village, there was also an expansion in women's income-generating activities, though mainly within their home, such as weaving and food processing. These activities have also come to be seen as 'work', and as separate from women's reproductive tasks, despite their actual location.[4]

Ritual tasks, however, cannot be categorized and analyzed as a form of 'work' simply because the same term in Balinese designates both paid labour and ritual activities. The more pertinent question is: What are the features of ritual-related tasks in Bali that make them a distinct category of work, different from both waged labour and unpaid domestic activities? The answer to this question has two dimensions.

First, ritual activity in Bali involves a vast expenditure of time and labour. As a practice-oriented religion (Geertz 1973: 177), Balinese Hinduism emphasizes the preparation and implementation of rituals as a very important manifestation of the followers' dedication to their ancestors, the gods, and spirits. As I shall illustrate in the following paragraphs, women often bear greater responsibilities in this field than the male members of their family. Given the multiplicity of women's roles, the time spent on ritual labour is set against other obligatory tasks, especially in the eyes of the women themselves.

Second, women's performance of religious activities is essential for the general well-being of their family members and also in maintaining the social standing of their household in the community. Mutual help in the preparation of rituals and gift-giving, exercised primarily by women, ensures the upkeep of inter-household relations (Nakatani 1997). Also, highly complicated sets of offerings, the fruit of arduous female labour, symbolize reciprocal relationships between humans and gods or between different humans and their common ancestors.

Hanna Papanek, in the course of trying to identify some of the factors determining the uneven distribution of employed women throughout the social hierarchy and the labour force, has come to advocate the concept of 'family status-production work' (Papanek 1989). This category of work refers to women's unpaid activities that may contribute to the upward social status mobility of their families. Papanek argues that middle- or upper-class families tend to strategically withdraw their female members from paid employment, and deploy them to 'increase the competitive advantage of households' (1989: 98). A prerequisite for this strategic choice is that the household in question does not have to rely on female waged labour for its subsistence. Women are instead involved in the indirect support of other, wage-earning members of the household, in the education of their children as an investment in the future, and in the implementation of religious performances as an investment in social relationships and local political or patronage networks.

The last two categories of 'family status-production work' are directly relevant to my present argument. What differentiates the Balinese case is that most Balinese women, contrary to Papanek's assumptions, are simultaneously involved in what she calls 'family status-production work' (i.e. the fulfilment of ritual obligations) and in income-generating work. Historically, Balinese women appear to have always contributed to the household economy by raising small livestock, trading vegetables and fruit, selling home-made snack meals and sweets, and carrying building materials for roadwork. Balinese men were, it is reported, generally reluctant to work for wages (Covarrubias 1937: 82, 86; Penbrook 1976: 77). Prior to the expansion of the government sector, therefore, it seems reasonable to propose that women may have had greater access to cash income than men did in rural areas.[5] Women also worked in rice fields alongside their husbands. It must be noted, however, that one's given status in the traditional hierarchy had important implications in the choice of work for both men and women. Only the women of low-ranking status groups would undertake crude and physical tasks, even today, though impoverished aristocrats would also do so under specific circumstances.

In the 1970s and 1980s, different types of work opportunities for women have been found in handicraft production, garment manufacturing, and tourism. Under various programs funded by the government or international aid agencies, handicraft industries were particularly encouraged as the most respectable form of female employment, for home-working women could still fulfil their roles as wives and mothers. Accordingly, a variety of handicraft productions became a vital source of income for women, and to a lesser extent, for men, in many villages in Bali. The village of my study was one of these.

The garment sector also witnessed a particularly rapid development since the early 1980s. The majority of the work force was constituted by women, recruited from villages through subcontractors. They usually took up piece-work at home (Jayasuriya and Nehen 1989: 340), but as the industry developed, increasing numbers of young female workers started to work in small establishments on the outskirts of Denpasar, away from their villages. In the 1990s, this sector suffered under the severe competition of other countries such as China and Bangladesh, but it still seems to retain its strength and serve as an important employment provider for young women.[6]

It almost goes without saying that tourism has been the most thriving sector in the Balinese economy during the past two decades. This sector offers prestigious and lucrative job opportunities for both men and women, although competition is extremely high. Even at my research location, a village situated in a relatively remote and mountainous area, tourist facilities have increased since the early 1990s and started to hire local men and women.

In the following analysis, therefore, women's roles in the ritual domain will be set against this background of an increase in potential and actual opportunities of income-earning. The next section will illustrate the details of women's ritual-related activities especially in the contexts of offering production, and life cycle rituals.[7]

THE CONTENTS OF RITUAL-RELATED ACTIVITIES IN BALI

It is no exaggeration to say that for the Balinese hardly a day passes that is not loaded with ritual performances of some kind. The timely implementation of numerous life-passage rituals, from pregnancy to death and beyond, for example, counts among parents' primary obligations towards their children, and also those of children, who eventually must repay their ritual debt to their deceased parents. People prepare and present the prescribed offerings for the shrines and temples in their compound, they are engaged in the maintenance and the enactment of annual ceremonies of the village temples for which they share responsibility, they hold life-passage rituals for their immediate household members or close agnatic kin, and help in the preparation of or attend the life-passage rituals held by members of related households and neighbours. In addition, there are other kinds of ritual obligations; some prescribed for special days in the traditional Balinese calendar and others incurred by membership in various social organizations, such as neighbourhood associations (*banjar*) and rice-irrigation societies (*subak*).

Figure 6.1 shows the frequency of ritual-related activities for members of a Balinese *satria* (the second highest 'caste') household over the course of one year. A distinction is drawn as to the participation of male and female persons on different religious occasions. For this household, ritual events filled one-third to a half of people's time each month, although the duration and intensity of the activities varied. As we can see from this figure, women's involvement is more frequently required than men's.

Figure 6.2 further illustrates this point. The data presented therein is based on 'ritual diaries' kept upon my request by members of eleven households of various status groups.[9] By this measure, women again appear to be more heavily involved in religious activities than men.

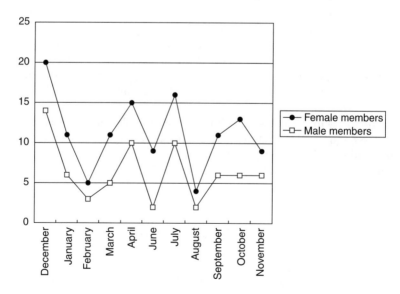

Figure 6.1 Frequency of participation in ritual labour (December 1991–November 1992).[8]

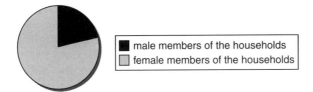

Figure 6.2 Proportion of time spent on ritual tasks by male and female members of 11 households.

It must be noted in this context that work in the ritual domain of life is rigidly divided along gender lines. As a rule, all types of religious responsibilities require the joint participation of a married couple, as only married persons are regarded as fully responsible members of the community. While a person can be replaced by another family member to make up a pair, cross-gender replacement is not accepted. In other words, separate tasks are allocated to men and women and preparations proceed separately for each sphere of tasks.

Women are made responsible for the production and presentation of offerings in all types of rituals and for the presentation of gifts to the sponsors of life-passage rituals, while men are in charge of setting up and decorating ritual venues and preparing meat for ceremonial feasts. To illustrate the intensity of religious requirements particularly for women, I shall now give a more detailed description of two types of ritual activities – offering making and life-passage rituals.

PREPARATION AND PRESENTATION OF OFFERINGS

In Hindu Balinese religious practice, no act of worship is complete without 'offerings' (*banten*). Offerings come in an enormous number of varieties, with differences in content, size, shape and function, depending on the specific producers, recipients and ritual context. Collective work sessions are organized for temple rituals or large-scale life passage rites. Women spend hours making containers and the ingredients of the required offerings under the instruction of an offering expert (*tukang banten*). Palm leaves are meticulously cut and plaited according to prescribed patterns, cooked rice is moulded into cone shapes, and coloured rice dough is shaped into various intricate forms representing all things in nature and is subsequently fried. Many other ingredients such as fruit and specific side dishes are all prepared before the final stage of offering-making (*matanding*), when all of the ingredients and components are arranged into the different groups of offerings that together make up a complete set (*bakti*), as prescribed by the specific occasion. The complete set of offerings is then presented to the gods or ancestors by male priests.

Women are also in charge of making and presenting various offerings for ceremonies within their own compound and to the compound members' ancestors. These offerings are less complicated than offerings produced for larger, communal rituals. For most households in the village of 'Singarsa' (pseudonym), where I conducted my research, the simplest daily offerings consist of several grains of freshly cooked rice placed on tiny squares of banana leaf (*banten jotan*). These are presented at around mid-day, shortly before a cooked meal is served to household members. There are also households whose women present more elaborate offerings or *canang* (small but beautifully made containers of plaited coconut leaf strips, filled with raw rice grains, flowers, a tree leaf and a betel nut quid)[10] every day. Some women produce from 25 to 75 *canang* by themselves, while others commission the making of such daily offerings to women in the neighbourhood, who bring a fixed number of *canang* every afternoon.

Ready-made *canang* are also available from women traders at the morning market. Their customers are women who want to present proper *canang*, especially on full moon and new moon, or on other days of special significance (for example, when they are holding some rite in the compound or when one of the family members has his or her birthday). Flowers and some other basic ingredients for making *canang* are also sold in the market. Women may also purchase the necessary raw materials for other offerings, including young coconut leaves to make offering containers.

The purchase of daily offerings is apparently a quite recent practice, but is now generally accepted in non-*brahmana* households as a convenient device for women to save time. Usually it is the wife of the household head who prepares and presents the daily *jotan* or *canang*, but any other female member of the household can also do the job. A menstruating woman should not engage in any offering making, even for her own use.[11] Therefore, when the wife has her period and no other female household member is available, the husband may prepare and present the daily offerings. Men, in any case, are more likely to take regular offerings to the rice fields, though it is their wives who prepare them.

The different and interlocking Balinese calendrical systems mark certain days as times of special ritual significance, when prescribed offerings should be made and set out at the relevant locations. The day of Kajeng-Kliwon, which occurs every 15 days, for example, is deemed a ritually dangerous day when evil spirits (*buta-kala*) make their presence felt. Special offerings to these nether-worldly forces (*segehan*) are placed on the ground outside the gates of each house compound. Even households who present only the simplest *jotan* offerings on a daily basis always prepare *canang* and *segehan* on Kajeng-Kliwon. It is also customary to present *canang* on every full moon (*purnama*) and new moon (*tilem*), even when there is no significant ritual on that day. On any of these special days, therefore, the number of offering sellers in the market doubles or triples.

Also, according to the Balinese *wuku* (permutational) calendar, a period of special festivities starts on the fourth day (Wednesday) of the 11th seven-day week, called Galungan, and ends on the seventh day (Saturday) of the 12th week, on Kuningan. This 10-day period commemorates the return of the deified ancestors to their former homes where the living welcome them with offerings and special feasts. Despite the existence of numerous other celebrations, villagers particularly look forward to the Galungan – Kuningan period, often regarding it as 'holidays' in the sense of a break from the daily routines of life.

These holidays, however, require a great deal of preparation. Five days before Galungan the women of the household start to make offering containers and religious ornaments by cutting, plaiting, and pinning palm leaves into various shapes. Some households start preparations even earlier by making special rice cakes (*jaja gina*) which have to be dried in the sun. Two days prior to Galungan, rice flour cakes called *jaja uli* are made. On the final day before the feast, women are busy assorting a variety of offerings; some to be placed on the grounds for nether-worldly forces, others to be presented to deities and ancestors in the family temple, and yet another type to be brought to the temple of deceased ancestors (*pura dalem*).

Meanwhile, men are busy decorating the family temple dedicated to their ancestors and the gateways of their compound with woven strips of palm leaves (*lamak*) and other dangling ornaments (*cenigan*) made by women. They also erect a long bamboo pole (*penjor*) decorated with rice sheaths, palm leaves, a coconut, fruits and cakes. This final preparation day is designated Penampahan, from *nampah*, 'to slaughter an animal'. Pigs are slaughtered and butchered by men for the Galungan feast on the next day. For this occasion, the sons and daughters who work in the cities or other family members who have settled elsewhere in Bali will all return to the home village. The entire village will be coloured by a festive mood, with special ornaments everywhere and the streets filled with more people and cars than usual.

On the day of Galungan itself, men and women put on newly made ceremonial attire; a white tailor-made shirt for men and a tight 'blouse' of colourful lace material (*kebaya*) for women. Children are also dressed up in their newest clothes. Families then visit the Pura Dalem together to present offerings and to worship. Afterwards they dedicate offerings to their ancestors in their family temples. If they have family members who have not been cremated yet, they must also take offerings to the graveyard. Having fulfilled these obligations, people just relax and enjoy informal conversation or play games.

About 5 days later, the preparatory activities start again for the Kuningan day, though on a smaller scale than for Galungan. The ornaments made for Galungan are replaced by different ones and new sets of offerings are freshly made. While normal activities such as office work, schooling, and weaving cease during this Galungan – Kuningan celebration, this period is likely to be further filled with various rites of passage that, again, require a considerable amount of labour.

'Family offerings' (*aturan*) are the offerings individually prepared in each household and brought to the village temples at their annual celebrations (*odalan*) as 'a symbol of its participation and its members' homage' (Stuart-Fox 1987: 180). The typical ingredients of such family offerings are half-cooked rice, a variety of nuts, *saur*,[12] fruits, different kinds of cakes, boiled eggs, and roast chicken, all of which are nicely piled on a silver base plate or attached by skewers to a soft trunk of a banana tree placed in the middle of the offering. The result is a fairly big, cylindrical structure of colourful components, crowned by a cut-out palm-leaf confection (*sampian*) and a pair of *canang* containing a nominal cash donation (*sesari*) to the temple.

Although it is still customary for women to prepare at least one or two kinds of cakes for this offering themselves, they also buy ready-made cakes of attractive colours and shapes to supplement what they have made at home. Such cakes are specially made as offering items and periodically begin to fill the morning market as major festive days approach.

It takes 2–3 hours for women to complete one set of family offerings, including buying and cooking necessary ingredients and putting them together into a proper shape. Men also contribute to the making of offerings by roasting chickens over a fire of dry coconut shells. When several different temples celebrate their *odalan* on the same day, as is the case in this village around the full moon of the fourth lunar month, all women of the household spend hours sharing tasks to prepare several sets of *aturan* at a time.

On the actual day of the full moon, the family offerings or *aturan* are brought to the temple shortly before the culminating point of the ritual, when the male *brahmana* high-priest recites religious formulas and invites the gods to come and consume the essence of the offerings. As in the case of daily offerings, it is almost invariably the female members of the household who 'bring the family offerings to the temple' (*maturan*). After depositing their offerings in the innermost court of the temple grounds, women stay on, surrounding the temple priest who performs the ritual. They then receive a few drops of holy water sprinkled by the priest, and retrieve their offerings to take them home as soon as the ritual is over. Were the mother to have her period and thus be polluted (*sebel*) at that time, a daughter who has passed puberty or some other female member of the household will stand in for her. The husband can also deliver the offerings, but this is rather uncommon.

MARRIAGE CEREMONIES

For life-passage rituals such as weddings, tooth-filing rites and cremations, the group of participants can be divided into three categories:
(1) Those who help with the preparations (*ngoop* or *ngayah*) and come
to attend the ritual (*saksi*); (2) people who help with the preparations, but
do not attend the ritual itself; and (3) those who only pay a formal visit
with gifts (*madelokan*) prior to the actual ritual.

The first category includes members of the agnatic kin group of the
host (those who recognize a common male ancestor of variable genealogical
distance) and of any other households who maintain regular ceremonial
ties with the host. Such ceremonial relationships involve rigorous
reciprocity. The two parties must observe a rule of mutual invitation to
life-cycle rituals and associated gift-giving (Nakatani 1997). The households who fall into this second category are not bound to the host household by an obligation of witnessing the ritual, and will help with the
preparations mostly because they are on good terms with the host as
close neighbours or long-term friends. A third category is the people
who are engaged through ceremonial gift-exchange without participation in the ritual event as such. This type of relationship, often described
as *masuka-duka* ('in joy and sorrow'), rarely transcends the boundary of
the hamlet (*banjar*) and is only observed at the time of marriage and
death. All other ceremonial occasions necessitate formal invitations,
which require the invitee's participation in the preparatory work.[13]

In the case of a marriage, the news of an impending ceremony is
typically spread through women's 'gossip' at morning markets and
bathing places. During the period prior to the temporary marriage
ceremony called *semayut makatelun*, which takes place three days after
a *de facto* marriage,[14] the family of the groom is busy preparing for
the ceremony and receive a large number of guests. A pair of male and
female representatives from every household who is on visiting terms
with the groom's household for ceremonial occasions comes to greet
them. Female guests bring wedding gifts (*padelokan ganten*) during the
daytime, while male guests pay their visits at night. They are all served
cigarettes and betel, coffee or tea, and sweets. Normally, the mother of
the groom receives the female guests, accepting their gifts with proper
greetings, while the groom, his father, and other senior male figures of
his descent group entertain the male guests. Households that are not
very close to the groom's family may send only female members as their
representatives.

Both patrilineal and matrilineal relatives of the groom come to help in
the preparation and to bring gifts.[15] Women make hundreds of sweets to
serve the guests, boil water incessantly for coffee and tea, and make
square place mats of palm-leaves for the ceremonial feasts. The offerings
required for the third-day ceremony are not so numerous, thus only

a *tukang banten* (offering expert) will see to it, perhaps assisted by one or two other women. *Jaba* (the lowest 'caste') women who assist in a *triwangsa* family's ceremony are especially busy, taking refreshments to the in-flowing guests, washing cups, and getting a new set of refreshments ready for the next group of guests. They also serve coffee and cakes to the ritual helpers-cum-guests, both male and female. When women of different status groups are working together, menial work is invariably performed by the *jaba* whereas women of higher status engage in offering making or other less physically demanding work. As in the case of temple ceremonies, men make bamboo trays and meat skewers to be used at the feasts.

On the day of the ceremony, male helpers come very early in the morning to cook the ceremonial meal. Some chop-up vegetables into tiny pieces and grate fresh coconut, while others mix seasonings. Still others engage in boiling pork or grilling meat on skewers (*sate*). At the same time, a suckling pig is roasted on the fire, along with numerous chickens, as a part of the offerings. Women too come early in the morning. Some are asked by the hosts to stay behind to help with the final preparations, while others are informed when the ceremony and subsequent feast will begin. The latter women go home and return later in proper ceremonial dress, while those who stay assemble offerings under the instruction of the *tukang banten*. When the offerings are ready and the holy water (*tirta*) made by the *brahmana* high-priest is brought to the compound, the ceremony starts. By that time, those who are supposed to witness the ceremony, which consists simply of the purification rite (*mabiyakala*) and the presenting of the essence of the offerings to the ancestors (*nganteb*), are all present. When the bride and groom finish *nganteb*, those present fetch some part of the offerings to eat on the spot. Because this communal act of eating the leftover offerings (*maparid*) consolidates existing ceremonial ties, the attendance of members of all related households is considered essential.

After the ceremony is over, ceremonial meals are served. Contrary to the usual Balinese custom concerning daily meals, four to five persons sit together and take food from one big square plate on a tray in the middle. The host must take care to ensure proper seating arrangements. Each group of people eating from one plate should be of the same status. Moreover, those who eat together must start eating at the same time and then finish more or less in the same instant, in order to avoid eating the 'leftovers' of the others.

The feast marks the end of the ceremonial procedure for the *semayut makatelun*. Almost the same procedure, including gift-giving and ceremonial feasts, is repeated when another ceremony, bigger in scale, is held later.[16]

A principle of reciprocity is enforced among households who exchange help in the fulfilment of ritual obligations, through mutual gift-giving, assistance in preparation and the mutual attendance of rituals. Precisely because of their reciprocal nature, the enactment of life-passage rituals can be regarded as a social enterprise as much as it is a religious event. Unlike temple ceremonies, the scale of ritual and its cost are assessed not so much by the elaborateness of the offerings as by the number of helpers and guests. To reiterate, the presence of all related households in such rituals is a prerequisite for the mainten-ance of ceremonial ties among them. Therefore, it is an important task for a major female figure of the host household (normally the mother of the groom) to carefully take note of whether everyone is there. In the case of a bigger marriage ceremony (*semayut gede*) which involves formal invitations, she must ensure that no one is forgotten on the invitation list and that all those invited have attended and brought gifts. Her responsibility also extends to the purchase of all the neces-sary goods for the ceremony and the efficient allocation of tasks to ritual helpers.

WOMEN'S PERCEPTIONS OF THEIR RELIGIOUS ROLES

In the course of my field research, it became a part of my daily routine to listen to women of all ages grumbling about the heaviness of their religious responsibilities. They typically expressed this sentiment by saying, 'there are always rituals (*karya wenten manten*)'. Despite the overall frequency of ritual events, certain days or months are more filled with ceremonies than others, as shown in Figure 6.1. During these times, women's lives become truly hectic.

In Singarsa, the fourth lunar month (*purnama kapat*) is favoured for both temple ceremonies and life-passage rituals, and thus the intensity of ritual activities is greatest during this month. In order better to cope with the associated demands on their time, the female members of the household divide the tasks. For example, a mother may make the family offerings while her three daughters bring them to separate temples, or a mother and a daughter may attend two different weddings scheduled for the same day. In this respect, the presence of adult daughters in a household can lighten their mother's burden consider-ably. This also means that married women and unmarried daughters tend to share the same view, that religious activities are much too frequent and time-consuming. An unmarried woman in her early twenties commented that:

> Balinese are always like this. We cannot earn much because we must work for rituals. If there are rituals, the expenses are great. For offering ingredients and gifts, for example. Besides, we cannot work [to earn money].

Another married woman in her mid-fifties was of a similar opinion:

> It takes me hours to make these offerings, from buying materials, cutting and pinning palm leaves to putting all the components together. Then five minutes later [when the offerings are presented at the ritual], they will be thrown away! It is just endless. Why are we doing this?

These and many other complaints stressed the fact that women must put aside other types of work while fulfilling religious duties.

The most typical of income generating activities in this village is cloth production, which has prospered as a major cottage industry in this area since the late 1970s. Most female residents of Singarsa, regardless of age or social status, are now extensively involved in this sector and achieve a relatively high income. Indeed, many households have come to depend to a considerable degree on women's earnings from the hand-weaving industry. While development of this industry has contributed to an improvement of living standards and general household facilities, the allocation of time and labour has become a crucial issue for female weavers (Nakatani 1999).

The following remarks by another unmarried weaver in her early twenties succinctly describes the dilemma:

> A little later Galungan comes, then Kesangga [the sixth lunar month when several temple celebrations take place]. I have not finished this cloth. It's a source of headache. There will also be a wedding where I must help out. If I cannot finish this piece before Galungan, I must borrow money first [to buy necessary ingredients for offerings].

As indicated by the above quotations, income-earning wives and daughters commonly pay for gifts and for the ingredients of offerings. Other than for major rituals requiring a large cash expenditure, it is mainly women who make decisions about what is to be brought as a gift or how much is to be spent on the purchase of offering ingredients, and it is they who take financial responsibility for these expenses. When their remunerative work is interrupted by ritual duties or completely stopped by a customary prohibition on weaving during ritual periods such as Galungan–Kuningan, women suffer income loss at the very same time as they encounter the great additional expenses incurred by these rituals. This dilemma is a great source of anxiety and frustration. The recent economic crisis has even intensified this situation, because the price of gifts and ingredients for offerings has doubled or tripled because of hyperinflation since 1998.

It is not my intention to suggest, however, that religious activities as a whole are perceived by these women only as burdensome and unworthy.

When women perform ritual preparations in groups for large-scale rituals, a lively and warm atmosphere characterizes their workplace:

> The women gossip and chat together in groups while making offerings, especially if this is for a larger ceremony. Thereby a contented, light-hearted atmosphere is generated, which lays the basis for attuning the thoughts imperceptibly to the art of fashioning offerings. Through their coordinated and united effort the women become increasingly absorbed in the work. This state of absorption is intensified by the detailed prescriptions that have to be followed in producing offerings and the emphasis that is placed on 'purifying thoughts' (*nyuciyang pikayun*) during the work. This mode of consciousness is contemplative in intent, the discursive activities being gradually silenced as the creator of the offering becomes engrossed in the art.
>
> (Hobart *et al.* 1996: 132)

Balinese villagers, including women, men and children, are generally enthusiastic about ceremonial occasions and enjoy festivities. Young women carry themselves proudly in their best and most attractive ceremonial clothing on their way to major temple ceremonies, even though they may also complain that they cannot complete their half-woven cloths because of this mission. Most women, if not all, draw a rewarding sense of satisfaction from the offerings they make. Though not expressed explicitly, the appearance of family offerings does have an effect on individual women's esteem. Those who are skilful, in particular, take pride in creating and presenting beautifully composed offerings.[17]

THE REWARD OF RITUAL WORK

It is equally important to note that villagers tend to resent the excessive commercialization of ritual-related work. In particular, they do not agree with 'offerings catering', a new business organized by female professionals who take orders for complete sets of offerings as required for a variety of rituals (Brinkgreve 1992: 135). According to the villagers of Singarsa, those who 'pay' for offerings or any other contribution to their rituals are only forced to do so because they cannot rely on unpaid cooperation from their descent groups or fellow villagers; in short, it reflects a deficit in their social support network.[18]

This line of thinking is closely related to their contention that ritual labour is to be highly valued as an idiom for expressing and reinforcing existing ties between households, as well as those between humans and divine beings. Theoretically, in the case of life-passage rituals and rituals for family temples, the host household can expect contributions of goods and labour from members of their own descent group and others with whom they have ceremonial ties. But if the host has a reputation of not helping out in other people's rituals, the degree of cooperation from those related households can be kept minimal, precipitating a labour shortage. On the other hand, when a ritual is held by a household whose members are known to be diligent (*anteng*) and ready to extend a helping hand to others outside their compound, a host of helpers will flow in from all corners of the village to make the ritual a crowded and lively event.

The 'crowded and noisy conditions' (*rame*) created by a large number of ritual helpers and guests is used as the main indicator to determine whether a given ritual is 'successful' or not (Warren 1993: 162). When someone returns home after attending a ritual, other family members will invariably ask: 'Was it crowded (*rame*) or quiet (*sepi, suung*)?'[19] Ritual obligations, especially those incurred by inter-household relationships, should therefore be fulfilled at any cost to ensure the future success of one's own rituals. In case of financial difficulties, for example, it is said that people can excuse themselves by begging the pardon (*matur sisip*) of the gods, or by bringing only as much as they can (*sasida-sidayaang*) to a public temple ceremony. However, people should not negate their obligations toward their neighbours, because the latter will invariably 'speak ill of them (*raosin*)'.

What does this observation imply for our discussion of the meaning and purpose of women's ritual labour? As already mentioned, women's presence at life passage rituals as gift-givers and ritual helpers is crucial for the maintenance of the social standing of the households they represent. If such acts are used to maintain or increase the social status of the household, then it must be asked further, who benefits most from women's socio-ritual labour?

As for the ritual sphere in Balinese society, it is not simply the male head of the household who enjoys prestige and associated rewards accumulated by means of staging successful, large-scale rituals which involve the participation of many guests and helpers. All members of the host household 'own the ritual'. Often the reason for a ritual's success is ascribed to the fact that the female members of the household have previously contributed much of their labour to the rituals of others.

Both men and women can gain credit for their skilful management of a ritual; by careful budgeting and efficient allocation of labour to different stages of offering production in the case of women, and by displaying skill in organizing the preparation of ritual meals in the case of men. The contributions of unmarried daughters are also valued in their own right. In other words, the result of family-status-production work by different members of the household does not simply enhance the prestige of the main male figure but can be ascribed to any individual of the household. All members of the household, regardless of gender and age, seem to fear the negative consequences of a neglect of ritual-related duties, and to value the regard or respect that may be received from fellow villagers as a reward for ritual diligence.

This does not, of course, imply that everyone is happy with the present situation, as is evident from the foregoing discussion. Women's attitude toward their heavy burden of ritual duties is ambivalent at best. On the one hand, they are aware that they contribute to the maintenance of their family's social status through their ritual labour. In this respect, their commitment to this category of work is not invisible at all. Most women also enjoy making offerings to some extent, and refuse to buy ready-made offerings or do not 'feel good (*tan becik rasane*)' when they do. On the other hand, they resent the fact that the responsibilities laid on their shoulders are often too much to handle, especially because the two types of their work, ritual and cloth production, are now in direct conflict as demands on their labour time. The ritual work does take up men's time as well, yet the demand for male labour is smaller. Women's offerings and ceremonial visits are indispensable, while male absence may be excused in certain contexts. And more significantly, the work sessions are usually organized so as to minimize the interruption of men's normal work schedule (Warren 1993: 153).

There is a further and important consideration. While women are integral and even definitive members of households (in that the concept of the 'household' more or less assumes a married couple at its foundation), the same does not apply, or not to the same degree, to the larger patrilines formed by a group of related households. For example, while women become members of their husbands' descent groups upon marriage, and contribute to the status of this larger group through their ritual labour, their membership can cease and their personal investment can be lost following a divorce.

UNEVEN DISTRIBUTION OF TASKS ALONG SOCIAL DIVISIONS OTHER THAN GENDER

One last point needs to be made concerning the unequal distribution of ritual tasks along the lines of social divisions other than gender. One of these divisions runs between groups of different status and another between urban and rural populations.

Regarding the first division, it is not easy to make generalizations about the effect of 'caste' status on the types and intensity of ritual obligations. Yet the residents of the village where I conducted my research often did make such generalizations. They suggested, for example, that *satria* households are much less constrained by ritual duties than *jaba* households, because they do not support the communal village temples. Since labour contribution toward communal temples is generally considered to be much greater than that toward one's own descent group temple, the *satria* families who are exempted from the former type of obligation are considered to be in a significantly privileged position.

In addition, *jaba* households carry a greater degree of commitment to ritual work on behalf of other households. This is because they have a number of *triwangsa* households to whom they must offer their unpaid labour (*ngayah*). As already mentioned in passing, the *jaba* households who are *braya* (tied by patron–client relationships) to the upper-caste host of a ritual must perform the most demanding tasks of all, both time- and labour-wise, in the preparation process. Compared to *triwangsa* households, who offer only limited help to their *braya* or even to households of equal standing, *braya* households devote much greater energy to their patron's rituals. It must be added, however, that their relationship is not simply one between exploiter and exploited. Theirs is certainly an unequal exchange, but for particularly close and devoted *braya* (called *braya arep*), *triwangsa* families can act as generous patrons. This patronage can take the form of finding employment for clients, providing them with rice and other food, or letting them use the patrons' facilities for their own rituals, and many other types of favours. Apparently, when a *triwangsa* group fails to offer any such favours or privileges to their *braya*, the *braya* may reduce their devotion and divert their attention and energy to another, more generous patron. Nevertheless, with women's cloth production now a crucial source of income for many *jaba* households, the requirement of female labour for their patrons' rituals carries a serious economic cost.

With regard to the second division with an impact on the distribution of ritual work tasks, it was observed that people in the village are often commissioned with offering making by members of their extended families living in the urban part of Bali. Men who have migrated to Denpasar or other cities with their wives and children still tend to follow the specific customs of their native village, especially in relation to ritual. For example, whenever they hold life-passage rituals for their children (e.g. third-month or sixth-month ceremonies) they either come back to the village to conduct these rituals or ask their families in the village to prepare the appropriate offerings and bring them to Denpasar.

In the case of one *jaba* group I knew well, the family in the village chartered two mini-buses and carried all the necessary offerings, together with a local high-priest (*pedanda*), to Sanur, where a ritual for a baby was to be held. Only the ceremonial meals were prepared on the spot. This arrangement was explained by stressing the fact that the way offerings are made in Sanur do not conform to village traditions, and that all the necessary materials were more expensive there.

The urban family would pay for the cash expenses on such occasions but not for the labour of their relatives. Even with the reasons given above, it is significant to note that members of urban families including women do not put aside their paid work for implementing rituals, while their rural counterpart is forced or 'strongly expected' to do so. The latter thus contribute their time and labour, to the detriment of their own subsistence activities, to ritual performances which do not necessarily enhance their own social position. We may be able to rationalize their actions in part by arguing that they are doing this as an investment in their own, long-term security. Often their family in the city has access to tourist income or stable monthly salaries, and may help them financially at a time of crisis. In recent years, a gap in economic status between urban and rural families tends to be widening, because access to foreign currency, which is unattainable for the majority of rural residents, is a most significant asset in the current situation. Herein we can see an emergence of a modern parallel to the seemingly 'feudal' patron–client relationships between upper and lower status groups.[20]

CONCLUSION

This chapter has examined Balinese ritual life as a sphere of work, with a special emphasis on women's labour contribution to ritual performances. To illustrate the heavy burden of their responsibilities in this sphere, a detailed description of two major categories of ritual-related activities, the preparation and presentation of offerings and the preparatory tasks involved in life-passage rituals, has been provided. In view of the great quantity and significance of the female labour required, ritual is clearly recognized as a distinct form of 'work' by the women themselves and by other villagers as well.

The time and labour women devote to rituals are set against other possibilities, such as remunerative activities. It can be said that this is an outcome of greater pressure placed upon women as income earners in the course of 'modernization'. Since the 1970s, a decided decline of the relative importance of agricultural sector has increased general expectation for women's engagement in non-farming employment. In the village under study, a rapid growth of handicraft production in the 1970s and 1980s coincided with, and further accelerated, a commodification of village life. Women's cash income has become vital not only for maintaining subsistence but for keeping-up with the prestigious display of newly acquired wealth, typically through modern housing but also through greater ritual extravagance.[21] In short, women's role as income-generating workers has not diminished the socio-cultural significance of their ritual work.

Women thus feel torn between the two types of work; directly remunerative and socio-religious. This is because they need to earn money in order to meet the additional expenses incurred by rituals, and yet, must put aside much of the fruit of these same income-producing activities for the sake of fulfilling their ritual obligations.

I do not wish to portray rural Balinese women simply as 'victims of patriarchy'. Although women pay a greater labour contribution than men to ritual performances, and often complain about it, they can take pride in enhancing the social status of their households, if not their own personal esteem. A lack of equality is more strongly reflected, however, in the general positioning of women in the performance hierarchy of ritual.[22] Women's ritual labour is skewed toward the end of ritual preparation, while men, especially the male priests, dominate the ceremonial stage of ritual. In view of the highly visual character of Balinese ritual, with its amazingly colourful variety of offerings – made mostly by women – it would not be justifiable to describe women's labour as 'invisible' (Tan *et al.* 1985: 262). What is not so visible, however, is the impact this tremendous task of ritual work has on women's lives, especially in a modern context.

Under the current condition of a national political crisis, with many local repercussions for the Balinese, I have observed a further intensification of ritual activities among both rural and urban families (see also MacRae, Chapter 3, this volume). With even larger-scale and more costly rituals staged to spiritually guard against the dangers perceived to be lurking everywhere at this moment of political instability, and with fewer and fewer people able to rely on farming as their main source of income (see MacRae, Chapter 7, this volume), the twin pressures on women, as ritual and economic workers, and on rural women in particular, is intensifying in equally dramatic proportions.

NOTES

1 A study of women's roles in Bali by Indonesian scholars (Tan *et al.* 1985) draws a distinction between 'economic' and 'non-economic' spheres of activity, the latter of which includes both domestic labour and 'social activities' (*kegiatan sosial*), i.e. ritual-related tasks. I propose to differentiate ritual work from daily household chores and child care, for the former is not contained within the domestic context.
2 There are also more specific terms for general types of 'ritual' such as *pacaruan* (blood sacrifices) or *rainan* (rituals held regularly on a specific anniversary date). Other than that, many rituals have a specific name as well, such as *masanggih/matatah* – the tooth-filing rite.
3 I am grateful to Hedi Hinzler for leading my thoughts to this point.
4 A change in the local concept of work is also noted by Rudie (1994: 209), who returned, about 20 years later, to the village of her earlier fieldwork of the mid-1960s in Malaysia. In that case, however, an earlier notion of work (*kerja*), which included a wide variety of activities ranging from material production and ceremonial tasks to housework, had been narrowed to cover only formal, permanent employment. Women who did not have such jobs reported that they had no work.
5 Korn (1932: 497), for example, notes the strong economic position of the wives and adult daughters to whom the men were said to be 'indebted (*in het krijt staat*)'.

6 On my last visit to Bali in 2000, I often heard urban-based, middle-class working women complaining over the shortage of domestic helpers. They were blaming garment factories for attracting village girls who, in turn, regard domestic assistance increasingly as degrading work.

7 The following description of ritual performances is based on field research in eastern Bali conducted between 1991 and 1993. The research was financially supported by the INPEX Foundation and the WOM/ACT Fund from the Royal Anthropological Institute. I also paid two short visits in 1998 (with Grant-In-Aid for Scientific Research from the Japanese Ministry of Education) and most recently in 2000. The general practice concerning rituals has remained more or less the same since my first research period, although some important changes will be specified in later sections.

8 The month of May is missing from this graph because I was not allowed to stay in the village during that month due to the national election.

9 I asked a female member of each sample household to keep records of all ritual events which required labour contributions of members of their household. The purpose of each event, its place, the tasks required, the name of the person who performed the task, and the duration of the task were written down for the month of October 1992.

10 What is commonly termed a 'betel quid' is composed of betel leaves (*piper betel*), the seed of the areca palm (*areca catecu*), and lime. As in other parts of Indonesia (Reid 1985), the chewing of betel has been largely replaced by cigarette smoking in Balinese villages, though many older Balinese still prefer it.

11 Some authors have argued that the ideology of female pollution reflects and, in turn, consolidates the categorical inferiority of women (Ruddick 1986; Branson and Miller 1989). I do not see a convincing causal link between the belief in female pollution and women's actual inferiority in status. It is true that women themselves note a certain sense of an unclean state, attached to their body, and occasionally resent it. Yet they also perceive this state as merely transitory and see it on a par with all other occasions entailing pollution such as death, which affects both genders. In some context, women even welcome their menstruation periods as a time of repose from endless ritual-related work.

12 *Saur* is a mixture of grated coconut, garlic, chillies and various other seasonings, including turmeric to colour it yellow.

13 An exception to this is the 'guests of honour', as it were, who are invited due to their respectable position in the village (e.g. the village headman, district head) or their high social standing. They do not participate in the ritual preparations but only come to attend the ceremony (with gifts). If one of the marrying couple is a public servant or school teacher, his or her colleagues are to be included in this category. When *brahmana* (other than the officiating priests) are invited to weddings at non-*brahmana* households, they are also entertained as formal guests without participating in the ritual work.

14 This *de facto* status begins when the bride is 'captured' in the case of elopement or when the bride is met by the groom in the case of marriage by 'formal request'.

15 The wedding gifts consist of uncooked rice (1.5–2 kg) and 'presents' (*kado*); nicely wrapped gift items such as glasses and ceramic plates. In former times, wedding gifts were home-made sweets and cooked food including rice, roast chicken and some side dishes. Wrapped gifts from the shops apparently replaced them in the mid-1970s or later.

16 It is said that *semayut makatelun* meets religious requirements for marriage, but another ceremony, *semayut gede*, is necessary for social purposes. The timing and the scale of *semayut gede* is entirely up to the groom's family, though they must choose an auspicious date.

17 Jensen and Suryani (1992: 99, 109) point to the inner feelings of peace and fulfilment experienced by the women when claiming their own family offerings after the blessing with holy water at a temple ceremony.
18 The practice of 'offerings catering' was already widely accepted in other areas of Bali, especially in the cities, at the time of my first research. In Singarsa, one *brahmana* woman was known to run that kind of business, but the orders were said to come from outside the village. More recently, it seems less uncommon to buy a fixed set of offerings especially for large-scale rituals such as a tooth-filing ceremony. But the way villagers talk about such practice is still tinged with mild scorn or reproach.
19 When the host household is forced to keep the cost for a certain ritual to a minimum, they will do so by limiting the number of invitations and reducing the scale of the ritual. In such a case, it is explained that the ritual is made *suung* ('kept quiet') intentionally.
20 Obviously, not all the urban migrants are financially successful. Their village family can be an important shelter in times of crises such as prolonged unemployment. Some rural Balinese who are primary producers have also benefited from the economic crisis because increases in the market price of their products kept up with general inflation levels, unlike the salaries of most urban Balinese (see Reuter, Chapter 8, this volume).
21 At the beginning of the 1990s, a general tendency toward holding more and more costly rituals was observed at all levels of society. I was able to verify this impression by comparing ritual expenses, in rice equivalent, of certain life-passage rituals between 1977 and 1978 (Poffenberger and Zurbuchen 1980: 126) with those I observed myself in 1991–1992.
22 Earlier ethnographies of Bali have also associated men (as the heads of the households) with the role of 'representing' households 'before the law and before the gods' (Covarrubias 1937: 156). As I argued elsewhere (Nakatani 1997), however, it is not clear in what sense the man is considered to represent his household or family, outside such jural-political contexts as the monthly meetings of the *banjar* (neighbourhood association). In my view, it is married women who most often represent their households through their ritual work.

REFERENCES

Belo, Jane (1953) *Bali: Temple Festival*, Seattle and London: University of Washington Press.
Boserup, Esther (1970) *Women's Role in Economic Development*, London: George Allen & Unwin.
Branson, Jan and Miller, D. (1989) 'Pollution in Paradise: Hinduism and the Subordination of Women in Bali'. In P. Alexander (ed.), *Creating Indonesian Cultures*, Sydney: Oceania Publications.
Brinkgreve, Francine (1992) *Offerings: The Ritual Art of Bali*, Singapore: Select Books.
Covarrubias, Miguel (1937) *Island of Bali*, New York: Alfred A. Knopf.
Geertz, Clifford (1973) *The Interpretation of Cultures*, London: Fontana.
Grijns, Mies *et al.* (1994) *Different Women, Different Work: Gender and industrialisation in Indonesia*, Aldershot: Avebury Press.
Hobart, Angela, Ramseyer, Urs and Leeman, A. (1996) *The Peoples of Bali*, Oxford: Blackwell.

Jayasuriya, S. and Nehen, I Ketut (1989) 'Bali: Economic Growth and Tourism'. In Hal Hill (ed.), *Unity and Diversity: Regional Economic Development*, Singapore: Oxford University Press.

Jensen, Gordon D. and Suryani, L. K. (1992) *The Balinese People: A Reinvestigation of Character*, Singapore: Oxford University Press.

Korn, Victor E. (1932) *Het Adatrecht van Bali*, Gravenhage: G. Naeff.

Kuhn, Annette and Wolpe, A. (1978) *Feminism and Materialism: Women and Modes of Production*, London: Routledge and Kegal Paul.

Manderson, Leonore (1983) *Women's Work and Women's Roles: Ecnomics and Everyday Life in Indonesia, Malaysia and Singapore*, Canberra: The Australian National University Press.

Mies, Maria (1982) 'The Dynamics of the Sexual Division of Labour and Integration of Rural Women into the World Market'. In L. Beneria (ed.), *Women and Development*, New York: Praeger.

Moir, Hazel (1980) *Economic Activities of Women in Rural Java: Are the Data Adequate?*, Canberra: Development Studies Centre, Australian National University. Occasional Paper No. 20.

Moore, Henrietta L. (1988) *Feminism and Anthropology*, Cambridge: Polity.

Nakatani, Ayami (1997) 'Private or Public? Redefining Female Roles in the Balinese Ritual Domain'. *Southeast Asian Studies* (Center for Southesast Asian Studies, Kyoto University) 34(4): 722–40.

Nakatani, Ayami (1999) 'Eating Threads: Brocades as Cash-Crops for Weaving Mothers and Daughters in Bali'. In R. Rubinstein and L. Connor (eds), *Staying Local in the Global Village: Bali in the Twentieth Century*, Honolulu: University of Hawaii Press.

Papanek, Hanna (1989) 'Family Status-Production Work: Women's Contribution to Social Mobility and Class Differentiation'. In M. Krishnaraj and K. Chandra (eds), *Gender and the Household Domain*, New Delhi: Sage Publications.

Penbrook, J. F. (1976) 'The Role of Women in Traditional Bali'. In B. B. Hering (ed.), *Indonesian Women: Some Past and Current Perspectives*, Bruxelles: Centres d'Etude du Sud-Est Asiatique et de L'Extreme-Orient.

Pittin, Renee (1987) 'Documentation of Women's Work in Nigeria'. In C. Oppong (ed.), *Sex Roles, Population and Development in West Africa*, Protsmouth: Heinemann.

Poffenberger, Mark and Zurbuchen, Mary S. (1980) 'The Economics of Village Bali: Three Perspectives'. *Economic Development and Cultural Change*, 29: 91–133.

Ram, Kalpana (1991) *Mukkuvar Women*, London & New Jersey: Zed.

Reid, Anthony (1985) 'From Betel-Chewing to Tobacco-Smoking in Indonesia'. *Journal of Asian Studies*, 44(3): 529–47.

Rogers, Barbara (1980) *The Domestication of Women*, London: Kogan Page.

Ruddick, Abby C. (1986) *Charmed Lives: Illness, Healing, Power and Gender in a Balinese Village*, Brown University, unpublished Ph.D. Thesis.

Rudie, Ingrid (1994) *Visible Women in East Coast Malay Society*, Oslo: Scandinavia University Press.

Saptari, Ratna (1995) *Rural Women to the Factories*, Amsterdam: University of Amsterdam, unpublished Ph.D. Thesis.

Stuart-Fox, David J. (1987) *Pura Besakih: A Story of Balinese Religion and Society*, Canberra: Australian National University, unpublished Ph.D. Thesis.

Suratiyah, Ken *etal.* (1991) *Pembangunan, Pertanian dan Peranan Wanita di Pedesaan Yogyakarta dan Bali*, Yogyakarta: Pusat Penelitian Kependudukan, Universitas Gadjah Mada.

Tan, Mely G. *etal.* (1985) *Peranan Wanita dalam Keluarga di Pedesaan Bali*, Jakarta: LIPI Project Report.

Van Baal, Jan (1975) *Reciprocity and the Position of Women: Anthropological Papers*, Assen: Van Gorcum.

Van Bemmelen, Sita *etal.* (1992) *Women and Mediation in Indonesia*, Leiden: KITLV Press.

Warren, Carol (1993) *Adat and Dinas*, Kuala Lumpur: Oxford University Press.

Young, Kate, Wolkowitz, C. and McCullach, R. (1991) *Of Marriage and the Market: Women's Subordination Internationally and Its Lessons*, London: Routledge. Second edition.

7 The value of land in Bali

Land tenure, landreform and commodification

Graeme MacRae

Once upon a time, according to a scholarly just-so story supported more by repetition than evidence, land was a resource of little import in the political economies of Southeast Asia (Gullick 1958: 125; Geertz 1980: 24, 171; Errington 1983; Warren 1993: 86; Wiener 1995: 44; Schulte-Nordholt 1996: 35). If this were ever true, it is no more. Times have changed and land is now central to many of the most critical conflicts in contemporary Indonesia.[1] As the proverbial real-estate agent, who flourishes wherever local economies meet the global market, says of land: 'God is not making any more of it' and, as population densities, standards of living and the demands of commercial development all increase, competition for land is becoming more intense.

In Bali, a small island with a long tradition of intensive agricultural land-use and high population density, land has been a critical issue since at least the 1930s (Robinson 1995: 56–57). More recently, the leasing and disguised purchase of land by foreign expatriate residents, growing demand from an expanding indigenous middle class, and the development of large-scale tourism resorts have intensified this pressure. The resulting scarcity of land has led to widespread public concern manifest in the island's main newspaper; in an editorial (Bali Post 1996) and a series of articles explaining aspects of land legislation (Windia 1996a–e) and even in an article in a national newspaper (Jakarta Post 2000) entitled 'Foreign land ownership erodes Bali's cultural identity.' Despite its central place in local concerns, however, studies of land use and land tenure in Bali have been few and far between, since the pioneering work of Dutch colonial scholars Gunning and van der Heiden (1926), de Kat Angelino (1921) and Korn (1924). The purpose of this chapter is to document the history of land tenure and use in and around Ubud, a thriving tourist town in south-central Bali, in the context of past and present land crises and, further, to use this material to reflect critically upon some scholarly assumptions about land and land-related social conflicts.

THE CURRENT CRISIS: LAND IN UBUD IN THE 1990s

The symptoms and key aspects of the current land-crisis in Bali may be summarized as follows:

1 A general scarcity of land, created in the first place by rising population, with direct effects on inheritance and resulting in a trend toward increasing demand and prices.
2 The effect of tourism and the international real-estate market, creating an additional layer of inflation of land-prices.
3 A progressive shift from traditional collective control of use and access to land to individualized private ownership.
4 A progressive shift of land (and labour) from subsistence agricultural use to tourism and other commercial uses.
5 Increased state intervention, in the form of systematic registration (*sertipikat*) and a more rigorous tax regime.
6 A rush on the part of owners to register their land.
7 Consequent loss of local control over land and opening of the door to foreign ownership.
8 The economic and social consequences of landlessness.
9 Cultural consequences of separation of village land from village *adat*.
10 Exacerbation of these effects in the areas where tourism is most dominant.

In my explorations of the villages in the Wos valley, upstream of Ubud, since 1993, I am frequently greeted with the question 'Do you want to buy land here?' Land-hunting has obviously become a significant motivation for foreign strangers to explore the bucolic byways of Bali. Even before the liberalization of laws restricting foreign ownership of land, foreigners had been involved for some years in *de facto* purchases made in the name of Indonesian (usually local) partners. Demand for picturesque rural house-sites and for scarce street-front land for commercial tourism enterprises in central Ubud, as well as the beginnings of a local speculative investment market, had led to a steady inflation in the price of land, beginning in the 1980s and reaching astronomical levels in the early 1990s, as shown in Table 7.1.

This quantitative inflation was accompanied by qualitative shifts in the relative valuation of land, and by corresponding shifts in patterns of wealth and poverty. Poor families, owning the least valuable agricultural land along river gorges, suddenly found themselves the recipients of offers they could not refuse from representatives of international hotel chains.[2] Owners of prime rice fields (*sawah*) in central Ubud were, at the same time, able to make a better income by selling or even leasing their land, investing the proceeds and living on the interest, than by growing rice on it.[3] Many others without these options continued to farm, earning

Table 7.1 Value of rice-field land, Ubud 1951–1996

Year	Land values (Rp./ara)	Rice prices (Rp./kg)	Rice/land ratio (kg/ara)
1951	500	Not available	
1957	333	Not available	
1959	1000	Not available	
1964	1140	Not available	
1965	2000	Not available	
1968	3830	Not available	
1971	7700	40	192.5
1980	200,000	238	840.3
1981	300/500,000	198/255	1176.5/1960.8*
1986	500,000	472	1059.322
1990	10,000,000	500	20,000
1993	32,000,000	1000	32,000
1996	20,000,000	1000	20,000

Source: MacRae 1997: Tables 2.9, 2.10.

Note
* The difference between these figures reflects different primary sources.

incomes which slipped ever further behind those of their neighbours in the tourism industry. The agricultural use-value of land has been progressively superseded by its capital-value, and this has had repercussions throughout the local economy.

By the early 1990s, land, along with certain other strategic resources, had become the prime determinant of a household's ability to compete successfully in the new tourism-based economy. Land can be used to generate profit either by building residential or commercial premises on it, renting or leasing it to others to do likewise, or simply by allowing its value to appreciate. This is, for the people of Ubud, a significant change from a generation ago, when land was valued primarily for its rice-producing potential and even this benefit was offset by the tax liability it attracted. The change from two generations earlier is an even more dramatic reversal; from when the tax liability was so feared by many people that they, according to oft-recited oral history, voluntarily turned over their land to the *puri* (royal house) of Ubud to avoid tax (MacRae 1997: 331).

TRADITIONAL LAND TENURE

The story of this change may be told, at its simplest, in terms of supply and demand. Until the late nineteenth century, the population of Bali was relatively small, less than one million in 1874 compared with almost three million at the time of writing, and land for subsistence was readily available to anyone prepared to move into virgin territory (Vickers 1989: 219).[4]

Local oral histories in this part of Bali (and elsewhere in Indonesia) are replete with stories of the founding of villages by people moving from another, more crowded area, clearing forest, and establishing subsistence-based communities (see also Howe 1980; Schulte-Nordholt 1996: 56). Although such land was nominally under the control of a local ruler (or in the mountains, the village), access to it was rarely denied and indeed, the authorities concerned welcomed the increase in human resources available to them.

Land was understood to be ultimately the property of the gods, with kings and local authorities exercising earthly rights in mediating between those of gods and ordinary mortals (Hobart *et al*. 1996: 49–56). Worldly tenure of agricultural land was achieved by clearing, use and occupation. Residential land was held in collective trust by the *desa*, an association of households defined socially and spatially. Socially it was defined by joint responsibility for the maintenance, physical and spiritual, of two or more temples dedicated to the deities associated with a specific area of land. Spatially, it was defined by common residence on an area of land bounded usually at the uphill and downhill ends by rice fields and on the cross-slope sides by river gorges (MacRae 1997: 190–94). Use-rights to residential land were conditional upon contribution to collective ritual obligations (Warren 1993: 141–42). Each household consequently had secure use-rights to residential land with associated garden space and access to agricultural land through outright ownership or a variety of tenancy and sharecropping arrangements.

Upon this primary system of village tenure was superimposed, albeit unevenly, the authority of the *puri*, princely houses with zones of political control which they sought endlessly to defend or expand. Such control was always tenuous and dependent ultimately on their ability to muster human labour power for military or ritual purposes, and this dependency on human resources was the undeniable fact on which the orthodoxy I am seeking to critique herein was presumably based. The problem with this prioritizing of human over material resources is that the ability of a ruler to command a large group of supporters was itself dependent on his ability to ensure the material subsistence of his supporters (Schulte-Nordholt 1996: 35). This in turn depended on secure control over land, especially productive rice-growing land and the irrigation water which fed it (Schulte-Nordholt 1996: 55–57).

Ubud lies within the area once under the dominion of the eighteenth century kingdom of Sukawati, which had upstream outposts at Peliatan and Tegallalang. By the late nineteenth century the entire area of what is now Kabupaten Gianyar was more or less settled and although nominally under control of Puri Gianyar, competition for control over it was intensifying between rival princes, especially those of Sukawati descent. The rapid expansion in the 1880s by the sub-kingdom (*pungawaan*) of Negara (near Sukawati), up the Wos Valley as far as Kelusa and Keliki, threatened the stability of the entire kingdom and most directly the closely related *puri* of Peliatan and Tegallalang. The latter combined forces, ostensibly on behalf of Gianyar, to defeat and destroy Negara (MacRae 1997, Chapter 6).

FROM THE SEA TO THE MOUNTAINS: THE RISE OF UBUD

Ubud was, until this time, a poor and peripheral outpost of Puri Peliatan, itself a *pungawaan* of Gianyar. It depended for subsistence on a small grant of local land from Puri Peliatan. But in the war against Negara, the head of Puri Ubud, Ck. Gede Sukawati, distinguished himself as an indomitable warrior, astute commander, and a man of great magical power (*kesaktian*). He took, as the spoils of war, the lion's share of the territory previously controlled by Negara; the majority of the Wos Valley, as local stories have it, 'from the sea at Ketewel to Taro in the mountains' (MacRae 1997: 330). This land provided the material (*sekala*) base, underpinned [in local thinking at least] by the supernatural (*niskala*) base of his personal spiritual power (*kesaktian*) and by an older mythological charter to Sukawati dominion over this territory, through which Ck. Sukawati was able to maintain the control over human resources necessary to maintain his power until the coming of the Dutch.

According to a consensus of contemporary oral history, Ck. Sukawati managed these far-flung resources in a manner which diverges somewhat from the widely accepted model of South Balinese land-tenure.[5] According to most accounts, the majority of farmland was *tanah pecatu*, land granted to farmers in exchange for various services to the village or their lord (the former was also known as *tanah ayahan desa*, the latter as *tanah ayahan dalem*).

Scholars have varied over the years in their interpretations of the exact nature of this relationship between land, the peasant farmers who work it, their produce, and their aristocratic patrons (de Kat Angelino 1921; Korn 1924: 127; Gunning and van der Heiden 1926; Boon 1977: 56; Geertz 1980: 176; Warren 1993: 63; Hobart *et al.* 1996: 55; Schulte-Nordholt 1996: 60, 129). All agree (at least implicitly), however, that *pecatu* was the dominant form of relationship between lord and peasant, land and labour in pre-colonial South Bali. The only other agricultural land, according to Schulte-Nordholt, was simply 'privately owned' (1996: 129–30). What is important for this discussion is that *pecatu* involves the granting to farmers of relatively unencumbered rights to the use and produce of land in exchange for labour obligations to the lord of the land.

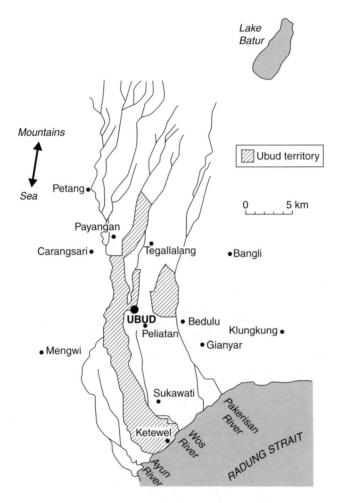

Figure 7.1 Ubud territory, late nineteenth century.

Ck. Sukawati (according to the oral accounts), rather than distributing land as *pecatu*, retained direct control, something akin to 'ownership', allowing local people undisturbed use for subsistence purposes, but claiming, instead of labour-service, a portion of the produce. The collection of the king's portion was administered by *sedehan* and either brought back to the *puri* or sold, on-site at low prices, much of it back to its producers. Described this way, the system seems much more like the relatively well-documented tenancy/sharecropping arrangements of the twentieth century (Robinson 1995: 256; Schulte-Nordholt 1996: 250–51) than any variant of the *pecatu* model, though it operated on a larger scale and a more permanent basis.

The harvest share claimed by the *puri* is also the subject of divergent opinion. Of my two most reliable informants, both former *sedehan* of different *puri* branches, one claimed that there was so much land that the *puri* could afford to be very generous and this portion was relatively small and flexible, dependent to a degree on calculation and voluntary submission by the farmers involved. According to the other, the *puri* took three parts to the farmer's one, a system known as *mpat* or *merapat*, the least generous but common division of the harvest in this part of Bali (Robinson 1995: 256).

This system of remote administration of the periphery was supplemented at the centre by an even more peculiar arrangement. A stock item of local historical knowledge runs something like this: 'The *puri* told people not to worry about working in the rice fields, all they had to do was go to the *puri* and they would be given food.' The ubiquity of this rather remarkable claim is matched by its extraordinary resistance to clarification, let alone verification. As far as I can make out, it refers to a general availability of cooked rice (*nasi*) in the palace kitchens and especially of grain (*beras*) stored in the palace granaries. The source of this never-ending supply of rice was the portion steadily flowing into Ubud town from far-flung harvests throughout the kingdom.

It seems likely that such a system may have begun in the provisioning of what was in effect a standing army, based in Ubud itself rather than outlying villages, which must have been on almost full-time alert during the last decade of the nineteenth century. If so, this system of provisioning may well have been a factor in the sustained willingness and effectiveness of this highly successful army. Most of my informants regarded the system as something which had operated in the remote past, but according to one of the more reliable ones, some semblance of it remained in operation until the land reform of the 1960s. The scale and regularity with which the contemporary *puri* is able to mobilize an army of civilian workers for its extravagant ritual campaigns may be a relic of the system. A further trace remains in the generous meals served by the palace kitchens. Members of the communities most closely linked by ties of hereditary ritual service to the *puri* may to this day be seen helping themselves in the *puri* kitchen.

A direct consequence of this system of labour management was that while many local people did not labour in the rice fields, neither did they acquire any established rights to them. Indeed, I heard the item of local oral history quoted above usually in answer to my questions as to why so few people (and especially certain *banjar*) own land in Ubud. The majority of land immediately around Ubud itself was, and much still is, controlled not by Puri Ubud, but the senior *puri* at Peliatan. Most of that which is now owned by local farmers, especially in the former Peliatan dependency of Padangtegal, was distributed by Puri Peliatan on a *pecatu* basis, while that owned by Puri Ubud is sharecropped.[6] In addition to sustaining an unusually effective army for over a decade, this system enabled Ck. Sukawati to maintain an export–import trade via his port at Ketewel, a small but well-qualified elite of religious, artistic and administrative specialists, and ritual production sufficient to maintain his status.[7]

This dual system of military and ritual centre, supported by the surplus of a productive rural periphery, can be viewed from the point of view of management of land or of labour, but neither view does justice to their mutual, if somewhat asymmetrical, interdependence in practice. Ck. Sukawati's success, and the relative prosperity of Ubud as a whole was built upon his ability to mobilize labour, but this was integrally bound up and utterly dependent on his control over the resources – productive, human and ritual – of a specific area of land.[8]

Many of the distinctive features of contemporary Ubud are held in local opinion to be the results of this system: The abundance and geographical spread of land held directly by the *puri*, the correspondingly widespread sense of loyalty to Puri Ubud throughout the Wos Valley, the landlessness of many Ubud people, as well as their disinclination for engaging in manual labour and corresponding talent for cultural and ritual production.[9]

LAND UNDER THE DUTCH

After the voluntary submission of Gianyar to the Dutch in 1900, Ck. Sukawati was allowed to retain relatively unrestricted control over his kingdom, supported no longer by his own military might but by that of the Dutch. With the need for military expenditure eliminated and with special exemption from taxes and retention of his private landholdings in recognition of his services in brokering the deal with Gianyar, he was able to continue to amass wealth, apparently without either excessive demands upon his sharecroppers or a reduction of his local largesse (MacRae 1997: 371).[10]

By the time Ck. Sukawati died in 1919, the situation had begun to deteriorate. Changes to the colonial tax laws and administrative boundaries began to erode his privileges, and the influenza epidemic of 1917 significantly reduced both rice production and population. The earthquake of 1917 also destroyed his favourite palace and presumably with it some of his standing in the eyes of his people. The earliest memories of his younger son, Ck. Agung, are of great material luxury, but they are soon replaced with images of a *puri* in internal disarray (Hilbery 1979: 9–15).

The effects of these changes on ordinary people in Ubud are not entirely clear. According to Robinson's account of Bali as a whole, the 1920s are generally regarded as having been a time of prosperity, fuelled by high prices for export cash-crops. At the same time, however, the introduction in 1919 of a requirement to pay taxes in Dutch currency and a more rigorous land-tax regime in 1922 were also the beginning of a new form of tax-induced hardship. A combination of increased cash-crop production, rising commodity prices, and the relative ease of tax evasion enabled many farmers to keep their heads above water and the state to maintain, and even increase its taxation levels through the 1920s. Yet there is also evidence of considerable hardship and the beginning of a pattern of transfer of land from smaller to larger landowners (Robinson 1995: 52–59). Accounts of both Gianyar and Mengwi, immediately east and west of Ubud, suggest that by the early 1930s indebtedness, poverty, hardship, and ultimately landlessness were extreme and widespread in this area (Robinson 1995: 53; Schulte-Nordholt 1996: 253–54; 288–90).

It is difficult to believe that Ubud was immune to these effects on all sides but it seems also that, at least in the 1920s, the land-tenure policies of the *puri* may to a degree have (intentionally or otherwise) protected ordinary farmers against the direct effects of taxation and the accumulated wealth of the *puri* may have acted as something of a collective buffer for the whole community.

Ck. Sukawati's successor as head of the entire *puri* was his eldest son, Ck. Raka, a man of abilities comparable to those of his father, but whose values and loyalties were greatly influenced by his education and patronage by the Dutch regime. In the space of a few years, he managed to lure Walter Spies to Ubud, take Gusti Nyoman Lempad's daughter as a concubine, organize the first tour of a Balinese dance troupe to Europe, collecting a French wife en route, and most importantly, to manipulate the division of his father's inheritance greatly to his own advantage, at the expense of all his siblings. By the time he moved on to the national political arena in Jakarta in 1932, not only was the inheritance but the *puri* itself divided by the inheritance dispute, but some of its members relatively impoverished and its vast landholdings fragmented between several competing sub-*puri*.

These sub-*puri*, deprived of much their previous economic security, their landholdings reduced, divided, and newly vulnerable to a less generous taxation regime, came to depend increasingly on their reduced landholdings to keep them in the manner to which they had become accustomed. If there was a time when the reputation of Puri Ubud as a rapacious landlord was established, it was through the practices of some of the sub-*puri*, especially that of Ck. Raka himself, during this period. Stories abound of abuses against anonymous villagers, against such notable local citizens as Gusti Nyoman Lempad, and even against *laba pura*, the land set aside for the support of temples.[11]

Farmers depended on cash crops, especially copra, coffee, pigs, cattle and rice for export to pay their taxes. The Great Depression dramatically reduced worldwide demand for and prices of these crops. Many farmers were unable to pay even when the colonial administration reduced its demands. People lived in fear of taxation and title to land became a liability, in many cases greater than its value as a subsistence asset (Robinson 1995: 54–59; Schulte-Nordholt 1996: 253; MacRae 1997: 376). These were the circumstances, beginning perhaps in the 1920s and certainly in the 1930s, in which it was said that, in Ubud, some people gave their land to the *puri* because they were 'afraid of taxes' (*takut pajak*).

What exactly happened is unclear from these accounts, but what is clear is that during this period, and as a direct result of this pressure, substantial amounts of land passed or returned from the control of farmers to that of the *puri*. It seems likely that this occurred through a variety of mechanisms referred to in the vague accounts of my informants. Some said that farmers simply 'gave' their land to the *puri*. Others said that farmers asked the *puri* for assistance in paying their taxes. The *puri*, likewise may have offered assistance to farmers in difficulties. In any of these circumstances the *puri* probably took possession of the *pipil*, the taxation records which served as a kind of *de facto* title to land.

Schulte-Nordholt (1996: 250–51) relates how these matters were managed by officials known as *sedehan*, who had become colonial tax-collectors but were, in local understandings, as they had been in pre-colonial times, agents of the *puri*. The interests of these *sedehan* coincided with those of the *puri* in relieving farmers of title to their land. Once again, the system in Ubud appears to have been similar, with the fact that the *puri* retained *sedehan* of its own to manage its landholdings, only adding to the potential misunderstandings (and exploitation of them).

Although the general exemption of *puri* from land tax was lifted in the reforms of 1919 and 1922, there is some evidence (in the form of local anecdote and Hilbery 1979: 19) that Puri Ubud may still have received special treatment, at least for some years. Such immunity would have facilitated their willingness to relieve farmers of their tax-burden by taking formal possession of their lands just as *sedehan* in Mengwi 'paid the land rent for others, thus gaining possession of the land' (Schulte-Nordholt 1996: 289n.86).

This, combined with the residual awe in which people held the *puri* as a whole, would also have placed the *sedehan* in a position to exercise considerable control over the terms of the subsequent relationship between farmer and *puri* in relation to the land involved. It seems likely that this also was the period in which the contemporary pattern of landlessness among sections of the Ubud population was more firmly entrenched, and also when the less-than-generous shareholding practices for which Gianyar was notorious (Robinson 1995: 256; Schulte-Nordholt 1996: 293) were developed.[12]

AFTER THE DUTCH: THE DEVELOPMENT
OF A LAND CRISIS

The Japanese interregnum of 1942–1945 replaced taxation in Dutch currency with direct appropriation of surplus production of foodstuffs, especially rice, and the forced production of additional crops such as cotton and sisal (Hilbery 1979: 24; Robinson 1995: 75). It also caused dramatic inflation of the prices of basic commodities, which had the side effect of allowing debts to be paid back with relative ease, thus enabling some small farmers to retain land which might otherwise have been lost to money-lenders. After the defeat of the Japanese, and the Independence struggle against the returning Dutch, the farmers returned to their fields, but once again political and economic turmoil prevailed.

Despite legislation in 1951 prohibiting harvest shares of less than 50 per cent to tenant farmers, old patron–client relations prevailed and many landlords, in Ubud as in the rest of Bali, retained much higher harvest shares (Robinson 1995: 252). As the 1950s progressed, there were several steep rises in the price of rice and productive agricultural land was the only guarantee of survival. Population had increased dramatically and average landholdings were a fraction of what they had been a generation previously (Robinson 1995: 251).

The resulting pressure for a more equitable distribution of land was one of the dominant political issues during this period. It was taken up most forcefully by the Communist Party (PKI) and its subsidiary rural organizations, notably Barisan Tani Indonesia (BTI), for which *land-reform* became a central aim (see also Darma Putra, this volume).[13] By 1960, they had managed to persuade the government to initiate a program of land redistribution. But the situation was to deteriorate further before the program reached Ubud.

In the early 1960s, the shortage of rice was exacerbated by plagues of crop pests and the eruption of Mt. Agung. Inflation reached crisis proportions, with the price of rice rising over 400 per cent in less than a year from late 1962 to 1963, further increasing the pressure on the government to reform relations of agrarian production. This was the time at which Ubud people recall eating the trunks of banana trees to survive and many young men took to the roads in search of employment or food.

Landreform

Landreform was ostensibly designed to reduce all large landholdings to a scale enabling landholders to still support their families comfortably while transferring legal title of the surplus to those, sharecroppers or tenants, who actually worked the land. The regulations allowed landowners to retain additional lands for the support of dependent kin and also to reserve land for *laba pura*. By skilful manipulation of these exemption rules, and other aspects of the system, many of even the largest land-owners were able to subvert the system and thus retain very high proportions of their land (Utrecht 1969: 79; Mortimer 1972: 18–19; Robinson 1995: 255–57).

In Ubud, the process did not begin until 1963. At this time the *kecamatan* (subdistrict) had a population of some 31,000 of whom the vast majority were farmers. The allowable limits were 7 ha of *sawah* (irrigated-) and 9 ha of *tegal* (dry-fields). Only 21 landowners reported holdings in excess of these limits. Between them they reportedly owned a total of over 1000 ha, which is about 28 per cent of the total productive land in the *kecamatan*. These landowners were, with partial exceptions, members of several related *puri* or their close retainers. Of this Puri Ubud itself reported 636.24 ha or nearly 60 per cent. The remainder was held by four related *puri*. Of the land reported by Puri Ubud Ck. Raka Sukawati personally owned over 250 ha or 24 per cent of the total reported.[14] These figures are summarized in Table 7.2.

Through judicious exploitation of the rules regarding dependants and *laba pura*, the top 21 landowners were able to retain 464 ha, over 43 per cent of their total reported holdings, the majority of it the more highly valued *sawah*. This left a surplus of 602.991 ha for redistribution to farmers. To receive this land, farmers had to pay a fee of the order of Rp. 15,000–30,000 (not much less than the market value of the land at the time) to the government which was passed on to the landowner as 'compensation' (*ganti rugi*). Thirty-three years later, in 1996, 467.77 ha (or just over 75 per cent) of this land had been redistributed to a total of 1529 farmers (although by 1996 only 1013 had obtained certificates giving irrevocable legal status to their ownership). The majority of *sawah* plots are in the range 0.2–0.4 ha which, if the land is good, is just sufficient to feed a small family.

In 1996 I found, to my amazement, that the process was still going on, managed by a staff of some six people in a small, stifling office in the Gianyar branch of the *Badan Pertanahan Nasional* (or BPN, 'National

Table 7.2 Excess land reported, land areas reported, redistributed and retained in the wake of *landreform*,[15] Kecamatan Ubud 1963–1996 (all areas in hectares)

Landowners	Reported Land Holdings	Concessions (for dependent family and temple land)	Balance (designated for redistribution)	Redistribution (achieved by 1996)
Top 21 owners	1067.055	464.064	602.991	467.77
Puri Ubud	636.24	N/A	N/A	N/A
Ck. Raka	254.89	N/A	N/A	N/A

Source: Landreform Office, BPN, Gianyar.

Land Agency'). Much of their work involves laboriously following through the processing of old claims and dealing with new ones, often brought by farmers who, after decades of submission to their landlords, have finally summoned up the courage to protect their land by application for proper title. In addition to this, cases of *tanah gelap*, 'dark' or 'obscured' land, not declared as excess by landowners, are still coming to light. These too are investigated thoroughly and if found to be true, lead to the summary confiscation of land. The extent of this *tanah gelap*, other circumstantial evidence, and reports from other areas suggest that the amount of land initially reported is at most around 75 per cent of true landholdings, which adds a further layer to the pattern of inequality both before and after redistribution (MacRae 1997: 393).

Another common practice employed by landowners to subvert the process was 'illegal transfers to relatives and dummies' (Mortimer 1972: 18). Robinson's research confirms that Bali was no exception to this pattern. One of his more graphic examples is from a village near Ubud in which the 'aristocratic' owners used a complex of false sales to disguise the extent of their holdings (Robinson 1988: 521). Several local people have told me privately that this was precisely what happened in Ubud and the consensus of more public oral opinion supports this claim, while falling short of asserting it in specific terms. The records of BPN and local *sedehan* confirm the transfer of increasing amounts of land from large (mostly *puri*) landowners to (what appear from their names to be) ordinary farmers, beginning well before *landreform*. While the nature of these transfers is not clear from the records, the balance of anecdotal evidence suggests that whatever the intention had been, *puri* landlords have since attempted to reclaim at least some of this land (Nusa 1996; MacRae 1997: 398).

After some 30 years the process of *landreform* is still incomplete, and appears only partially successful. At best it reduced the upper extreme of landholding inequality and ensured that most farmers have at least some access to land of their own, but it has not created a real basis of equality in landholdings. Furthermore, many of the gains have since been offset by further population increase and consequent subdivision of already marginally small holdings. And, as subsequent events have shown, *landreform* merely set the scene for the greatest transformation of all.

FOREIGN MONEY: TOURISM, INFLATION AND COMMODIFICATION OF LAND

The population-driven inflation in the value of land referred to above has coincided with and been accelerated geometrically, especially since the mid-1980s, by the development of tourism and the associated growth of a resident expatriate community. These developments have had a number of effects, both direct and indirect on land use, land value, and land tenure. First, the growth of the tourism sector has led to a compre-hensive shift of both land and labour from agricultural subsistence to tourism-based commerce (MacRae 1997: 47–49, 71–73). Second, it created a demand for street-frontage land through which restaurants and shops could have most direct access to the tourists on the street. Accommoda-tion was provided initially within existing family compounds. Families whose residential land fronted onto main streets had an immediate advantage, but as the tourism zone spread into surrounding agricultural land, farmers began converting or selling their fields for more profitable tourism uses (see Figure 7.2).

Third, it created a market for quiet secluded residential sites with views, preferably of mountains or rivers and with access to cool breezes. This combination of qualities occurs mostly along the edges of the steep river gorges, land which previously was the least valuable on account of its difficulty to access and cultivate, reduced sunshine hours, and often poor water supply. So while the uses of land have been stood on their head in the space of a generation, in an environment of general inflation, so also have the relative valuations of different categories of land been drastically transformed. Needless to say, such transformations have provided unexpected opportunities for some and losses for others.

In effect there began, for the first time, a true real-estate market based on the value of land as capital, rather than as a subsistence resource. The prices which entrepreneurs were prepared to pay for land were determined no longer by its ability to produce rice but directly by the expected returns from the tourism enterprises or residential property which could be built upon it. By the mid-1980s this return was more than could be made grow-ing rice and the rate of conversions, sales and leases increased dramatically. Fortunes were made through sales of relatively unproductive but strategic-ally located land. Some of these fortunes were subsequently lost through extravagant expenditure on non-productive consumer items and gambling.

New classes emerged: The cash-rich but land-poor unemployed peas-ant, the tourism entrepreneur using investment capital or partnership with landowners to obtain access to land on which to seek a return on his investment, immigrant labourers, real-estate brokers and speculators, the disgruntled former landlord seeking to evict his former tenants from land redistributed to them by *landreform*, and the well-heeled foreigner looking for land on which to build a house or establish an export business.

As the quantity and quality of tourism increased, so did the flow of for-eign cash into Ubud, while the supply of prime land dwindled and prices inflated astronomically. It was at this stage that farmers, struggling to keep up with the rising general cost of living, began to joke about being better off selling their land, banking the proceeds, and living off the interest. Many took the joke seriously and have done just that.[16] As might be expected, these changes have also led to conflict over use and particularly ownership of land.

(a)

(b)

Figure 7.2 The meeting of the landscapes of tourism and agriculture.

LAND CONFLICTS: THE AYUNG GORGE

The deep gorge of the Ayung river, just west of Ubud, has long been a site
of conflict; a natural border between rival kingdoms whose decisive battles were often fought on its banks (McPhee 1947: 92; MacRae 1997: 299,

303, 324). The villages along the east bank of the gorge were established in the nineteenth century as defensive outposts of Puri Peliatan. Since then it has become the site of conflicts of another kind.

When the Canadian composer Colin McPhee announced that he wished to build a house in Sayan, on a spectacular site overlooking the river, he inadvertently opened a Pandora's box of conflicts and confusions in the local community. He wanted to lease the land for 10 years and when it was rumoured that Rendah (the presumed owner of the land)

> would profit considerably [...] a long and bitter dispute arose over the ownership of the land. The village claimed it had always been village property. Chokorda Rahi, the prince, suddenly appeared [...] to say that the land actually belonged to him, had been given to him long ago by his father, in the palace at Ubud. The land had merely been loaned to Rendah [...] Rendah however insisted that the land had been given outright to him by the Chokorda in return for money he had once loaned.
>
> (McPhee 1947: 81–82)

The legal status of the land was recorded in a palm-leaf document called *pipil* which 'No one had seen [...] for ages, and it took a month to find'. When it was eventually found, the matter turned out to be less than straightforward and

> the Chokorda had to retreat, baffled. This *pipil* [...] turned out after all to be made out in favour of Rendah's elder brother, the *klian* (headman), with items – the coconut trees remained the property of Chokorda Rahi: the crop was his; one-fifth of it went to Rendah in payment for watching the trees.
>
> (McPhee 1947: 81–82)

This was in 1933, and over 60 years later, essentially similar dramas were still being played out as local entrepreneurs, usually in partnership with foreign capital, have tried to gain access to prime land overlooking the gorge, by means both fair and foul.

In early 1996, a local newspaper ran a story in which it was claimed that some Balinese *puri* were attempting to reclaim land previously granted, in some cases several generations previously, to their dependants. The article cited a specific lawsuit between Puri Ubud and the aggrieved 'owner' of a prime development site overlooking the gorge (Nusa 14.04.1996). My personal experience of such stories is limited to witnessing the parade of petitioners to the Landreform Office seeking assistance in their problems with former landlords, and to one more direct experience: I was sitting on the verandah of a friend's house when a young man rushed in, visibly distressed and gasped, 'A *cokorda* is coming at midday.' My host excused himself, changed his clothes and they hurried off together. The young man was from a family with long-standing links to my host's family. They lived in a village overlooking the Ayung gorge. They were hereditary clients of a branch of the *puri* living on land granted to them long ago. They were in fact thinking of selling their land and were in the process of seeking proper certification of it. The *cokorda* in question was of the younger generation and well-known for supporting certain expensive habits by selling land reclaimed from unwary former clients of his ancestors.

My host assembled his worldly-wise and heavily-built brother and a relative from another village who had already lost a substantial amount of family land to the same *cokorda*. Together they hurried to the scene. The *cokorda* never turned up, warned I was told, by his 'eyes' in the village. The family hastened to complete the certification process and when he did arrive some weeks later, the land was legally secure and he could only ask indignantly why they had not trusted him, their hereditary lord, to look after their interests instead of turning to 'outsiders'.

It was precisely to avoid conflicts of this kind, and urged on by government advertizing, that people applied in droves through the 1990s, to obtain indisputable legal title to their land, a procedure which ironically frees their land from customary restraints on alienation and opens the door to its inevitable commodification.

STATE AND REAL ESTATE: *PAJAK* AND *SERTIPIKAT*

The main thrust of Dutch economic policy in Bali was to pay for its own administration and the primary means for this was taxation. While they levied a bewildering variety of taxes, the main one was on productive land. To provide a basis of this, they began a system of surveying and registration of land, in the name not of its 'owner' but of whoever was working it. The unrealistic levels of Dutch land tax caused significant hardship, indebtedness, and ultimately loss of land during the 1930s.

The Indonesian state inherited this system which it continued to work, half-heartedly and inefficiently, through the 1950s. The *landreform* program of the 1960s was enacted under a comprehensive piece of legislation known as *Undang-Undang Pokok Agraria* 1960 (UUPA). While *landreform* was its most immediate aim, this legislation had several other ancillary purposes, including the prevention of foreign ownership. It was also a *de facto* step toward reorganizing the state's imperfect knowledge of land tenure and facilitating the systematic transfer of land from *adat* (collective traditional) control to that of national law. It created provisions and procedures for the 'conversion' (*konversi*) of land from its existing status under local village *adat* to a new status of private ownership (*hak milik*) subject only to national law. This conversion of

status is effected by the issue of a 'certificate' (*sertipikat*) which identifies
the land according to its area and boundaries, provides legal title, establishes its status as a taxable entity, and enables it to be bought and sold
free of *adat* encumbrance. Once certified, any land becomes legally
alienable in principle, regardless of the opinions of local *adat* or community
sentiment.

The vast bulk of land subject to *konversi* is agricultural land, but the
same principle applies also to residential land. Village residential land
(*tanah pekarangan desa*) is, under the *adat* system, owned by the village
and is in effect 'leased' in perpetuity to the household occupying it
subject to performance of the *ayahan* (unpaid labour) duties required by
local *adat*. Once certified, however, it too is theoretically freed from *adat*
control and may be bought and sold. As Warren (1993: 293) points out,
this cuts across and undermines the whole basis of village solidarity and
citizenship. In practice, however, there are very few cases in Ubud of
tanah pekarangan desa being sold and these cases are exceptional in
various ways.[17]

Other categories of land remained notionally exempt from registration
and taxation: Temple lands (*laba pura*), land granted to village officials
(*tanah bukti*), and village agricultural land (*tanah ayahan desa*). In fact they
became property of the state, but in practice continued to function as if
they were owned by the village.

In Ubud, certification of land is not systematically recorded on the
land records, but evidence of it begins to appear in the late 1970s. The
consensus of local opinion supports the common sense supposition that
it increased steadily through the 1980s building to the peak which
I observed in the mid-1990s. By this stage the frenzy was driven not only
by the astronomical inflation of prices, but advertizing on government
television, urging people to 'secure' their land by having it certified. The
Government is assisted and encouraged in this task by the Australian
Government and the World Bank.

The 'Land Administration Project' is a tripartite venture involving the
Indonesian Government, the World Bank and the Australian aid-agency
AUSAID. Its stated aims involve the registration of large amounts of
land, to establish a 'solid reliable database' of land information, and to
transfer skills to the National Land Agency (BPN) (see *Inside Indonesia*
1998). Although the project is based in West Java, I met, in mid 1996,
a BPN staff member who had been involved with it and seconded to Bali
to apply his new expertise to specific problems there. He was hoping to
go to Australia for further training the following year. Critics of the
project, both within and beyond Indonesia, are explicit in their belief
that it is part of a larger agenda to free-up land for sale.

After we register our land, who will get the comparative advantage?
[...] Having a certificate puts you in the capitalist arena. But you will

be a weak participant [...] The rules will result in unequal land distribution.

(Noer Fauzi, interviewed in *Inside Indonesia* 1998)

In Ubud, it is clear that this is exactly what has happened, with rich and poor alike selling land, in some cases resulting in impoverishment. More recently, however, there has arisen a widespread aversion to selling, especially to outsiders, and a shift to leasing land for anything from 10 to 30 years, at prices not much less than market values. Thus the people of Ubud are attempting to have their land/cake and eat it too – using it as a capital resource but retaining ultimate ownership of it.

CONCLUSION

Some of the conclusions to be drawn from this account are fairly obvious. First, the predictable pattern of increasing scarcity and hence price of land. Second, the systematic changes in land use and land value associated with the general economic shift from subsistence-based agriculture to tourism-based commerce. These have had secondary consequences in terms of employment and the opening up of new avenues of socio-economic mobility, with some previously wealthy groups losing their automatic dominance and others having at least the opportunity for considerable gain.

What is less obvious, but has become particularly apparent through attention to the historical process, is the role of land ownership in creating and maintaining the unique position of socio-cultural dominance of Puri Ubud. It was land, won in war, which provided the springboard for their rise to power. It was land, on which they paid little tax, which enabled them to retain a relationship almost unique among the royal houses of Bali, with their local community. It is land, hugely inflated in market value, which they are today exchanging in order to invest in the symbolic capital of ritual leadership in Ubud and beyond (MacRae 1999: 144–45).

The material presented here suggests also some more general points for Balinese, Indonesian and Southeast Asian studies. First, that the *landreform* process in Ubud was at best only partially effective and remains to this day incomplete. Second, that the *pecatu* model of land-tenure and land use was not universal throughout pre-colonial South Bali. Finally, that while the relative value of land and labour have indeed tended to become reversed during the twentieth century, this has never obscured from the oral historians of Ubud, and should not obscure from us, the vital role played by land in the material support of the labour upon which the power of nineteenth century rulers was based.

Should we be disinclined to take this last point seriously, it is worth noting that, at the time of writing, there are reports of landless Javanese farmers occupying plantation lands they believe to be traditionally theirs and the new President made promises to once again redistribute state land to the landless. The urban unemployment created by the Asian economic crisis has exacerbated this trend and the pressure on rural land is increasing as people return to their villages in search of subsistence (Bachriadi 2000), although there was in late 1999 little sign of this around Ubud. In Ubud to date, the foreign exchange generated even by reduced levels of tourism has so far insulated most people against this, but many successful tourism entrepreneurs are now diversifying their investments by purchasing land. Likewise, the recent devaluation of the Rupiah has made land in Bali even more affordable to foreigners. So the value of land continues to rise, as it did during the 1950s, despite the general economic downturn. A further, long-term downturn in tourism would make very visible once again the ultimate dependence of labour on land and the new levels of inequality based on ownership of land in which case the voices of the landless and the farmers, muted since 1965, may be heard again in Bali.

NOTES

1 The ongoing political crisis since May 1998 has obviously superseded all other problems, but even within this context, conflicts over land continue to erupt (e.g. Indonesian Observer 2000; Jakarta Post 2000; Wirata 2000).
2 Such land is relatively unproductive (of rice) by virtue of restricted sunlight, often poor water supply, and the most labour-hungry. Its value to the hotwires lies in its often spectacular views, seclusion and exposure to cool breezes.
3 I thought this was a joke farmers made at their own expense until I did a rough calculation which confirmed its literal truth (MacRae 1997: 78).
4 Although population density was low compared with the present, it has always been high by Southeast Asian standards – one of the reasons why land was perhaps more politically important in Bali than scholarly orthodoxy would suggest (see also Hobart *et al*. 1996: 54).
5 I discussed land-tenure practices, past and present, with dozens of (mostly) men, especially older ones. The majority had only partial knowledge but the vast majority shared in the broad outline of 'consensus' referred to here. More detailed explanations came from a few men who were old enough to remember the pre-WW2 period and who had been involved professionally in the management of land on behalf of either the *puri* or the state. These positions (known as *sedehan*) were usually inherited, so that the men I interviewed had a good idea of the systems administered by their fathers as well. Especially well informed and helpful were I G. M. Sumung of Taman Kelod, I W. Lungsur of Ubud, and I K. Teler of Padangtegal.
6 This is the explanation for the contemporary status of Padangtegal; relatively wealthy in land and ritually independent of Puri Ubud. Padangtegal was from the start, and remained, a direct dependency of Puri Peliatan, from which its people received *pecatu* land and eventually the option of ritual independence.

7 This elite included refugees from other kingdoms, especially from the destruction of Ubud's ill-fated ally, Mengwi (MacRae 1997: 325).

8 Henk Schulte-Nordholt notes the mutuality of the relationship which he expresses in terms 'mobilized manpower' as a manifestation of 'property' rather than the reverse (1996: 35). He also describes the *pecatu* system as a 'material basis for followership' (Schulte-Nordholt 1996: 129).

9 This at least is the picture painted by the majority of my informants, including the best-informed ones. There is a contrary opinion, claiming that beneath the appearance of loyalty is an underlying lack of respect for the *puri* as a result of their harsh and unforgiving attitude in revenue extraction. This opinion is also well represented, but usually by people with their own reasons to dislike the *puri*, and usually without the support of much in the way of evidence. It is my opinion that the better documented extortion practices and unpopularity of Ck. G. Sukawati's son and heir, Ck. Raka, are extrapolated to the *puri* as a whole in some of these accounts.

10 According to van Kol (1914: 346–48), Ck. Sukawati was, by 1914, the wealthiest of the kings of Bali. Robinson (1995: 256) reports the Gianyar region as having the least favourable sharecropping regimes in the 1930s, but this referred both to a later period and probably more specifically to the notoriously oppressive regime of Puri Gianyar itself.

11 I use the terms Puri Ubud and 'the puri', as do local people, contextually, to refer to several levels of aristocratic authority: the entire establishment of interlinked sub-*puri*; the pair, Puri Saren and Puri Saren Kauh, in which greatest ritual authority is concentrated, to either of these two or to other branches acting independently in specific contexts, or even to the actions of individual *cokorda*. While this may be confusing to the reader it is consistent with local usage which emphasises not specific socio-political structures but the ritually based authority common to all levels and parts of the *puri*.

12 According to a contemporary informant, relying on stories from his father and uncle, standard sharecropping practice in Ubud moved progressively from *mepat* (1/4 to the farmer), through *lon* (1/3rd to the farmer) and *nandon* (2/5th to the farmer), to *piat pada* (half to the farmer). Those working on *puri* land, however, enjoyed a relatively generous 50 per cent share (although this view was not shared by other informants and was at best probably offset by additional ritual obligations).

13 I defer here to standard Indonesian spelling of *landreform* to indicate its specifically local practice.

14 My quantitative knowledge of *landreform* in the Ubud area comes from the official records of the process, which are written in school exercise books tied into bundles with string and stored in a dusty, glass-fronted cabinet in the Landreform Office of the BPN, Gianyar. I am grateful to the staff of this office for their good-humoured resignation to my intrusions. The more qualitative aspects of my knowledge are the result of countless conversations with farmers and other people in Ubud old enough to remember the process, as well as more formal interviews with some of the surviving officials involved in the process.

15 The BPN records consist of a number of books and files, none of which are complete and which are not totally consistent with one another. The figures presented here have been compiled from a number of these sources and represent a certain amount of selection, editing and interpretation.

16 Land and interest calculation taken from MacRae (1997).

17 I am only aware of two such cases in Ubud. One involves a small portion of street-front land sold for a restaurant. Another involves a family in dire circumstances, both materially and ritually, who sold part of their house yard.

REFERENCES

Bachriadi, D. (2000) 'Land for the Landless: Why are Democrats in Jakarta not interested in Land Reform?' *Inside Indonesia*, 64 (October–December 2000).

Bali Post (1996) 'Masalah Pertanahan Makin Serius', 5 July 1996.

Boon, J. A. (1977) *The Anthropological Romance of Bali*, 1597–1972, Cambridge: Cambridge University Press.

Errington, S. (1983) 'The Place of Regalia in Luwu'. In L. Gesick (ed.), *Centres, Symbols and Hierarchies: Essays on the Classical States of Southeast Asia*, New Haven: Southeast Asian Studies, Yale University.

Geertz, C. (1980) *Negara: The Theater-State in Nineteenth-Century Bali*, Princeton (N.J.): Princeton University Press.

Gullick, J. M. (1958) *Indigenous Political Systems of Western Malaya*, London: Athlone.

Gunning, H. C. J. and van der Heiden, A. J. V. (1926) 'Het Petjatoe: En Amstveldenprobleem in Zuid-Bali'. *Tijdschrift voor Indische Taal-Land-en Volkendkunde*, 66: 329–94.

Hilbery, R. (1979) *A Balinese Journal, 1973–1979*, Honolulu: Southeast Asian Studies Program Paper no. 7, University of Hawaii.

Hobart, A., Ramseyer, U. and Leeman, A. (1996) *The Peoples of Bali*, Oxford: Blackwell.

Howe, L. E. A. (1980) *Pujung: An Investigation of the Foundations of Balinese Culture*. Edinburgh: University of Edinburgh, unpublished Ph.D. Thesis.

Indonesian Observer (2000) 'Ex-Bali Governor undergoes Police Interrogation'. 3 November 2000.

Jakarta Post (2000) 'Prolonged Land Dispute finishes with Death'. 16 December 2000.

Kat Angelino, P. de (1921) 'De amstveldenen petjatoe-pengajah in Gianjar'. *Kolonial Tijdschrift*, 10: 225–65.

Kol, H. H. van (1914) *Uit Onze kolonien: uutvoerig reisverhaal*, Leiden: A. W. Slijthoff.

Korn, V. E. (1924) *Het Adatrecht van Bali*, Den Haag: Handelsdrukkerij 'de Ster'.

MacRae, G. S. (1997) *Economy, Ritual and History in a Balinese Tourist Town*, Auckland: University of Auckland, unpublished Ph.D. Thesis.

MacRae, G. S. (1999) 'Acting Global, Thinking Local in a Balinese Tourist Town'. In R. Rubinstein and L. Connor (eds), *Staying Local in the Global village: Bali in the Twentieth Century*, Honolulu: University of Hawaii Press.

McPhee, C. (1947) *A House in Bali*, London: Victor Gollancz.

Mortimer, R. (1972) *The Indonesian Communist Party and Land Reform, 1959–1965*. Clayton: Centre for Southeast Asian Studies, Monash University.

Nusa (1996) 'Setelah Kuasa dan Wibawa Puri-Puri Bali Hilang'. 14 April 1996.

Robinson, G. (1988) 'State, Society and Political Conflict in Bali, 1945–1946'. *Indonesia* 45 (April 1988): 1–48.

Robinson, G. (1995) *The Dark Side of Paradise: Political violence in Bali*, Ithaca and London: Cornell University Press.

Schulte-Nordholt, H. (1996) *The Spell of Power: A History of Balinese Politics*, Leiden: KITLV Press.

Utrecht, E. (1969) 'Land Reform'. *Bulletin of Indonesian Economic Studies*, Canberra: Australian National University Press.

Vickers, A. (1989) *Bali: A Paradise Created*, Hardondsworth (U.K.): Penguin Books.

Warren, C. (1993) *Adat and Dinas: Balinese communities in the Indonesian state*, Oxford and Singapore: Oxford University Press.

Wiener, M. (1995) *Visible and Invisible Realms: Power, Magic and Colonial Conquest in Bali*, Chicago and London: University of Chicago Press.

Windia, W. (1996a) 'Identitas Tanah'. *Bali Post*, 14 June 1996.

Windia, W. (1996b) 'Mengamankan Tanah Lebih'. *Bali Post*, 21 July 1996.

Windia, W. (1996c) 'Warisan Tanah'. *Bali Post*, 30 July 1996.

Windia, W. (1996d) 'Mengamankan Tanah Catu'. *Bali Post*, 7 August 1996.

Windia, W. (1996e) 'Pembebasan Tanah'. *Bali Post*, 22 September 1996.

Wirata, P. (2000) 'Bali called on to Protect Ancestral Lands and Religious Sites'. *The Jakarta Post*, 14 December 2000.

8 Mythical centres and modern margins

A short history of encounters, crises, marginality, and social change in highland Bali

Thomas A. Reuter

The central highland region of Bali is the principle homeland of a disadvantaged minority group on this rather prosperous Indonesian island, a people locally referred to as 'the Mountain Balinese' (*wong bali aga*). While southern Bali has long been a prominent research site for western social scientists and popular as an international tourist destination, few foreign visitors had paid much attention to the broader significance of Bali Aga culture when I first began my study of the island's highland region in 1992. A focal aim of my subsequent publications has been to remove some of the veils of biased representation that have situated the highland Balinese at the fringe of Balinese society (see Reuter 1998a–c, 1999a–b, 2000, 2002, in Press). In this chapter, I focus on how the position of the Bali Aga within Balinese society has changed repeatedly during times of crisis, including the Indonesian financial and political crisis since the fall of Suharto in 1998. The analysis is designed to support three hypothesis that have general implications for the study of social change.

First of all, the position of the Bali Aga within Balinese society has not been entirely 'marginal', unless marginality is defined exclusively in political economy terms. Seen from a symbolic economy perspective, however, it appears that the Bali Aga have been active co-producers of their own social status and have secured a number of specific privileges for themselves, particularly in a domain of ritual authority. I therefore argue that studies of social change need to pay attention to shifts in the distribution of symbolic, and not just material resources. What this implies is more than just a Foucaultian take on resources, wherein knowledge (a symbolic resource) is recognized as an essential ingredient of power. Rather, I am suggesting that the accumulation of symbolic resources can serve a diversity of underlying interests, some of which are not classifiable as material interests. Hence a Western, materialist value orientation cannot serve as a universal yardstick for distinguishing between elite and disadvantaged groups in non-Western societies, or for assessing the outcome of a particular struggle between such groups. Instead, resource gains and losses must be discussed within the terms of the (changing) symbolic value systems of the participants themselves.

Inspired by the way my Balinese informants themselves think about social change, I shall emphasize that some of the most distinct and dramatic transformations in Bali Aga and Balinese society have been the result of specific historical encounters with newcomers or new ideas. Encounters with outsiders or significant shifts in an already established relationship between the Balinese and the outside world have tended to produce or trigger specific local crises, such as the one that Bali is currently experiencing. Such crises always involve disruption of an established flow of resources, and often also the introduction of a new type of symbolic or material resource. Hence my second argument about social change, taking a resource theory perspective, is that new forms of competition over resources may arise following the sudden arrival of new competitors or resources on the scene. 'Newcomers' can be ideas as well as people. Local encounters with new ideas are particularly relevant to symbolic resources such as ritual authority, some of which may be losing their currency in the changing value systems of a modernizing Balinese society.

It is important to note that the Bali Aga have not become a militant minority or, in turn, a violently oppressed people. The competitive element in their relationship with an ever-changing Balinese political elite has long been held in check by drawing a value distinction between ritual and political spheres of authority, and by each of the two parties limiting their claims to only one of the two types of resources associated with these separate value spheres. My third argument about social change is that a 'dual authority' model – or some other form of pluralist value system with an equivalently diversified symbolic resource economy – can help to prevent a social crisis from escalating by restricting resource competition.

Admittedly, such cooperative agreements are subject to change and never free of transgressions. In the present case, for example, the prerogative of the Bali Aga to claim a distinct social identity and symbolic resource, as Bali's first settlers and ritual custodians, came under extreme pressure during the New Order period and thereafter. Nevertheless, they have also been able to regain some of this lost ground during the economic and political crisis since Suharto's downfall, and this has been accomplished without violent confrontation. At a time when interethnic, religious and community conflicts are engulfing much of Indonesia and many other parts of the world in a tidal wave of futile violence, the present case study thus offers some hope that social change can be accomplished peacefully, even under crisis conditions. The key to this may be our ability to differently 'value' different people and resources, rather than pursue a false hope for unity under a single, 'universal' set of values.

BEYOND POWER: THE BALI AGA AND WESTERN NOTIONS OF MARGINALITY

> We guard the mountain of life, the temples of Bali's origin; we are the old trunk that supports the fresh tip. If we neglect our [ritual] duty, the world shall rock and all its peoples shall tumble.
>
> (Bali Aga elder, Sukawana, 1994)

Marginalizing discourses concerning the Bali Aga have long been promoted by both traditional and modern Balinese political elites, and often enough with the unwitting support of colonial and national governments. These marginalizing discourses have tended to employ the geographical remoteness of Bali's central highland region as a focal metaphor for constructing its inhabitants as a historically and culturally distant and backward people. In view of the inequalities and silences produced by these discourses I have consistently endeavoured to emphasize the perspective and counter-discourses of the mountain people, and the importance of their contribution to Balinese history and society as a whole. At the same time, however, it was problematic to reconcile this 'marginality' of the Bali Aga with the fact that their very distinct cultural heritage has persisted throughout many centuries of opposition and survived numerous incorporation attempts, some of them in recent times. Ultimately, the only way to resolve this problem was to challenge the political-economy bias within Western notions of marginality.

The problem of incongruence concerning Bali Aga marginality can be rephrased simply in the form of two questions: If the Bali Aga were so marginal and powerless, why were they not absorbed into the dominant culture of southern Balinese polities over the last six-hundred years? And, if they were not without power after all, why then did they remain politically marginal? Note that in both questions, the focus is on political power.

The few earlier anthropological studies that had considered the Bali Aga at all had chosen to answer the first of these questions. It was assumed that they were indeed without any power, and had escaped cultural incorporation by virtue of the natural isolation or economic insignificance of the highland region. This 'isolation hypothesis' is questionable, has been unduly influenced by biased southern Balinese portrayals of the Bali Aga, and reflects a lack of knowledge about their society. And as I have argued elsewhere, the hypothesis is also unsustainable in view of what we now know about the early economic and political significance of the highland region (Reuter 1998c, 2002).

I was able to establish a more plausible explanation of their collective resistance to acculturation on the basis of a systematic study of the regional level of Bali Aga social organization. The research revealed that highland Bali, for its people, is a sacred landscape carved up into more than ten separate yet interrelated ritual domains (*banua*). Each of these domains is defined by a regional network of ritual alliance centred upon a sacred site of origin with a major temple. These alliance systems – some connecting as many as 50 different Bali Aga villages – have been crucial in facilitating their quest to maintain a distinct heritage and ethnic identity in contrast to the mainstream culture and identity concept of lowland Balinese.

While the Bali Aga had clearly profited from this 'powerful' network of inter-village alliances in some ways, this profit was not measurable in terms of political power as such. One could say that their alliance networks were like a social muscle that was never really flexed to take such political action as would have been required to remedy the politically marginal condition of the Bali Aga. In short, a portrayal of the Bali Aga as a more well-organized and cohesive society only begs the second of the two questions above: Why was this organizational power not used politically?

One answer is that the available organizational power was used – though only in a limited, defensive way – to secure a degree of political autonomy for the highlands throughout pre-colonial history.[1] Another response is that it could not be used in a more offensive manner for fear of retaliation from southern Balinese kings. Still another interpretation would be that Bali Aga social organization has been too egalitarian to permit an effective mobilization of force.

All of these answers may hold some truth. In the end, however, a satisfactory explanation for the Bali Aga phenomenon can only be derived from an ethno-historical analysis of Balinese models of identity, and of the special and changing place the highland people have occupied therein.

From this perspective it soon becomes obvious that political power was not the only resource at stake. The history of the Bali Aga is not just a political one. It has also been a history of struggle for status, and for status as an end in itself. A labelling of the Bali Aga as 'marginal', conceived purely in political-economy terms, is thus too limited a perspective to explain the phenomenon at hand. Bali's resource economy has been a multi-dimensional field of social action; differentiated on the basis of a value distinction between political and ritual authority. Hence the issue of competition between the Bali Aga and a changing Balinese political elite over the resource of political power could be prevented from arising in the first place or, at least, became but one issue in a more complex game of resource competition.

POLITICAL AND RITUAL AUTHORITY: MANAGING ENCOUNTERS AND CONFLICTS THROUGH RESOURCE DIVERSIFICATION

The Bali Aga have been a centrepiece in the historically conceived mosaic of Balinese identities, and there are two simple reasons for this. First of all, the Balinese think of their identities as a history of successive encounters between earlier and later arrivals. The more significant of these encounters are often described as distinct historical crisis points. Each group of newcomers had to acknowledge those who had come before them, but only some of them were indeed powerful or clever enough not only to establish a place for themselves in Balinese society, but to gain political control of the island. Furthermore, the category 'Bali Aga' points toward the very first of these 'significant encounters' that is still remembered clearly and still carries meaning for contemporary Balinese identities. It is essential to reflect briefly on this exemplary and legendary first encounter and archetypal social crisis before turning to an analysis of subsequent changes and crises in Bali's social history.

The highland Balinese are thought of as the island's indigenous people or first settlers. They have been important primarily as the symbolic counterpart to the pre-colonial political elite of the island's coastal princi-palities, because Bali's kings and nobles all identified themselves as illus-trious 'newcomers' with an external point of origin – the legendary Javanese empire of Majapahit. Bali's dualist model of identity thus builds on the idea of a transformative encounter involving the arrival of power-ful newcomers at a locality already occupied and claimed by indigenous others. This scenario obviously evokes a powerful potential for social or even military conflict, unless and until the initial crisis of the encounter between the two groups can be resolved conceptually.

There is nothing in this scenario to suggest that the earlier people must survive such an encounter with more powerful newcomers other than as a memory, except insofar as sacred origins are generally valued in Bali and in other Austronesian-speaking societies (Reuter 2002). The people whose ancestors first cleared the forest and cultivated the land tend to be respected because the spirits of these ancestors still guard the land and ensure its fertility, and given that they – as their descendents – have privileged ritual access to the spirits of the founding ancestors. This does not amount to a guarantee for survival, let alone for the long-term maintenance of first-settler privileges, but it does present the option of integrating an earlier people by peaceful means.

The procedure for this is the institutionalization of a basic division between the values of 'sacred origin' and 'alien power' and between the privileges of ritual and political authority.[2] Admittedly, it is histories of human encounters that create cultural values, rather than the reverse, insofar as the most socially determining values are always defined by the victors. But I shall argue that such values, once they have gained popular acceptance, may well have an effect on the outcome of subsequent historical encounters. In support of this argument I return to examine the Balinese case in more detail.

The particular stranger kings of this island are said to be the descendants of noble warriors from the Hindu Javanese empire of Majapahit, who gained political control of the island following their fourteenth-century invasion of Bali and defeat of its last indigenous king, Mayadanawa.[3] This last 'local' king was subsequently described as a monster of half-human, half-animal shape, and the Majapahit invasion as an act of liberation from tyranny (see Reuter 1999a). Disregarding the fact that Hindu kingdoms had already flourished on the island for more than 600 years prior to this event, the conquest was later constructed as the beginning of Hindu civilization on the island, and the indigenous Bali Aga as the remnant of Bali's more distant and savage past. Although it may seem ironical at first, this portrayal of Balinese origins has been a contributing factor in assuring the persistence of a distinct and presumably 'indigenous' Bali Aga culture.

The highland people were a logically necessary counterpart to the self-image of Bali's stranger kings. Fellow Balinese in general have long valued the past represented by the Bali Aga (civilized or not) as a mythical time when the divine creators of the world and the ancestral founders of human society still walked the earth. Furthermore, the permanent abode of these invisible creator or ancestor beings is assumed to be in the vicinity of the highlands; on the peaks of Bali's volcanic mountains or in the sky above to which they point. Finally, the mountains are also the sacred source of water for southern Bali's all important rice irrigation system.

It may well be that the people now known as the 'Mountain Balinese' had little choice but to bow to the greater military might and accept the political dominance of a new and 'foreign' Majapahit aristocracy in Bali. While there is evidence of some early military resistance to the new rulers, they have long tended to restrict their political ambition to the more humble goal of minimizing the local political influence of coastal kingdoms in the mountains (Reuter 1999a). But the Bali Aga have also had some positive reasons for accepting Bali Majapahit's political authority: In return, they themselves have been able to lay claim to a limited sphere of ritual authority in relation to Bali as a whole.[4]

Even today, the festivals of ancient Bali Aga temples in the heart of the mountains provide occasion for important rituals aimed at maintaining the productivity of agricultural land throughout the island. These fertility and harvest rituals are celebrated each year in honour of Bali's original ancestors, and timed to mark the turning points between the two seasons of agricultural production (the full moon of the fourth and tenth Balinese lunar months respectively). It was the ancestors of the Bali Aga who first cleared this land and whose spirits still protect it. And, as their descendants, it is they who must maintain the spiritual link to the island's origins. The temple festivals attract tens of thousands of worshippers from southern Bali, and the number of visitors in modern times, if anything, has been increasing due to improved accessibility. As well as the result of a successful and united struggle for autonomy, the Bali Aga's continuing custodianship of the sacred mountains is thus also on account of the voluntary recognition of their special ritual status and duty by other Balinese, most notably the island's traditional rulers.[5]

This twofold division of traditional authority – between indigenous custodians of the land and water in the mountains and politically powerful newcomers at the coast – is found frequently in other Austronesian societies, in one form or another. The complementary relationship between a ritually privileged 'lord of the land' and a materially privileged 'stranger king' (Sahlins 1985) has been referred to as 'dual sovereignty' (van Wouden 1968) or 'diarchy' (Cunningham 1965; Needham 1980; Valeri 1982). Other authors have focused more exclusively on the politically more prominent newcomers within this dyad ('the power of strangers', Barnes 1996), or on the historically variable process of 'installing the outsider on the inside' (Fox 1994).

The existence of this cultural theme among Austronesian-speaking societies is neither a coincidence nor an irreducibly 'cultural' idiosyncrasy. Its foundations, I suggest, may lie in the common historical experience of these related peoples; a history of migration across the islands of Insular Southeast Asia and the Pacific in countless successive waves. Each wave of immigrants encountered settlers who had arrived earlier, and who became 'the original people' from their perspective.

Akin to Austronesian-speaking peoples in many other island societies of the Southeast Asia-Pacific region, the Balinese thus are no strangers to the experience of cross-cultural encounters. Over many centuries they have been compelled to develop practical and conceptual strategies for coping with the periodic arrival of sometimes powerful and dangerous, but often simply fascinating newcomers seeking to trade at their shores, or choosing to make Bali their new home. What seems to have emerged from their endeavour to negotiate the sometimes drastic social changes precipitated by such critical encounters is the idea that 'society' necessarily encompasses at least two categories of people with separate origins. 'Earlier' or relatively more 'indigenous' people are distinguished from others who have arrived more recently and are more obviously of foreign extraction. Despite the regulating effect of this cultural model, however, each of these historical encounters has had its own specific, variable, and often unpredictable outcomes.

If Balinese portrayals of their own society have envisaged a social whole forged from repeated encounters among different peoples, the encounter between Bali Aga and Bali Majapahit has been the 'first' and the most important of these encounters until the early twentieth century.[6]

This identity model acknowledges difference, inequality and conflict, but also speaks of a perpetual effort to regulate the passage of powerful newcomers and powerful new ideas into the mythical core of Balinese civilization. Its emphasis on historical change as a necessity of life has a twofold advantage. The model allows for maintaining a sense of connection to a sacred past and provides a basis for cooperation or 'restricted competition' with earlier arrivals.[7] It also values the positive potential of what is foreign and different. Overall, the model recognizes the inevitability of competition as well as the need for cooperation in a culturally diverse society.

The distribution of symbolic and material resources in a society operating under a value system of twofold authority may be described as a system of complementary inequality. It is therefore not appropriate to describe the Bali Aga as 'marginal', as we normally understand the term. The temptation to do so arises, I shall argue, because contemporary western observers have an inappropriately materialist conception of what counts as an important resource, together with an inappropriate spatial idiom to describe the distribution of resources between 'centres' and 'margins'. From this perspective, the Bali Aga would appear to have been 'marginal' for as long as they have existed as a separate category of people. This is because a conventional conception of marginality foregrounds power and wealth and disregards the fact that, in other societies, ritual status may be recognized as a primary resource equal in value, if not superior to material resources.

I shall argue that 'marginality', in this modern and materialist sense, begins to become useful as an appropriate way of describing the social condition of the Bali Aga from the time when traditional Balinese power structures were replaced with the much more effective administrative apparatus and modern idiom of a Dutch colonial and Indonesian state.

COLONIALISM AND MODERNITY IN BALI: THE RISE AND LIMITATIONS OF A MATERIALIST MODEL OF CENTRES AND MARGINS AND THEIR INTER-RELATIONS

It is inappropriate to assume that their colonial encounter was the beginning of relevant history for post-colonial societies. Pre-colonial and post-colonial ideas of identity, therefore, cannot be separated completely, and the former can be expected to have shaped the latter to some degree at least. In the Balinese case, the local, pre-colonial model of identity did not distinguish between people so much in terms of 'centres' and 'margins' as of a dynamic and time-focused notion of encounters between earlier and later arrivals. It would be contrary to the spirit of this same temporally oriented model, however, to suggest that traditional Balinese conceptions of their society have remained unaffected by the major crises in the island's more recent history, that is, by colonial and post-colonial encounters with the world beyond. In short, I shall argue that contemporary Balinese models of their own society are a hybrid of pre-colonial and modern forms of thought and interaction.

The effect of encounters with the colonial and Indonesian state on Balinese society was not the same as that of earlier encounters, such as the one between Bali Aga and Majapahit. The Dutch were not a related Austronesian people. Instead they introduced a system of political administration and a cultural model of society that was almost completely alien at the time. They did not have the intention of treating Bali as their new homeland, nor did they see a spiritual need for connecting with the Bali Aga, as the island's original people and custodians of its sacred mountains and ancient temples. Nevertheless, they did have a practical need to establish some form of local collaboration with at least some groups in Balinese society. Contemporary Bali's hybrid model of identity and system of power and status distribution originates from these early forms of collaboration.

The social crisis and changes in resource construction and distribution subsequent to the Balinese encounter with the Dutch had a specific and generally detrimental effect on the social status of the Bali Aga, which can be summarized as follows. The fiercely independent communities of the Bali Aga initially served as useful examples of traditional Balinese 'village republics' for the Dutch (Korn 1933). These communities presumably had been so obscure as to be able to escape the yoke of 'oriental despotism' that had been imposed on the less fortunate commoner people of southern Bali by a host of greedy and opium-addicted kings and nobles. But all too soon the Dutch abandoned their policy of 'liberating the common people' in favour of a system of indirect rule, in collaboration with the same 'petty tyrants' they had criticized earlier on. An original interest in and admiration for the Bali Aga vanished almost completely in the wake of this policy change. On their sporadic excursions from the larger towns of the coastal regions – built around the palaces of Balinese kings but now reconstructed as colonial administrative centres – foreign researchers no longer came empty handed to the mountains, if they came at all. They carried with them a luggage of southern Balinese cultural preconceptions about the Bali Aga, heaped upon them by a traditional local elite who, once defeated and tamed, had become very useful as political accomplices, tax collectors, key informants and cultural brokers.[8]

For the Bali Aga, the effect was clearly negative. The *Regent* and former king of Bangli, for example, was able to claim ownership of land in the highland district of Kintamani and in other Bali Aga villages to the south to an extent that had not been possible until then. The reinstated rulers of southern Balinese regencies were generally able to extend their political control through the Dutch colonial administration system, especially in the area of taxation (see Reuter, in Press; compare to MacRae, Chapter 7, this volume).

While the Dutch established themselves much later in Bali than in other parts of the Indonesian archipelago and did not stay on the island for very long, their foreign ideas certainly did. Collaborators became perpetrators in their own right as many Indonesian colonially-educated administrators became political leaders and civil servants in a new and independent Indonesian state. The result was a permanent transformation of traditional Balinese power structures and associated cultural identities.

This transformation has had two important features: It created a new type of local political and economic elite with unprecedented power, and it led to a partial decline in the relevance of ritual status as a culturally valued symbolic resource. The more specific effects of modernization on the differentiated resource economy of Bali require detailed discussion, however, especially given that the transformation concerned was not a total one.

A modern form of government and an associated state discourse of modernity became integral aspects of Balinese worlds with the rise of a new and independent Indonesian Republic after the second world war; a post-colonial state created in the image of the Western nation states of this time. The degree of local participation and empowerment in a gradual process of 'modernization' under the auspices of the Indonesian nation state has varied across different sectors of Balinese society, with the Bali Aga among those left the furthest behind. While the aspiration of owning television sets, cars or other modern commodities, may be shared by most contemporary Indonesians, only a small minority of people have been able to influence what modernity would mean for their society as a whole. In short, Balinese society changed in terms of the distribution of resources between different groups and also in terms of the types of resources available within a new symbolic and political economy.

The most active promulgators of modernist discourses and prominent social representatives of a recently acquired modern identity are the new and rather small political and economic elite of Indonesia and its local subset in Bali and other provinces. The latter are not powerful newcomers in an ethnic sense, and they need not be. It is sufficient that they are a cosmopolitan group who have domesticated the once foreign (Western) project of modernity and seek to install it within their own society. This process is thought of as initiating from the 'modern centres' (*pusat*) of power and reaching out to the 'traditional periphery' of rural and isolated regions.

The power of this new political and economic elite is unprecedented in Balinese history. Under the Dutch and even more so under Suharto's New Order regime, the administrative gaze of the state has penetrated deeper into the personal affairs of its citizens, and far deeper into the mountains of Bali and other rural regions, than any traditional ruler ever could have contemplated (Warren 1989). In addition, the predominantly rural, agricultural economy of pre-colonial Bali was soon eclipsed by a tourism industry located mainly in the urbanized southern region of the island. This change in the mechanics and economics of power has led to an unprecedented concentration of wealth in the hands of a few, notwithstanding the rise of a modestly-sized new middle class in Bali and elsewhere in Indonesia.

Bali's modern elite of politicians, administrators, and business people lend support to the materialist concept of society espoused by the Indonesian state and by key players in the global economic system, but not uniformly so. Modern-day power holders do not constitute an entirely homogenous group. Its members include a considerable subset of traditionalists who have managed to retain not only their Balinese values but also some of their earlier power. Bali's privileged certainly include many newcomers to the chambers of power, and generally these are people admitted on the basis of newly acquired wealth or political influence. But many among Bali's traditional aristocratic elite also managed to survive and reinvent themselves by securing a privileged position in the new political administration and economy, without necessarily relinquishing entirely an earlier and more traditional idiom for the legitimization of their power (see MacRae, Chapter 7, this volume).

Other traditionalists who failed (wholly or in part) to make the transition work in their favour have sought refuge in claiming the status of being the more 'original' or 'traditional' Balinese in juxtaposition to the most recent 'newcomers' and champions of modernity (not the least in a context of selling tradition to cultural tourists). Many among Bali's traditional Majapahit ruling class have been pushed toward a more religious role in their forced retreat from a newly emerging modern political and economic scenario. In other words, they have adopted a position structurally similar to the one previously occupied by the Bali Aga under the traditional model of dual authority. In some cases, the residual authority of the Bali Aga in matters of ritual has been eroded as a result.[9]

Ritual authority in general does not convey the same sense of allure or consolation it once did for individuals excluded from the domain of political power. It has remained important, however, as an alternative way of organizing people in modern-day Indonesia. Political repression during the New Order period gave ritual or religious modes of organization and authority a special significance. The latter were tolerated while more overtly political or economic forms of association, such as genuine opposition parties or trade union movements, were subject to persecution and state-violence. Like the Bali Aga under a dominant Bali Majapahit political system, many of the people excluded from partaking in the authority of the modern, authoritarian state became active in religious organizations. And like the ritual domains of the highlands, these religious forms of organization formed a social muscle that was never fully flexed to release its potential of power until the time of Suharto's downfall.[10]

The changes that have occurred in Balinese society since independence have been fundamental, unprecedented and highly significant. Seen from a different angle, however, some continuities with pre-colonial society are also apparent. To begin with, members of the modern and urbanized Balinese power holders are still 'stranger kings' in a sense. Their local power, again, is drawn explicitly from a privileged association with ideas of foreign origin and from privileged access to the new resources of the nation state and global economy. And even my informants from among Bali's new political and economic elite delighted in explaining to me that human society depends on a balance between power and sacredness, the modern and the traditional. These kinds of ambiguities in popular attitudes toward social change were characteristic not only for Bali but for all of Indonesia during the Suharto period, and similar ambiguities persisted even in the discourse of the New Order state itself.

Modernity was clearly a state agenda, and those Indonesians who were presumably 'yet to be modernized' (*belum moderen*) tended to be people in such geographically remote localities as the mountains of Bali. During the New Order period, these marginal groups (from the modern state's perspective) were depicted as excessively 'traditional' (*tradisional*), in the negative sense of being too 'backward' (*tertinggal*) or 'not yet regulated' (*belum teratur*) enough to be able to comprehend and embrace the presumably benevolent development plans of the government (see Lowenhaupt-Tsing 1993). Nevertheless, a state-friendly and controlled traditionalism was also valued as a resource pool of indigenous Indonesian cultural capital, to be harnessed for a nationalist struggle against wholesale Westernization and, in some cases, to be traded as a valuable commodity on the global tourist market. Some of the most revealing state-produced images of the idea of 'tradition', in this positive sense, have been cultural theme parks, such as the *taman mini budaya* in Jakarta, wherein marginal culture has been transported to, and is fully controlled by the power of the political centre. In this limited sense then, a long-established model of dual identity, reconceived in terms of a new tradition-modernity distinction, may have played a significant role in the construction of Indonesia's national culture.

Looking from the perspective of a global distribution of power and knowledge, it may be tempting to accept modernity as a universal project with a culturally homogenizing influence on all human societies, and hence to describe the Bali Aga of central Bali (or others like them) as politically marginal people on a marginal island in a marginal nation within a globalizing world. But the very sense of contradiction in this act of socio-spatial positioning, in allocating Bali's cultural periphery to the island's geographical (and mythical) centre, presents an admonition.

The western spatial metaphors 'centre' and 'periphery' may or may not have precise equivalents in local, popular or state discourses about power. Even where they do, this does not justify a moral endorsement. As Craig Reynolds (1995) and Deborah Tooker (1996) have argued, western perceptions of the 'centres' and 'margins' of traditional states in Southeast Asia have carried an element of complicity. Endorsing portrayals of smaller polities as the outer layer of a mandala, for example, as peripheral and lack-lustre replica of a more powerful and 'exemplary' centre, has meant that so-called marginal groups 'have been defined from the perspective of dominant political groups', leading to a 'reaffirm[ation of] existing power structures' (Tooker 1996: 324). A similar aspect of endorsement accompanies contemporary readings of modern nation states in the region, so long as power is taken to be the 'central' concern of human life.

It is important not to endorse local discourses blindly where they aim to disadvantage certain sectors of a society, nor to overestimate their efficacy in shaping the construction and distribution of various resources within that society. And in any case, to locate people like the Bali Aga at the periphery of the world would only reinforce the spatial idiom and materialist perspective of a global discourse in which power and wealth now form the centre of all concerns and fragile culture is perched precariously at the fringe. Indonesians may seem to be adopting some aspects of this model, but it is not a foregone conclusion that theirs will be identical to our own models of modernity. Only insofar as this kind of materialist discourse now does hold sway in Bali, is a classification of the Bali Aga as 'marginal' appropriate.

Therefore two questions remain: How materialistic are the discourses of modern Balinese power holders concerning the Bali Aga, and how effective are these discourses and the interventions they justify in making them actually marginal?

THE MAKING AND CONTINUING USEFULNESS OF A MARGINAL PEOPLE

It may be of some use to develop a general social theory of 'marginality' for the analysis of the modern condition of the Bali Aga and other ethnic minorities in Indonesia, and in modernizing nation states around the world. It is regrettable, however, that many 'marginality studies' in contemporary anthropology seem to view political marginality (power-lessness) as the only issue of real importance. And while it is generally recognized that power is culturally constructed, only a few ethnographic studies have emphasized that the mechanics and concept of power itself can be culture-specific and variable (see also Geertz 1995; Wiener 1995). Instead, marginality studies have attempted to identify universal aspects in the political narratives of modern nation states.

Various narratives of modernity are assumed to be similar because the non-western nation states in which they are produced are themselves assumed to be the products of a global process of cultural homogenization that originated in a historical process of Western imperialist expansion. Indonesia, for example, is often portrayed and judged by political commentators in the western media not as a political system with a history and destiny of its own but as the still imperfect replica of a Western democracy. Anthropologists have not sufficiently criticized this 'global' (here: 'culture-less') approach to contemporary non-western societies, even though they may have been in a position to do so. I am therefore advocating a more culture-specific concept of marginality that pays attention to local models of society and to an associated distribution of *status* (rather than just political and economic resources) in these societies.

One important insight conventional marginality studies have had to offer is that the condition of political marginality is a co-production, insofar as underprivileged minority groups tend to object to hegemonic discourses and resist outside interventions, or even to utilize them through a process of appropriation (Lowenhaupt-Tsing 1993). The following analysis of the making of Bali Aga marginality has been designed in view of these considerations. A strong focus on the cultural specificity of Balinese and Bali Aga models of society is combined with an inter-actionist approach that acknowledges the active participation of marginal people in the construction of such models.

In modern Bali, and specifically during the New Order period, the label 'Bali Aga' has tended to conflate notions of physical, historical and cultural remoteness. Its social referents came to be regarded as prehistoric survivors from a distant past, and as 'survivors' only on account of their protected location in the remote mountains. Their distinct customs – falsely presumed to be 'primitive' – were taken as evidence of their lack of exposure to the influence of a presumably more 'civilized' and refined Majapahit culture centred in the royal courts of the Balinese lowlands.

This positioning of the Bali Aga in a forgettable past was reliant upon an act of selective amnesia. The historic significance of the mountain region in the development of Balinese civilization has been systematically ignored by most modern Balinese. This is remarkable, considering that there are several hundred royal inscriptions (*prasasti*) to bear testament to the importance of mountain communities during the approximately 600 years before the Majapahit invasion, when Balinese dynasties had already established a complex Hindu civilization on the island. Although they are quietly acknowledged as first settlers and as custodians of the most ancient temples on Bali even today, the mountain people have not been acknowledged as contributors to 'Balinese civilization' in the classical, let alone the modern sense.

Curiosity about the details of current Bali Aga cultural practices has been limited among fellow Balinese (until recently, see below). Most often they have been portrayed instead by means of a negative description: 'The Bali Aga do not cremate their dead, do not distinguish between different castes, do not recognize Brahmana priests, do not use Sanskrit prayers, do not have wet rice agriculture, do not use refined Balinese language, have no literature or literacy, and do not elect village leaders on the basis of aptitude' (these statements have been collated from interviews with urban Balinese). In other words, any difference (actual or imaginary) between the two groups has been interpreted as a deficiency on the part of the mountain people. Wherever Bali Aga traditions are more complex than those in southern Bali, the relevant information has failed to filter through.[11]

Modern narratives about the Bali Aga thus have built upon traditional cultural criteria and added others, to construct a new scheme of differentiation. Most importantly, the people of the highlands were counted among those Balinese who were still remote from the ideals of Suharto's project of modernization and development.

In recent years, for example, Bali Aga villages have been identified by local Balinese authorities as appropriate targets in relation to a nation-wide government initiative for the advancement of Indonesia's economically and socially most backward communities (*desa tertinggal*, lit. 'villages left behind [by progress]'). In Bali Aga villages this has meant that some people have had to destroy their traditional wooden houses with earthen floors, and to replace them with concrete structures. The new dwellings are said to be more hygienic or 'healthy' (*rumah sehat*) than traditional homes, and government loans were provided to fund their construction. The affected families were often left with no other choice than to sell land, trying to meet the repayments for a forced life-style change.

Indonesian tertiary students, to provide another example, are required to take part in compulsory community service internships (*Kuliah Kerja Nyata* or *KKN*).[12] These group internships are a means by which the government has been seeking to proliferate progressive ideas at a local level wherever development is seen to be retarded. In Bali, it is the communities of the Bali Aga who have been allotted the dubious status of being among the most-favoured KKN sites and, by implication, the most under-educated sector of society.

These and other forms of negative targeting were made possible by exploiting the development agenda of the New Order state. Modern conceptions of Bali Aga marginality during the Suharto period were formed by a specific state discourse on modernity, with 'development' (*pembangunan*), 'education' (*pendidikan*), and 'progress' (*kemajuan*) as its key metaphors (Warren 1991).[13]

A rhetoric of distance, denial of history, negative descriptions, negative targeting and other marginalizing strategies have been unleashed upon the Bali Aga primarily by local representatives of the modern Indonesian state. Urban Balinese stake holders with positions in the modern political administration system have been able to use these marginalizing strategies as a license for intervening in Bali Aga affairs with the borrowed power of the state.

It should be noted, however, that the types and effect of such interventions also reflected significant differences between the agendas of Bali's half-modern, half-traditional elite and those of the New Order state as a whole. The main conflicts between the interests of a Java-centric, Muslim-dominated, and authoritarian Indonesian state and regional Balinese interests centred on the issues of 'religion' (*agama*) and 'tradition' (*adat*). Local Balinese power holders were keen to protect the distinct character of Bali as a Hindu society with a distinctly Balinese cultural tradition. Some further discussion is required to explain the nature of this conflict and its consequences for the Bali Aga, who became caught up in it.

Under Suharto, the concepts *adat* and *agama* were as pivotal to nationalist discourses concerning Indonesia's future as were notions of modernity and development. This combination was ambiguous in itself and also led to numerous conflicts of interpretation between Jakarta and the outer regions. On the one hand, the outside forces of modernity were to be tempered and civilized, once again, by promoting the value of an indigenous 'Indonesian tradition'. On the other hand, tradition and religion were perceived as potential obstacles to national unity unless they could be reconstituted according to the needs of a modern state. Regional traditions were to become part of a national culture, in keeping with a state-sponsored idea of 'unity in diversity' (*bineka tumbal eka*). A struggle began between regional leaders, who tended to assert their cultural or religious distinctiveness in the name of diversity, and the Jakarta administration with its desire to preserve national unity.[14]

The dominant compromise policy of local power holders in Bali was to assert the distinct interests of Bali as a whole, but to suppress diversity within. In a way, the state thus provided regional power holders with a mandate to intervene in the traditional and religious affairs of local minority groups, particularly those in marginal or 'disorderly' regions, and for eliminating the extremes of cultural and ethnic diversity they apparently represented. Nevertheless, this elimination of local diversity was also a way to unify the regions in relation to their own efforts to resist absorption within a national mono-culture. For the Hindu Balinese it was particularly important to show a united front, for example, in their (successful) quest to gain recognition for Hinduism as a state-endorsed religion.

The power of the New Order state thus presented itself to the Bali Aga and other disadvantaged groups with a Balinese face, as it was wielded and manipulated by provincial and local politicians and administrators. The interventions experienced by the Bali Aga as the most imposing were related to the political struggle over tradition and religion. Government policies on these matters were (and still are) implemented through the provincial and local branches of state-controlled institutions such as the BPPLA (*Badan Pelaksana Pembina Lembaga Adat*) or 'Agency for the Implementation and Cultivation of Traditional Institutions', and the PHDI (*Parisada Hindu Dharma Indonesia*), the Brahmana-dominated and government-controlled religious institution that officially represents all Hindus in Indonesia.[15]

State discourses and specific interventions through these and other administrative bodies took a diversity of forms and elicited an equally broad range of local responses, from accommodation, appeasement and opportunism to non-cooperation, subversion and public protest. While the Bali Aga have had limited chances of success in competing with other Balinese in the borrowing (or purchasing) of state power as such, they did manage to appropriate some elements of state discourses to defend their own traditions against interference. For example, they have welcomed calls by PHDI for a simplification of ritual procedure. Bali Aga people have long been opposed to what they describe as extravagance in southern Balinese ceremonial life. The casteless Bali Aga also claim (perhaps rightly so) to have a more democratic form of village government, in the spirit of the Indonesian constitutional principle *Pancasila*, than what is to them a neo-feudal southern Bali. In general, however, the Bali Aga have not become organized as a modern political faction, and their efforts to tap into the symbolic power of the state by adopting some of its narratives are mostly related to specific issues arising in a local context. Some specific examples of Bali Aga experiences of, and responses to state interventions may illustrate how these negotiations have unfolded.

One of the changes the BPPLA has tried to impose in highland Bali (and less so elsewhere) relates to its efforts at standardizing the organization of the Balinese 'customary village' (*desa adat*). Bali Aga communities differ very significantly from those of the south in their organization. Most importantly, they feature a council of paired elders (*desa ulu apad*) who are ranked in order of seniority (Reuter, in Press). The common critique is that this kind of leadership selection it is not based on aptitude and formal education. Little attention is paid to the fact that a leading position in these councils is only obtained by persons who have had many years of experience and practical learning as junior council members, and that an individual lack of aptitude is absorbed through the collective nature of local decision-making. Suggestions of dismantling their village councils have been rejected or circumvented by most Bali Aga communities.

The New Order government's real concern may have been that a seniority-based system of succession to positions of community leadership was impervious to the influence of institutions like the BPPLA, which elsewhere in Bali 'approves' and 'educates' village *adat* leaders until today. Villages in southern Bali are headed by a single *klian adat* and his assistants, rather than a large council of elders. These *klian adat* have to be literate in Bahasa Indonesia and, until the recent fall of the Suharto regime, had to support the ruling Golkar Party, before being approved as candidates by the authorities. Once 'elected' (as well as 'selected'), they have to attend educational sessions chaired by the BPPLA branches in district or regency capitals.

Local responses have not always taken the form of unrelenting resistance. Many Bali Aga villages accommodate the wishes of the government by electing a *klian adat* as well as maintaining a full council, or by allocating the office of *klian* to an elder of a particular rank. Other villages have indeed decided to disband or modify the council of elders itself. Such cases are rare and tend to indicate not only external pressure but internal conflicts among political factions in the villages concerned (Reuter 2002b).

During the late-New order period, the BPPLA officially declared its intention to force the Bali Aga further into line. In a 1993 statement of their development plan, the authority's steering committee proclaimed that they wished

> to integrate the social structure, culture and Hindu religion of old Balinese [Bali Aga] villages into that of the appanage villages [villages under the cultural influence of the Majapahit courts] so that in the long run the cultural difference between them becomes less acute.
>
> (*Hasil-Hasil Pesamuhan Majelis Pembina Lembaga Adat, Daerah Bali*, Denpasar, 26 February 1993, Item 3, p. 35)

The committee's vision of a culturally homogenized Bali, in which there is apparently no room for the idiosyncrasy of Bali Aga traditions, reflects a specifically Balinese agenda as well as a national agenda of administrative streamlining. The less obvious Balinese agenda, as I suggested earlier, has been to promote internal homogeneity in Balinese *adat* and Hindu *agama* in order to be able to present a united front to the outside as a Hindu minority in a predominantly Muslim nation.

A different set of interventions has originated from the religious institution PHDI, the organization which had begun to rationalize and homogenize Hindu religion and ritual practice in order to gain national recognition for Hinduism (Bakker 1995). This national agenda has inclined some PHDI leaders to be critical of the local variability of religious practices in Bali. Again, it has been the Bali Aga whose traditions showed the greatest discrepancy from the norm.

One specific and important issue relates to temple architecture. Many Bali Aga communities do not have 'the three Hindu village temples' (*kayangan tiga*, i.e. a *pura dalem*, *pura bale agung* and *pura puseh*) that are officially required as the most essential places of worship according to PHDI guidelines. In addition, individual Bali Aga temples do not contain all of the shrines that are deemed to be essential elements in temple design in southern Bali. Hence, the leaders of the temple committee of Pura Pucak Penulisan, for example, have suffered repeated criticism because this important Bali Aga regional temple does not feature a *meru*, a tall shrine with a multitiered roof, or a *padmasana*, a stone seat dedicated to Sang Hyang Widi, the paramount Hindu deity promoted by the PHDI (in response to a monotheism requirement for state-accepted religions under Suharto's *Pancasila* doctrine, which has been problematic for Hindus).

The most serious religious issue for the casteless Bali Aga, however, concerns their lack of recognition of the role of Brahmana priests (*pedanda*). In one incident, the regional temple at Penulisan was visited by a group of worshippers under the ritual leadership of the Bupati (regency head) and a *Brahmana* priest from Bangli. Locals were outraged about the outsiders' attempt to ritually appropriate their temple, and responded by constructing the visit as a ritual defilement. The 30,000 members of the temple congregation first allowed and then responded to this violation of local tradition and authority by holding an elaborate three-week-long purification ceremony culminating in a ritual 'bathing of the deities' (*melasti ring segara*). This ritual protest created such publicity and embarrassment for the unwelcome visitors that they have never since returned.[16]

In another incident, the dominant faction in a Bali Aga village – under the leadership of the administrative village head (*kepala desa dinas*) – called in a *pedanda* to officiate at a village ritual. In this fashion the group's leader managed to enamour himself to the political leader of the regency, the Bupati of Bangli. (The *pedanda* whom they invited was the same relative of the Bupati who had led the fateful visit to Penulisan.) As a reward, the faction's hold on the important office of *kepala desa* remained virtually unassailable throughout the New Order period. This was because the Bupati had the power to reject all candidates put forward by rival factions in the village.

Attempts to passively involve the Bali Aga in modern forms of state-sponsored ritual have also led to considerable local resentment. In one case, the *kepala desa* of a mountain village reported to the council of elders during a local meeting how he had been ordered to Bangli to receive *tirta* ('sanctified water') from an annual blood sacrifice ceremony (*taur agung*) sponsored by the Bupati. This ceremony is held in Bangli and other regency capitals on the day before *nyepi*, the southern Balinese new year festival. 'Where did you throw it?' the elders asked, given that *nyepi pemerintah* ('the *nyepi* of the government calendar') is not observed in this and other Bali Aga villages, and that, hence, the *tirta* had no specified use. 'With respect', said the *kepala desa*, 'I just put the bottle on my kitchen shelf, opened it and – let the water evaporate!' Government pressure does not dissipate quite as easily, and the laughter in the assembly over this small victory only accentuated the gravity of the situation. The *kepala desa* later urged the village elders that they should instruct people to show consideration for the religious authorities by not working or commuting too much on *nyepi*, when everyone in Bali is supposed to stay at home.[17]

The preceding discussion has revealed significant changes in the status of the Bali Aga with the advent of colonialism in Bali and even more so with the establishment of an independent Indonesian nation state. Their symbolic capital as ritual custodians of the island's sacred mountain temples has been retained, for whatever significance it may still hold in modern Bali.[18] Even this limited success has not been achieved and cannot be maintained without a struggle. A major cause of escalation in the struggle of the Bali Aga to retain their limited privileges has been the inward movement of the former 'newcomers' from Majapahit into the realm of indigenous ritual custodianship, following the (partial) disempowerment of the latter at the hands of the colonial and Indonesian state. The relevance of the remaining symbolic capital of the Bali Aga is also shrinking in the context of an increasingly modern and materialistic Balinese society, so that many of their younger generation may no longer care to continue the struggle to hold on to it.

Traditional notions of 'the indigenous' and 'the foreign' have acquired a whole range of new and different meanings in the five decades since Indonesian independence. Post-colonial Bali has been swept by its own waves of newcomers, both Javanese and Western. Increasing numbers of poor, economic immigrants and wealthy investors are coming from Java and other neighbouring islands to seek their fortune in Bali's thriving tourism industry (see Vickers, this volume). Tourism, in turn, attracts about two million foreign visitors each year. It is not surprising then that the Balinese are feeling more invaded than ever and are reacting with an unprecedented attitude of xenophobia (see Darling, this volume). In this atmosphere, for persons to be of Balinese (let alone Bali Aga) origin may be sufficient grounds for their allocation to a post-modern category of the island's 'indigenous people'.

My discussion of the changing fortunes of the Bali Aga also shows that there are a number of continuities between traditional models of Balinese identity and modern discourses, especially if we consider how state discourses are moulded to the agendas of local power holders and also meet with resistance and suffer adjustments at the margins. The main continuity of Balinese politics of identity lies in a historical experience of perpetual exposure to outside forces, and in a preoccupation with the cultural management of these encounters between ever new categories of 'foreigners' and 'genuine Balinese people'.

Although a distinction between the indigenous and the foreign is given ever new meanings, old and new idioms of social distinction merge in the thinking of modern Balinese and in the modern experiences of the Bali Aga alike. For the present time at least, pre-colonial Balinese concepts of dual authority relating to a wider Austronesian cultural heritage still seem to inform contemporary Balinese thought to some extent, and thus remain relevant as a counterpoint to more materialistic readings of Bali's over-all resource economy. In short, the representational landscape of post-colonial Bali still reflects an on-going concern with non-material values, and a struggle over symbolic resources for their own sake. Nevertheless, it cannot be ignored that this struggle is now taking place on a social playing field marked by much greater (and still increasing) economic and political disparities than ever before, and that a global materialist worldview has become a significant influence on modern Balinese thought and lifestyles.

GLOBALIZATION, POST-MODERNITY, AND AUTHENTICITY: A RETURN TO EARLIER MODELS OF IDENTITY?

Indonesia's political crisis since 1998 can be viewed as a belated popular response to 32 years of oppression and exploitation at the hands of former president Suharto and his Java-centric New Order regime. But external, if not global, factors were also at play in the events of 1998. Perhaps the main trigger for the public unrest that eventually led to the dismissal of Suharto was the impact of the Asian economic crisis on Indonesia at that time. In general terms, the influence such global events are having on Indonesia points toward a more fundamental dilemma: How viable is the idea of establishing a 'modern' and 'democratic' Indonesian nation state in this 'post-modern' and, perhaps, 'post-democratic' period of global capitalism?

From this perspective, we must question whether the current weakness of the Indonesian nation state is symptomatic only of its own political history or of an increasingly powerful and global economic and financial system. And somewhat apart from their disempowerment at the hands of a global economic system, it is equally significant that Indonesians are increasingly exposed to, and participating in a global popular culture and in mass consumerism. What this may spell for Bali and for Indonesia as a whole is very difficult to predict. Nevertheless, a number of interesting trends and recent developments seem to suggest a return to cultural and religious identities in Indonesia, as in other parts of the world.

Cultural, ethnic and religious identities have become highly politicized in Indonesia from the very beginning of the *Reformasi* period. As the New Order lid of repression lifted, lingering regional conflicts and ambitions began to surface or escalate. This contemporary phenomenon is again not unique to Indonesia. The renaissance of neo-traditional identity concepts – as the new key idioms for defining political struggles – is a global trend, as many people now prefer to view themselves as Basques, Croatians or Balinese, for example, rather than citizens of a Spanish, Yugoslav or Indonesian nation state.

This return to regional cultural identities may be, at least in part, a response to the diminishing relevance and scope of national political institutions in the wake of globalization. World system and globalization theorists have questioned the very idea of the nation state as a distinct and autonomous unit, by pointing to global processes of economic integration (Appadurai 1990). Nation states, the 'locals' in today's world, are indeed held hostage to the interests of multinational capitalism to such an extent that democracy is being undermined. Global economic pressures are such that differences between the policies of the major political parties of many nation states have become more or less cosmetic, in the eyes of many voters.[19]

In debt-ridden Indonesia, the government's scope for implementing a specifically 'political' program is especially limited, but there has also been a general and worldwide decline in the relevance of political ideology as a mode of social mobilization since the end of the Cold War (see also Darma Putra, this volume). More often now, the battle lines of social conflict between different groups of people seem to be drawn in the ink of cultural identity, which may include ideas of ethnicity, race, religion, or a combination of all these.[20]

As far as Indonesia is concerned, and whatever its local and global causes may have been, the weakening of state authority and nationalist sentiments since 1998 has been accompanied and accentuated by the rise of particularly violent intercommunity, interethnic, interreligious, and separatist conflicts throughout the archipelago, from Central Kalimantan, Sulawesi and the Moluccas to West Papua and Aceh. In a last ditch attempt to give some semblance of order and control to this flow of power away from the central government to the regions, Presidents Adurrahman Wahid and Megawati Sukarnoputri have since introduced new or amended legislation which promises to provide increased regional autonomy, and hope thereby to curb a swell of separatist sentiments.

Bali has witnessed some of this new wave of violence as well, for example, in the 'Ash Thursday' riots following the failure of Megawati's initial bid for the presidency and the repeated local militia attacks on ethnic Javanese immigrants (see Vickers, this volume). My impression, however, is that most Balinese are relatively sympathetic to, and content with the central government's offer of increased autonomy. But many also fear that Bali will be divided and the more easily ruled by Jakarta because the current autonomy proposal is directed at Bali's individual regencies (*kabupaten*), rather than the province of Bali as a whole.

Balinese are thus struggling to transform their long-running struggle for a separate status – as an Indonesian people with a distinct culture and religion – into a more openly political struggle for autonomy. This struggle is taking place within the context of nation-wide changes in the distribution of political power which, in turn, have been influenced by global economic change. Another dimension of globalization's local impact, however, is the increasing commercial marketing, transience, and arbitrariness of cultural identities around the world, in Indonesia, and especially in Bali.

It is somewhat ironic, but perhaps not accidental, that cultural identities are becoming more and more important in a brave new world of ethno-politics, even as they are becoming more and more difficult to justify in view of a global convergence in people's actual cultural practices. An interesting local example is the fast growing number of foreign tourists who, following the example of Mick Jagger and Jerry Hall, decide to 'get married the traditional Balinese way'.[21] In the light of such a glaring alienation of culture for commercial purposes it is becoming difficult for many Balinese to portray their culture as a primordial aspect of their being. Moreover, this process of culture-alienation is not a one-way street. Many among urban and even rural Balinese are themselves becoming trans-cultural in their daily practice, by adopting more and more elements of a cosmopolitan way of life.

The alienation and commercialization of cultural experiences does not mean that culture ceases to be an issue. The opposite may be the case. Experiences of cultural alienation and arbitrariness create a crisis of identity and raise a fundamental issue of 'cultural authenticity'. One common response is to embark upon a quest to regain a lost sense of authenticity in the form of a sometimes militant 'neo-traditionalism'. This kind of search for a reconstituted sense of authenticity, it seems, is under way in Bali.

Many among the disenchanted and now predominantly urban population of southern Bali are beginning to look for their 'original' and 'authentic' cultural roots (*budaya bali asli/bali tulen*), among other things, by reinventing the idea of being 'Bali Aga'. This process of reinvention has taken two basic forms.

One interesting phenomena is that a growing number of Balinese commoners are beginning to reconstruct themselves as Bali Aga, in a modern sense of being simply and genuinely 'Balinese'. As a result, numbers of southern Balinese visitors at the festivals of even minor Bali Aga temples have been skyrocketing since the 1990s. I have spoken with members of these visiting delegations on numerous occasions. Many of them explained to me that they were tired of defining themselves as the descendants of 'Javanese immigrants' or that, in other words, it had all been a big mistake to seek affiliation to a Majapahit origin (*kawitan jawa majapait*). Now, one man said, it was 'time to remember that we are really Balinese, while there is still a real Bali to be found, here in the highlands' (interview with a southern Balinese visitor at the festival of a village temple in Sukawana in 1999).

Another indicator of change is new usages of the term 'Bali Aga', and new understandings of Balinese identities in general. As the media sector gained unprecedented liberty in Post-Suharto Indonesia, for example, new journals and newspapers with a distinct 'traditional culture' orientation began to mushroom in Bali from 1999 onward. One of these is a daily newspaper by the name of '*BALI AGA: Koranya Krama Bali*' ('Bali Aga: The newspaper of the Balinese community'). The subtitle suggests a new concept of 'being Bali Aga', now synonymous with 'being Balinese'.

More generally, the new genre of 'traditionalist' newspapers and magazines illustrate the popularity of a renewed quest for Balinese cultural authenticity. One of the most popular of these publications is the monthly magazine *SARAD*. In a recent editorial, its producers claim that rapid social change in recent decades

> demands of the people of Bali that they are constantly watchful unless they wish to lose their sense of self-worth in the end.
>
> (*SARAD*, July 2000 [Year 1(No 7)], p. 3)

This watchfulness is directed at what is described as 'outside interference' or 'infiltration'. In the title of the above-mentioned article, for example, the traditional village community (*desa adat*) is described as the 'last [line of de]fence of Bali[nese culture]' (*benteng terakhir bali*).

There is often much confusion and debate as to what does and does not actually cause damage to 'Balinese culture'. Renewed state intervention is clearly recognized as one of the potential threats:

> The traditional village is subject to continuous state intervention. From Dutch and Japanese colonialism to the New Order and even the present Reformasi, the powerful are all too diligent in disrupting the autonomy of traditon[al institutions]... [...and are] 'raping tradition' (*Desa adat tak putus diintervensi negara. Sejak kolonial Belanda dan Jepang hingga Orde Baru dan reformasi kini pun begitu getol mengoyak otonomi adat. [...dan] 'memperkosa adat'.*)
>
> (*SARAD*, July 2000, p. 14–15)

For others, the greater threat is the latest wave of newcomers in Bali. Among them are the many poor Javanese immigrants, often criticized for not contributing financially to ritually-defined local communities because they are not Hindus (see Vickers, this volume). Equally threatening, though in a different and perhaps more flattering way, are a growing number of western expatriates, who are seen as overly eager to 'become Balinese' (whatever the financial cost):

> If Balinese people originating from Majapahit five centuries ago could form a family tree with many branch lineages that have been passed on to the present, then to what clan group are foreigners who have become Balinese people [expatriates] going to be allocated to? (*Bila orang-orang Bali asal Majapahit lima abad lalu bisa membentuk pohon keluarga dalam soroh-soroh yang diwarisi hingga kini, lantas soroh apakah orang asing yang kini menjadi orang Bali ini mesti dimasukkan?*).
>
> Jung Iryana, *SARAD* 1, No 7(July 2000): 58

Many of the articles in traditionalist journals focus on such threats to Balinese cultural authenticity, and contain long deliberations on how Balinese scriptures and traditional philosophical principles may be applied to contemporary life situations in a meaningful way. Authenticity is not envisaged as the absence of social change so much as a continuity of underlying values. It is frequently noted, for example, how well Balinese tradition fits in with a demand for the protection of basic human rights, and with other such modern value concepts as are cherished now by the majority of contemporary locals. Indeed, most of the articles in traditionalist publications can be described as genuine reflexive efforts to find new solutions on the basis of old, but arguably timeless ideas. Until now, only a minority of Balinese have chosen to adopt a more violently xenophobic response to social change, and only a very few are willing to promote this kind of approach openly and in public.

Few among the Bali Aga have felt a need to join this quest for renewed authenticity until now, but it may not be long before some of them will. Many of my younger informants who live in major cities appear concerned to find the money more so to cover their mobile phone and other modern life-style expenses, than to help pay for the next temple festival back home in the highlands. The transition to an urban and modern way of life is generally accompanied by a distinct sense of alienation, though heavily ameliorated by a simultaneous sense of liberation from the strictures of life in a tightly knit village community. Major social problems among city-dwelling Bali Aga are just beginning to take shape, especially among a group of young adults, aged 25 years and older.

Many of these young men and women are now of an age where they are urgently expected to marry and become fully active as members in their home communities. Some are criticized for failing to attend important village gatherings and festivals on a regular basis. Others are quite keen to revert to what they describe as a more simple, social and orderly way of life, only to find that they are often unable to achieve a full reintegration into village society. Many long-term absentees, for example, lack the ritual skills and knowledge to fulfil their duties, or find it difficult to claim their local rights as community members.[22] Others manage to observe their duties and preserve their rights by returning home frequently, but this alternative form of 'absenteeism' is often frowned upon by their urban employers.

There is no evidence to suggest that the world of the Mountain Balinese has ever been marginal in the sense of being 'small' and 'isolated'. The preceding discussion has further shown that their world has witnessed a series of expansions in its encounter with colonialism, the modern state, and globalization. Many Bali Aga have relocated to the urban centres of Bali and beyond in recent decades, in search of education, employment opportunities or a more 'modern' lifestyle. Others accepted government offers of land and have transmigrated as farmers to the more sparsely populated outer islands of Indonesia. A few have even lived and studied in western countries. All this has affected life back home in the villages. The majority of those who have left the highlands still return regularly as a matter of filial or ritual duty, and thus act as an extension to the world of those who stayed behind. In any case, most villagers now have access to modern electronic media and are increasingly compelled and equipped to reposition themselves in ever changing national and global contexts.

But what impact does increased contact among societies in global and national contexts really have on their cultural uniqueness – seen in relation to the value of this uniqueness in local symbolic economies, in tourism, and beyond? Whatever prognosis may be proposed for the future of cultural diversity, it is important to avoid an essentialization and reification of culture. Like colonial imperialism, the more recent technology-driven process of economic 'globalization' has affected the world as a whole. Global interaction is not simply an encroachment of western modernity upon other societies, that would necessarily precipitate a decline of their cultures. Ultimately, cultural boundaries can be said to be 'softening' only upon the essentialist assumption that they have been 'harder' at some time in the past.

The present study of Bali's changing symbolic economy shows that this has not been the case, especially for the Balinese, who have been able to look at and negotiate their ambivalent experience of modernity, and even post-modernity, as one more of an already familiar type of encounters with foreign peoples and ideas. This may explain in part why Bali has weathered the current crisis in Indonesia without much physical violence, and with local symbolic violence also tempered by the value differentiations that define the multiple stakes of its symbolic economy. The muteness of the Bali Aga, which had reached its zenith during the New Order period, may be coming to an end, perhaps, as Balinese in general are finding more of a voice in the chorus of national politics and new ways to reclaim their own culture from the warehouses of global tourism and global consumer culture.

NOTES

1 Bali's pre-colonial rulers, for example, did not manage to establish effective control over the day-to-day running of local and regional affairs in the high-lands, and even Suharto's repressive New Order regime found it difficult to do so. In addition, southern noble houses or other outsiders had almost no land-holdings in the highlands at all until the colonial period and only very few even thereafter (see Reuter 2002a).
2 Note that while both forms of authority involve a claim to symbolic resources, only political authority directly presupposes and in turn supports the control of material resources. The material benefits of ritual authority are indirect and very limited by comparison.
3 The ancestors of Bali's Brahmana clans are said to have come from Java as well, upon invitation of the new rulers. Upper-caste (*triwangsa*) groups other than the Brahmana and Bali's royal houses are said to be the descendants of the retinue of lesser nobles in the invading Majapahit army, or members of the demoted branch houses of the latter.
4 While this dual identity construct may be regarded as the product of a tacit agreement with mutual benefits for the two parties, it should also be pointed out that the vast majority of ordinary Balinese commoners have been denied access to both ritual and political authority as a result. In recent decades, there have been attempts by many commoner groups (*wong jaba*, 'outsiders') to lay claim to a Majapahit origin as well, in competition to the traditional elite of the three upper castes (*triwangsa*, *wong majapahit*, or simply *jero*, 'insiders'). This trend has been in keeping with the growing power of those *jaba* people who became members of a modern economic and administrative elite.
5 The rulers of Klungkung, who also claimed to be the paramount kings of Bali, for example, maintained close ties with the Bali Aga people and temple of Lake Batur (Pura Ulun Danu Batur). The rulers of Mengwi, likewise, maintained close ritual ties to the mountain temples Pura Pucak Manggu and Pura Pucak Antap Sai (see Reuter 2002a).
6 This encounter was only the first to be widely remembered and broadly signifi-cant for Bali as a whole. Note, however, that Bali Aga groups whose members lay claim to political authority in a local context also tend to construct them-selves as the descendants of (earlier) 'royal immigrants' rather than 'indigen-ous' Balinese, even though they may still claim a position of precedence in relation to the more recent newcomers from Majapahit in a wider context of identity. This suggests that a dual distinction between earlier and later people can be applied recursively. Note also that some named groups in southern Bali, such as the blacksmith or *pande wesi* clan, have consistently claimed a pre-Majapahit origin as well, and again in connection with a claim to a number of specific ritual privileges.
7 One reason why such cooperation may have been necessary and possible is that 'people' were perhaps as important a resource as was land in many cases, at least until recently (see MacRae, Chapter 9, this volume).
8 See Vickers (1989) for a more detailed account of the general impact of the colonial encounter on Balinese society.
9 One example of how former Majapahit aristocrats have tried to appropriate the Bali Aga's status of ritual custodianship are the repeated attempts of certain

noble houses (*puri*) to gain control over important regional temples in the mountains, such as Pura Balingkang and Pura Pucak Bon (see Reuter 2002a).

10 While personal connections to fellow members in social or religious networks outside the state perhaps did not yield as many political benefits as did connections to powerful and corrupt individuals within the state, there were some material benefits nonetheless. Particularly in its final years, the New Order state could not easily ignore or repress the interests of large and well-organized groups of people, and was increasingly forced to buy them off rather than risk their politicization. Suharto's Islamic turn in the 1990s and the subsequent transfer of large sums of money to mosque-building and similar projects in neighbouring Java (Hefner 1997) is one example to illustrate this general trend.

11 These stereotypes do not reflect the opinion of all Balinese. Those who have regular contact with Bali Aga people tend to entertain much more balanced views.

12 Ironically, the acronym 'KKN' nowadays stands more often for the English loan words *korupsi, kolusi, nepotisme*, and is often used with specific reference to corruption, collusion and nepotism under the late Suharto administration.

13 While the Bali Aga were no longer explicitly juxtaposed to Bali Majapahit in such state discourses, the myth of a Majapahit-inspired civilizing mission did not vanish entirely. Most notably, the notion of a historical continuity between the ancient Javanese empire of Majapahit and the modern Indonesian state was promoted as a means of strengthening nationalist sentiments and in order to justify the continuing political centrality of Java in the New Order state.

14 Note that under the dictatorial rule of former president Suharto, *adat* and *agama* also provided a last bastion for local political resistance (in an outwardly 'apolitical' idiom) because other attempts to publicly express dissent were met with violent oppression.

15 A predominance of Brahmana is still evident among the ranks of the PHDI, but this is beginning to change (cf. Pitana 1995). Note that there is also considerable factionalism and disagreement about the future of Balinese Hinduism among the different Brahmana groups themselves. More specifically, not all Brahmana groups are represented within PHDI and many on the outside may disagree vehemently with PHDI policies.

16 Not everywhere has there been such well organized and effective resistance. For example, some Bali Aga villages in western Buleleng have changed their religious practices almost to the point of abandoning their Bali Aga identity, at least publicly.

17 A local version of *nyepi* (*nyepi desa*) is celebrated in these villages at different intersections of the Balinese lunar-solar calendar, sometimes up to three times in a single year. To be fair, it should be added that the specific traditions of some non-Bali Aga villages are also quite unique, and have suffered equally from the cultural homogenization mission of state authorities.

18 As mentioned earlier, most of the important regional temples of highland Bali are still controlled by the Bali Aga.

19 According to some of my informants' experience, the same may also apply to the initially more critical and distinguishable minor parties of post-Suharto Indonesia. Once they reached government, I was told, there has been a tendency for such parties to adopt the same *Realpolitik* approach they had been criticizing earlier on. Whether this assessment is accurate or not, it reflects the rising disenchantment of voters even in this nation

state, where such a diversity of political parties at least have had a chance to arise in the first place.
20 There is no denying that many of these conflicts involve economic issues, but this does not take anything away from the fact that the preferred method of social mobilization is to appeal to cultural identities.
21 A very modern 'Bali Aga' friend of mine is running one of these new businesses, and very ironically so, under the name of 'Puri (palace) Weddings'. Many of her own family and friends back in the village find the very idea of such a business distasteful and morally compromising.
22 I know of several cases where long-term absentees, upon their marriage and return to their village of origin in the highlands, were refused the usual right to claim a plot of village land for building a house.

REFERENCES

Appadurai, A. (1990) 'Disjuncture and Difference in the Global Cultural Economy'. In M. Featherstone (ed.), *Global Culture: Nationalism, Globalization and Modernity*, London: Sage Publications.

Bakker, F. L. (1995) *Bali in the Indonesian State in the 1990s: The Religious Aspect*. Paper prepared for the 'Third International Bali Studies Conference' at the University of Sydney, 3–7 July 1995.

Barnes, R. H. (1996) *The Power of Strangers in Flores and Timor*. Paper presented at the international conference on 'Hierarchization: Processes of Social Differentiation in the Austronesian World', Leiden: International Institute for Asian Studies (IIAS), 17–19 April 1996.

Cunningham, C. E. (1965) 'Order and Change in an Atoni Diarchy'. *Southwestern Journal of Anthropology*, 21: 359–82.

Fox, J. J. (1994) *Installing the 'Outsider' Inside: An exploration of an Austronesian cultural theme and its social significance*. Paper prepared for the First International Symposium on Austronesian Cultural Studies. Unversitas Udayana, Denpasar: 14–16 August 1994.

Geertz, H. (1995) *Sorcery and Social Change in Bali: The Sakti Conjecture*. Paper prepared for the 'Third International Bali Studies Conference' at the University of Sydney, 3–7 July 1995.

Hefner, R. (1997) 'Islamization and Democratization in Indonesia'. In R. Hefner and P. Horvatich (eds), *Islam in an Era of Nation States: Politics and Religious Renewal in Muslim Southeast Asia*, Honolulu: University of Hawaii Press.

Korn, V. E. (1933) *De Dorpsrepubliek Tenganan Pagringsingan*, Santport: Mees.

Lowenhaupt-Tsing, A. (1993) *In the Realm of the Diamond Queen: Marginality in an Out-of-the-Way Place*, Princeton (N.J.): Princeton University Press.

Needham, R. (1980) *Reconnaissances*, Toronto: University of Toronto Press.

Pitana, I Gede (1995) *Priesthood and Warga Movement: Observing Socio-Cultural Changes in Bali*. Paper prepared for the 'Third International Bali Studies Conference' at the University of Sydney, 3–7 July 1995.

Reuter, Thomas A. (1998a) 'Houses and Compounds in the Mountains of Bali'. In J. Davison (ed.), *Indonesian Heritage: Architecture*, Singapore: Editions Didier Millet, pp. 38–39.

Reuter, Thomas A. (1998b) 'The Ritual Domains of the Mountain Balinese: Regional Alliance and the Idea of a Shared Origin'. In J. J. Fox (ed.),

Indonesian Heritage: Religion and Ritual, Singapore: Editions Didier Millet, pp. 82–83.

Reuter, Thomas A. (1998c) 'The Banua of Pura Pucak Penulisan: A Ritual Domain in the Highlands of Bali'. *Review of Indonesian and Malaysian Affairs*, 32 (1): 55–109.

Reuter, Thomas A. (1999a) 'People of the Mountains – People of the Sea: Negotiating the Local and the Foreign in Bali'. In L. H. Connor and R. Rubinstein (eds), *Staying Local in the Global Village: Bali in the Twentieth Century*, Honolulu: University of Hawaii Press, pp. 155–80.

Reuter, Thomas A. (1999b) 'Communicating through the Invisible: The Paradox of Association and the Logic of Ritualised Interaction on the Island of Bali'. *Anthropological Forum*, 9 (1): 39–63.

Reuter, Thomas A. (2000) 'Der Umgang mit dem Fremden auf Bali: Betrachungen zu den Auswirkungen der Globalisierung im Hinblick auf kulturspezifische Interpretationsmodelle'. In B. Hauser Schäublin and K. Rieländer (eds), *Bali: Kultur – Tourismus – Umwelt: Die indonesische Ferieninsel im Schnittpunkt lokaler, nationaler und globaler Interessen*, Hamburg: Abera Verlag.

Reuter, Thomas A. (2002a) *Custodians of the Sacred Mountains: The People and Culture of Highland Bali*, Honolulu: Hawaii University Press.

Reuter, Thomas A. (2002b) *The House of Our Ancestors: Precedence and Dualism in Highland Balinese Society*, Leiden (Netherlands): KITLV Press.

Reynolds, C. (1995) 'A New Look at Old Southeast Asia'. *The Journal of Asian Studies*, 54 (2): 419–46.

Sahlins, M. (1985) *Islands of History*, Chicago: University of Chicago Press.

Tooker, D. (1996) 'Putting the Mandala in its Place: A Practice-based Approach to the Spatialization of Power on the Southeast Asian Periphery – The Case of the Akha'. *The Journal of Asian Studies*, 55 (2): 323–58.

Valeri, V. (1982) 'The Transformation of a Transformation: A Structural Essay on an aspect of Hawaiian History (1809–1819)'. *Social Analysis*, 10: 3–41.

Vickers, A. (1989) *Bali: A Paradise Created*, Harmondsworth (UK): Penguin Books.

Warren, C. (1989) 'Balinese Political Culture and the Rhetoric of National Development'. In R. Higgot and R. Robison (eds), *Southeast Asia: Essays in the Political Economy of Structural Change*, London: Routledge and Kegan Paul.

Warren, C. (1991) 'Adat and Dinas: Village and State in Contemporary Bali'. In H. Geertz (ed.), *State and Society in Bali: Historical, Textual and Anthropological Perspectives*, Leiden: KITLV Press.

Wiener, M. J. (1995) *Visible and Invisible Realms: Power, Magic and Colonial Conquest in Bali*, Chicago & London: University of Chicago Press.

Wouden, F. A. E. van (1968) *Types of Social Structure in Eastern Indonesia*, The Hague: Martinus Nijhoff. First published in 1935.

9 Unity in uniformity

Tendencies toward militarism in Balinese ritual life

Diana Darling

MICROPHONES

One day in September 1996, I found myself seated on the ground with about 70 other women in the inner courtyard of the Pura Puseh temple in Tegalsuci, a village in northern Gianyar.[1] It was around 9:30 a.m., and we were only beginning to warm up. The mountain mists here are chilling in the morning. The floor of the inner sanctum (*jeroan*) was strewn with new mats laid over the black volcanic sand. As the sun strengthened, the top crust of the sand turned a soft pale grey, but if you lifted the edge of a mat with your finger, the sand beneath was dark, damp and cold.

We had been there since morning, as we had been the day before and would be for the next 2 weeks. The village was preparing for a colossal temple festival. In Tegalsuci's local *adat* ('customary practice'), most temple work is done by the young people's association. The married men of the *banjar* also have fairly regular *adat* duties; but the women are so busy looking after their livestock, children, husbands, and businesses, that they are normally allowed to prepare their quota of temple offerings at home.

So it was not really routine for us to be showing up for temple duty like this, freezing in our new clothes, and wondering what was going on at home or in the fields or at the shop. My own thoughts were occupied with finding something in the temple that I knew how to do. But by mid-morning, as the day warmed up, we had settled in quietly and there was something blessedly serene about sitting there together making offerings, engaged in what really did feel like holy work.

Then suddenly the air went thick and grainy with a horrible noise. We looked up and saw our supervisor, the village's junior priest, sitting on a little pavilion right next to us and talking to us through a loudspeaker, his words so garbled by the device that we could barely understand what he said.

For me anyway, everything had suddenly changed. With the flick of a microphone switch, we were transformed from 70 adults, doing our best to be good spiritual citizens, into a herd of labourers sitting on the ground, corralled in a courtyard.

Microphones and loudspeakers, commonly referred to as '*mik*', have become integral to modern Balinese ritual. You hear them barking in the sunlight at processions and cremations, droning invisibly at weddings, and roaring above people's heads at temple festivals. The pretext for loudspeakers is that they are necessary for coordinating large groups of people over large areas, but there is more to it than that.

The amplification of ritual is a sort of modern banner or drum, announcing one's festivity (or religiosity) to all the world. Besides, the Muslims do it. I heard from some Balinese that 'if Muslims broadcast their prayers, Balinese Hindus ought to as well'. As to the apparent idiocy of using a loudspeaker to speak to someone only two metres away, there is also a totalitarian glamour about the loudspeaker that some people find irresistible. It calls attention to the person using it, and puts him (rarely her) in an elevated, indeed amplified position over other people. It precludes dialogue. It is an instrument of command. Its sound is a kind of projectile.

UNIFORMS

Another trend in modern Balinese ritual life, this one inspired by a grand cremation in the royal house of Pemecutan in 1985, is the fashion of wearing black for funerary rites. Prior to this, people wore whatever colour they liked at any ritual. If you looked good in a black shirt (or, for women, a black *kebaya*), you could wear it to temple festivals and weddings without arousing any comments except admiring ones. But those who saw the Pemecutan cremation on television were struck by the powerful visual effect of hundreds of people dressed in black. The fact that it was on television surely added an extra measure of chic.

People in Ubud say that soon after this, when Puri Ubud held its next cremation the word went out that everybody was to wear black.[2] By the mid-1990s, the fashion had become island-wide, and in Tegalsuci it was expressly forbidden to wear black at any ceremony except death rituals. This trend, by the way, was recently denounced in an article in the Balinese daily newspaper *Nusa*, which deplored the rise of ritual uniforms (*penyerageman*) and pointed out that black is the signature colour of Vishnu the Nurturer, and in Hinduism, has nothing to do with death.[3]

Meanwhile a second trend arose for men to wear white at large temple festivals, and for various female task groups (*sekaa teruni*, *banjar isteri*) to wear colour-coded uniforms (*stelan*). This presumably gives processions a smarter look and somewhat fulfils the recommendation by religious authorities to avoid one-upmanship in temple dress, in deference to less prosperous members of the community.

It also makes a vivid public statement about the strength of Balinese Hinduism. A truck full of men in white headscarves, for instance, has a more aggressive visual impact than a truck full of men whose headscarves are (as they used to be) white, red, black, batik, and blue brocade.

There is something distinctly martial about this new look. Some Balinese justify it by saying that it reinforces group identity, important these days as demographic pressures and modernization encroach upon the trad-itional order, and Indonesia's national fragility lends new meaning to regional and local identities. In some way, it is an expression of the same heraldic use of colour by the major political parties – from Golkar yellow, PAN-blue, PDI-red & black to the green of the Muslim parties – but it lacks the almost joyful celebration of plurality on parade during the 1999 election campaign in Bali. This may still be debatable, but there is another and much more emphatic expression of this new martial atti-tude in Bali; the revival of *pecalang*.

PECALANG: A NEW PEOPLE'S ARMY?

Here is another anecdote. Earlier in 1999, after having been away from Bali for several months, I returned home to a flurry of gossip. My hus-band (who is from Ubud) told me that Ubud was going to have *pecalang*. 'What's that?' I asked. '*Adat* police', he responded, and then after a pause, 'I'm not sure what it's all about.'

He then went on to explain that when he was a kid, there were men referred to as '*pecalang*' (or *pacalang/pacalangan*) who went out on patrol in a black-and-white chequered hip cloth (*saput poleng*) on the new-years-day of *Nyepi*, to report anyone seen out on the street or otherwise trans-gressing the rules of that abstemious Balinese holy day. As people became more inclined to observe *Nyepi* by their own volition, he said, the need for this '*adat* police' became obsolete, and it all died out about 30 years ago. Indeed, when I later asked some anthropologist friends about this, none had ever heard the term. But now the idea has come up to have *pecalang* patrol the streets again, and every night.

'Every night? Why?' I asked. 'They say it's to strengthen the *desa adat*', he said, meaning the village as caretaker of local customs and tradition. 'That's a nice idea,' I conceded (foreigners in Bali are unwittingly con-servative and automatically approve of preserving the *desa adat* and anything else that smacks of traditional culture). 'But what are they going to do, exactly?'

He told me that it was all rather vague. The idea had been floated by 'someone close to the puri' at a meeting of the leaders (*klian*) of the four neighbourhoods (*banjar*) of Desa Adat Ubud. Each *banjar* was to contribute 14 volunteers who would take turns in pairs on patrol. There would be no pay, but the *pecalang* would be able to get food at the *puri* kitchen, and they could use the *puri*'s *bale bengong* pavilion as their command post (*posko*).

'The interesting thing', he continued, 'is that suddenly each of four *banjar* received a set of 14 uniforms – red head cloth, chequered *saput poleng*, and black t-shirts with writing on the back – and none of the *klian* knew who had ordered them'. 'It sounds like the *puri*,' I said. My husband frowned. 'You can't say that: it's not certain,' he said, a bit severely.

Still, it is not hard to imagine any *puri* being flattered to have brightly-clad *adat* soldiers milling about. What palace would not like to have a palace guard? Besides, Puri Ubud – one of the progenitors of 'cultural tourism' and perhaps its most successful operative – is a functioning agency of *adat* authority (see MacRae, Chapters 3 and 7, this volume). Ubud's *desa adat* leader (*bendesa agung*) is from Puri Ubud and is known as an energetic promoter of huge temple festivals and a patron of temple- and barong-renovations. As Graeme MacRae (1997) has shown, his range of religious-development activity extends throughout the Wos River valley, with influence as far as Pura Sumeru in Java, and most recently to temples in Kalimantan. What finer expression of cultural authority than to have a swarm of cultural police around the place, leaning out of its *bale bengong* at the central crossroads of town?

Over the next month or so, I began to find out more about *pecalang*. In Tegalsuci, for example, it turned out that the term was well known after all. Although I didn't know at the time that this is what they were called, *pecalang* had been on the scene at least since that big temple festival in 1996 at the beginning of this chapter. They were the guys who, in that same red, black, and *poleng* uniform, stood around at the temple gate, directing traffic and sending improperly dressed tourists over to me at the visitors' booth so I could give them a sarong and collect their donations. I also learned that, up here in the mountains, a village's *pecalang* were sometimes called on by neighbouring villages to police the potentially unruly crowds of young men at a local *drama gong* or *joged*-dance performance (see Kellar, this volume).

When members of Megawati's party, PDI-P, held their big rally in Bali in 1998, it was *pecalang* from all over the island who – in their providential colours – acted as security guards. And recently, while reading Henk Schulte-Nordholt's (1996) *Spell of Power*, I came across a footnote in which *pecalang* are referred to as 'palace spies'. Meanwhile, every temple festival you drive past these days has *pecalang* at the main gate. We also began to notice that they wear *kris*, traditional Balinese daggers.

Stories about the revival of *pecalang* in Ubud began to trickle in. Someone heard that they were being instituted in response to a dispute about some bar in town, thought to be frequented by drug-dealers and whispered to be protected by the army. Someone else said that the bar was just doing too well and people were jealous.

Someone else again, a klian *banjar*, said the idea to have *pecalang* was because there were so many 'outsiders' (*orang luar*) in Ubud these days. 'What do you mean – tourists?' I said, pretending not to know what he meant. 'No, no – newcomers (*pendatang*). You know...', and here his voice dropped, '...Muslims. We have to strengthen the *desa adat*.'

This 'strengthening of the *desa adat*' was beginning to sound like a sinister refrain – especially in view of the proliferation of militia groups in many other parts of Indonesia after the fall of Suharto.

QUESTIONS

It is useful to ask; What is the reason for *adat* police in the first place? Whom are they supposed to be policing? To whom do they answer? Does *adat* need to be policed? And what is meant by 'strengthening the *desa adat*'? Against what? What are the attributes of a strong *desa adat*? These are questions that the people of Ubud might ask of their leaders, but they are of general interest as well, I think.

I suggest that *pecalang* signify a latent militarism that is somewhat congruent with Balinese ritual culture. One sees weapons, banners, ceremonial soldiers and followers throughout Balinese pageantry – most vividly, in the sacred *baris gede* warrior dance, performed in the innermost temple courtyard (see Reuter 2002: 121). Hindu literature is full of metaphorical battles. Moreover, Bali's famous collectivism thrives in a social climate that enjoys homogeneity and seems not to mind (much, yet) submitting to compulsory obligations imposed by authorities, whether those authorities be a traditional elite, the group itself, or an overwhelmingly powerful outsider. This submission is mostly accepted gracefully as the price of that great treasure in life, social harmony.

But one must beware of seeing *pecalang* only in a folkloric light, as a kind of modern *baris gede*. Symbol and reality are not entirely separate, but if you dress young men up as *adat* police, arm them, and send them out into the night to defend the *desa adat* (whatever they may think that means), you may be asking for trouble. If indeed the goal is social harmony – and with Bali's economy dependant on tourism, the stakes are not only social and spiritual, but also material, political and cultural – then it is important to recognize the ambivalent and provocative nature of physical power, lest the *pecalang* shoot themselves in the foot with their *kris*, as it were.

The rise of *pecalang* in Bali and full-blown militia elsewhere (a recent media report counts at least 32 militias in Indonesia, each claiming anywhere from a thousand to 500,000 followers) may be in response to some sense of menace.[4] The pace and scope of change in late-twentieth-century Indonesia is shaking the country's foundations; it is hard to think of an aspect of life that is not affected. In the case of Bali, the threat to the familiar way of life is construed by Balinese as coming from outside the traditional culture; from tourism and from social and economic challenges brought by other (non-Balinese) Indonesians (see Vickers, this volume). This sense of menace is obscured by the commercial need to present a facade of normality, that is, that 'traditional Balinese culture' is well and thriving, and more recently, that 'Bali is safe' (especially for tourists). The response is a convoluted theatricality in which the rise of *adat* warriors is supposed to send the message that Bali is invincibly tranquil. It is possible that the young men patrolling their village lanes are not fully aware of the purpose they are serving.

Another possibility is that militias are proliferating in response to a power vacuum in post-Suharto Indonesia. That the state, and particularly the army, seems to be no longer the only agent capable of exercising force, may be received as a welcome change by many who suffered persecution under the New Order regime. On the other hand, it is a matter of some concern that the military-like exercise of force appears to be widely regarded as an appropriate means for all kinds of social groups to realize their socio-political ambitions.

This consideration, especially in the context of a volume on the muted worlds of Bali, prompts the question: Who benefits by the militarization of Balinese culture? In this regard, the remarks of a Balinese observer are particularly interesting:

> The Balinese people who live in tourist areas are caught between two cultures – that of international tourists and that of domestic migrants from outside Bali. Local resources, such as the *desa adat* with its *pecalang*, are given no role at all; they are only exploited and used to support and reinforce the ruling authorities.
>
> (Wirata Dwikora 2000, my translation)[5]

This raises more questions: What role could 'the *desa adat* with its *pecalang*' play in tomorrow's society? What can traditional culture offer in response to the new challenges of these times? And in regard to 'strengthening the *desa adat*': Do the ruling authorities and the population share the same vision? Do their interests coincide?

What indeed is the nature of social harmony? Does it depend on the inviolability of cultural forms? Does social harmony need to be enforced by armed men, even nice young men in *adat* dress? Might it arise instead from good-will?

Considering the events following 11 September 2001, it is clear that Bali is not alone in facing fundamental questions about the degree and nature of security required for social stability, nor are its different social groups unique in looking to traditional forms for a culturally legible language in which to advance their interests – nor even in believing that their success depends on defending their identity by the use of force, if need be. Perhaps the real question is whether social harmony is possible in a milieu of a xenophobic identity politics, or whether identity is most securely grounded in the fact that we are all human beings.

NOTES

1 The *pura puseh* (lit. 'navel temple') is one of the 'three temples' (*kayangan tiga*) found in most Balinese villages, and is traditionally associated with the origin and the founding ancestors of the settlement.
2 Ubud has many '*puri*', a term referring to a Balinese royal house or one of its many branch houses. 'Puri Ubud' in this chapter refers to Puri Saren, which is considered Ubud's main palace.
3 'Haruskah Warna Hitam untuk Upacara Kematian?' *Nusa*, 19 July 1999, p. 16.
4 This anonymous report was posted in instalments from 15 to 21 May 2000 on *Indonesia Daily News Online* (IndoNews@indo-news.com), in the section 'Indo News', under the title 'Laskar-Laskar Tak Berguna' (see their archive under Xpos, No. 16, III, 18 May 2000). For a fascinating account of the history of these and similar organizations, I refer to Philip King's work on 'Satgas', the security forces of Indonesian political parties (King 2000).
5 '*Oleh dua budaya – dari turis-turis internasional dan migran domestik luar Bali – inilah masyarakat Bali di kantong-kantong pariwisata itu dijepit. Potensi-potensi lokal yang ada – desa adat dengan pecalang-pecalangnya – tidak diberikan peran apa-apa, tetapi melulu dieksploitasi dan dimanfaatkan untuk mendukung dan memperkuat rezim yang berkuasa.*' Putu Wirata Dwikora, 'Diskriminasi di Bali' *Kompas Cybermedia*, 4 June 2000.

REFERENCES

King, Philip (2000) *Securing the 1999 Indonesian Election*, Wollongong: CAPSTRANS Occasional Papers, University of Wollongong.
MacRae, G. S. (1997) *Economy, Ritual and History in a Balinese Tourist Town*, Auckland: University of Auckland, unpublished Ph.D. Thesis.
Reuter, T. A. (2002) *Custodians of the Sacred Mountains: The People and Culture of Highland Bali*, Honolulu: Hawaii University Press.
Schulte-Nordholt, H. (1996) *The Spell of Power: A history of Balinese Politics, 1650–1940*. Leiden: KITLV Press.
Wirata Dwikora, Putu (2000) 'Diskriminasi di Bali'. *Kompas Cybermedia*, 4 June 2000.

10 Indonesia in transition

Concluding reflections on engaged research and the critique of local knowledge

Thomas A. Reuter

The essays in this collection have illustrated how global or national crises impact on local societies and how their responses are shaped by the local social divisions, inequalities, and associated tensions these societies bring into the bargain. In short, what can be observed is a two-way process of interaction between differently positioned but significantly connected groups of human subjects. In the course of these concluding reflections, I would like to draw out some of the epistemological and ethical implications of this observation for social science in general, and for studies of social inequality and change in particular.

The intricacies of the process by which national or global crises are locally received and mediated are not always spelled out. Crisis-reporting by the mass media, for example, tends to be driven by a popular taste for the sensational and often fails to situate the dramatic changes of today adequately within local historical and cultural contexts. Much of the recent research literature on Indonesia, on the other hand, can be highly commended for shedding light on this intricate interplay of local and inter-local processes of social interaction, and the present volume is a further contribution to this end. A number of studies of marginal populations in Indonesia (see Chapter 8, this volume), for example, have revealed how futile it is to distinguish between the introduction of external influences and the internal dynamics of a society, as these two processes are never operating in isolation. It is very useful to think of the histories and current condition of local societies in terms of their embeddedness in a national or global context – so long as we remain conscious of the two-way interaction this inevitably entails.

Contemporary Bali is a perfect example to illustrate this point. National political uncertainty since the collapse of the New Order regime of former President Suharto in 1998 has encouraged people here and elsewhere in Indonesia to examine, challenge, or reconstruct patterns in the distribution of wealth, power, and social status that had been established during Suharto's 32 years in office. This process of renegotiation has brought violent upheaval to some parts of the country, as is illustrated by recent events in Aceh, Ambon, Kalimantan, Sulawesi, and West Papua. The island of Bali, where social change has been similarly profound but not as violent in its manifestations, has received very little attention in numerous 'crisis reports' by the Western media over the last 4 years, and when it did, it was on those few occasions when violence had flared up after all. Even the academic literature has tended to focus more on the most obvious crisis spots in Indonesia. The effects of the Asian economic crisis and of the subsequent crisis in the political system and economy of Indonesia have nonetheless been felt strongly in Bali, and in ways that are at once typical and unique.

I propose that understanding local, Balinese responses to changing national political and global economic landscapes is an on-going challenge and an important opportunity, with implications well beyond the confines of Balinese Studies. In the first part of these concluding reflections, I shall discuss the kinds of challenges and opportunities that may be involved in studying local processes of social change in Bali and elsewhere. I shall then argue that we too may need to change – our theoretical perspectives and methods, that is – in order to meet these challenges and opportunities.

One of the benefits of studying 'local' struggles for socio-political change in the wake of a wider crisis is that it may help us to gain a more balanced, accurate, and dynamic perception of the local society concerned, and of its positioning within wider arenas of interaction. But there is also a cost attached to focusing our attention on social conflict and change: The approach and role of (still predominantly Western) researchers in the social sciences may need to be re-examined and modified in this particular kind of research setting to make more room for critical and political engagement.

The focus on social tensions and struggles in Balinese society in this volume, for example, has inadvertently drawn attention to groups of people who have been denied access to power, wealth or social status, and whose frustrated ambitions may meet with hope and opportunity or may experience renewed setbacks during the current period of turmoil. It has been widely argued, on both epistemological and moral grounds and in very general terms, that social researchers can no longer claim to be objective and dispassionate scientific observers and should rather commit themselves to a specific moral position that is openly critical (e.g. Marcus and Fischer 1986). Under the more specific circumstance of researchers studying and commenting upon the struggles of disadvantaged groups of people, this general demand for critical engagement acquires a special sense of urgency.

The fate of others is closely intertwined, and their interests all too often in competition with our own; in the current context of globalization no less so than in an earlier historical context of Western colonialism. Most researchers, since the 1980s, have therefore openly argued or implicitly taken the position that it is impossible to escape the moral implications of social science research by pretending to be a disengaged and innocent bystander. On the other hand, it has also been very difficult to build a credible epistemological and ethical foundation for such a new, engaged and critical social science. Researchers are still sorting through their options in the aftermath of a serious crisis of their own, precipitated by the post-modern, post-colonial and feminist critiques of social science in recent decades. In the second part of this chapter, I shall consider some of these options by reflecting on how an undeniable demand for critical moral engagement in the social sciences can be met, particularly when studying crisis-affected societies, without having to succumb to the inherent limitations of a moral subjectivism.

TIMES OF CRISIS: CHALLENGES AND OPPORTUNITIES

It is necessary to exercise some caution in trying to define what actually constitutes a crisis. In the Indonesian case, we may well ask where the real crisis is to be located historically. Was the period of political oppression under the New Order not the time of more profound crisis than the post-Suharto period, despite the mirage of stability that the Suharto government managed to project to the outside world? And why should we describe the current struggle for democracy and justice, for all its violent manifestations, as a time of crisis rather than a time of hope and much needed reform (i.e. a genuine *Era Reformasi*)? Is it because Indonesia could become a less predictable partner for Western-dominated international political alliances, or a more difficult site for business investors hitherto accustomed to state guarantees of a cheap and docile labour force, soft environmental regulations, and lucrative deals with corrupt politicians?

These questions pose a serious challenge, and one for which I have no easy answers. As far as Bali's internal power and status struggles are concerned, I sincerely fear that the real crisis is a continuous one, and that many of the victims in today's crisis may turn out to be the same people who also suffered from poverty, political oppression and social discrimination under the New Order regime. As far as the prognosis for Balinese society as a whole is concerned, much will depend on what will happen to the New Order notion of 'development', especially in relation to the tourism sector of the Balinese economy. Regional autonomy may prove advantageous in that it provides an opportunity (but no guarantee) for Balinese to stop some of the excesses of an earlier development policy, but it may also intensify regional competition for development and produce a lack of cohesion in responding to island-wide environmental and social problems. In this and many other ways, Bali is at least as vulnerable now as it was before the political change of 1998.

The social changes that have actually taken place in Bali so far, in response to Indonesia's national crisis, are but the beginning of a process, the outcome of which cannot be predicted yet with any certainty. This volume has illustrated how social tensions have surfaced in the Era Reformasi, in a diversity of ways and contexts, both in Bali's political economy and in a local politics of representation. But the case studies have also shown that the idea of a 'crisis' (generally defined as a period of patent instability), while it may serve as an adequate answer of the question 'why now?' of social change, does not really shed much light on the 'why' component thereof. Even if we are prepared to consider the current situation as a legacy of the lingering crisis embodied by the authoritarian New Order government, many of the locally observed tensions and struggles still seem underdetermined. For example, while Kellar was able to demonstrate the profound impact New Order ideology has had on Balinese perceptions of gender roles, Nakatani's paper demonstrates simultaneously how very much 'Balinese' many gender-related issues have been, and continue to be, for local women. What relative importance, then, can we attribute to the outside influences that arise from Bali's relationship with larger worlds and their crises, and how dramatic is their local effect?

While the outcome of the present crisis may be too soon to call, it cannot be denied that Bali's political economy has witnessed a series of major transformations in the wake of earlier crises, triggered by Dutch colonization, modern state formation, and growing Balinese dependency on global networks of cultural and economic exchange. While all of these transformations can be described as 'gradual' processes (to varying degrees), there have also been specific or 'critical' events that have had a sudden and profound impact on Balinese lives.

The modernization of Bali's economy, for example, has been a gradual process, but the Asian economic crisis of the late 1990s was felt as a distinct event nevertheless. Was this momentary effect possible only because of an earlier gradual change? The local repercussions of the Asian and Indonesian economic crisis, it could be argued, were indeed most severely felt by those employed in a modern and largely export or tourism-oriented Balinese economy. But the pattern was really much more complex. Some of those working in the 'traditional' agricultural sector were indeed shielded from the effects of local inflation on food prices, which fits the pattern, but 'modern', cash-crop agriculture also profited from the increased export value (in Rupiah terms) of the goods they produce, including cloves and coffee. A number of modern, export-oriented manufacturing businesses profited similarly from a devaluation of the Rupiah, while tourism and other modern enterprises suffered the negative effects of slowing economic growth in the region, coupled, in Indonesia, with reduced foreign investment due to national political instability and mismanagement. In short, while modern, globalizing economies have gradually become more dependent on external markets, the local impact of a particular regional or global economic crisis can be very specific and very mixed, even within the modern sector itself.

A similar argument can be made about political crises. Following in the wake of the Asian economic crisis, there have been a number of major and minor political crises in the region, not exclusively but most notably in Indonesia.[1] Again, it soon becomes obvious that the answer as to the 'why' of the Indonesian crisis is an Indonesian answer, even though the Asian economic crisis may in part answer the 'why now' question. And, once again, we may ask how sudden and dramatic the local impact of this second, political crises was felt to be, in Bali and elsewhere in Indonesia.

The collapse of Suharto's New Order regime, subsequent uncertainties about the legitimacy of former Vice-President Habibie's interim rule, about the erratic policy shifts of President Wahid, and concerning Megawati's commitment to Reformasi have had a destabilizing effect on the political and administrative establishment throughout the country, at national, provincial and regional levels. Many previous alliances of mutual benefit – between leading state officials or members of the Golkar Party in Bali and local economic or cultural elites – collapsed or became unstable. As political power changed hands, the ensuing mood of openness provided opportunity for people who had been economically disadvantaged, excluded from political participation or culturally marginalized to voice their concerns openly for the first time in many years (see, for example, the report on workers' protests in Vickers, this volume). At the same time, however, there is no reason to conjecture that the new power holders – many of whom are members of Megawati's party (PDI-P), which gained an overwhelming majority in Balinese elections – are any less susceptible to involvement in a renewed culture of corruption and money-politics similar to the one that had characterized the earlier establishment.

A somewhat different set of questions arises in relation to the impact of recent global and national developments on the 'representational' or 'knowledge economy' of Bali or other local societies. In the current period of turmoil, the representational economy of Balinese society is certainly witnessing a dramatic increase in activity – as different groups engage with existing knowledge structures in order to gain, retain, or expand their control over a range of cultural resources (sometimes with of very practical motives in mind). Greatly increased freedom of the press in Indonesia and a proliferation of new and more diverse newspapers and magazines are the two developments that are very relevant to this trend, and both happened quite suddenly. But this volume has also shown something of the immense variety of idioms and symbolic frames, from literature and journalism to the performing arts and ritual, in which different sectors of Balinese society express their various ambitions. Some of these idioms, however, are not new at all and are specifically Balinese, as are the issues that are being discussed.

To be able to identify what constitutes a significant social change in public discourse on this island requires a good understanding of Bali's symbolic economy prior to the current period. A symbolic economy is an emergent and negotiated set of knowledge constructions based on a host of representational practices and discursive strategies. In the Balinese case, this construction attained some degree of coherence and also oppressiveness due to the rise of a dominant, New Order-sponsored idiom of representation. With the support of a local political elite, who were able to wield the power of the Suharto state locally, an alliance of traditional and modern cultural elites in Bali has managed to create and convey a compelling vision of the island's culture and history, not only to other, less vocal Balinese, but also to the world at large (see Chapters 3 and 8, this volume). Less privileged groups in Balinese society have not been invited to contribute to this vision, have been cast in a negative light, or have simply been ignored and thus marginalized.

Bali's politics of representation has been multifaceted; reflecting the diverging and overlapping interests of traditional and modern status and power holders who often, but not always, have been the same people. The dominant discourses of New Order Bali therefore drew upon a mixture of traditional and modern idioms to generate a hybrid language of social distinction, so as to provide a rationale for the various inequities still prevailing in contemporary Balinese society. An example is education in general, and literacy in particular. Originally used as a marker of caste-based privilege and later as a means to tap the power of the Dutch colonial state, education under Suharto became a yardstick for distinguishing between 'modern' and 'backward' groups within Balinese society, but with members of the upper castes still over-represented within the first and privileged of the two categories. In view of the local issues involved (such as caste) and the local idioms that merged into them, the contribution of New Order influence to the Balinese knowledge structures of the time, therefore, must not be overestimated, though it was clearly significant. Likewise, it is improbable that whatever dominant idiom of public discourse may emerge in the post-Suharto era will be able to determine completely what is said in Bali, or how it is said.

A further challenge in the study of historical 'crises' is that they may involve encounters (and sometimes violent ones) between different peoples with very different cultures and technological means. Post-colonial studies of Bali, for example, have documented some of the many political and economic changes and discursive shifts that took place in Bali following the specific event of the military intervention of the Dutch in Bali, and with the more gradual establishment of an indirect system of colonial rule (see, for example, Vickers 1989). The Asian economic crisis and Jakarta's political crisis could be classed, similarly, as Balinese encounters with powerful outsiders or outside influences (in a new guise or under different circumstances).

As Margaret Wiener, has pointed out, however, such encounters involve much more than just the impositions of an external influence on passive and helpless victims at the distant margins of a colonial, global or national power–knowledge system (Wiener 1995). Representations of Bali in the discourses of the nation state and in texts produced by Western commentators have long been, and continue to be, intermeshed with a local politics of representation.

The power and representational idiom of the Dutch colonial or modern Indonesian states have been systematically borrowed and appropriated by Balinese agents, through a complex system of political complicity that has had its origins in the Dutch policy of indirect rule. Foreign discourses, in turn, have also been shaped and elaborated through the cultural brokerage of privileged Balinese allies and 'key informants'. At the same time, alternative visions of Bali, like that of the Bali Aga, have also persisted – sometimes challenging and sometimes supporting those of more privileged Balinese – just as Balinese discourses as a whole have simultaneously supported, appropriated and subverted those of the colonial or modern state.

The research of the contributors to this volume affords a more open view of Bali's symbolic economy not as a single but as a multiple co-production of knowledge, reflecting a continuous negotiation of competing strategic interests as well as a common and communicative interest in cooperation, in interactions not only among the Balinese themselves but also in Balinese encounters with the larger world. This observation leads on to the second set of questions I would like to reflect upon; questions concerning the role of social science research in general, and the study of social inequality and change in particular.

Where a forceful realization of their strategic interests by one group at the expense of others is in evidence, there may seem to be a clear and distinct need to subject local power–knowledge systems to critical analysis. Even then, a move toward a critical analysis of local knowledge and power structures is problematic in that it could be construed as a renewed foreign intervention and an imposition of knowledge in its own right. As I have just suggested, however, there is no such thing as a simple and pure imposition of knowledge, because knowledge is intrinsically communicative. This is a significant point in relation to questions about the legitimacy of a critical moral engagement in social science.

In the following section I shall argue, on the foundation of a basic epistemological assumption, that engaged research and critical knowledge are necessary and can be legitimate and mutually beneficial under certain historical conditions. The assumption herein is that all knowledge arises from intersubjectivity (rather than any single subjectivity) or, in other words, that it is always more or less 'co-produced'. The specific character of a body of intersubjective knowledge, nevertheless, depends on the historical conditions of its production. 'Legitimate' knowledge can be produced only under the historical conditions of a relatively level economic and political playing field, where it can be genuinely 'co-produced' by way of free interaction and argumentation rather than being 'imposed' to some greater or lesser degree.

REPRESENTATION, POWER AND SOCIAL SCIENCE: IS IT LEGITIMATE TO PURSUE A CRITICAL KNOWLEDGE OF OTHER SOCIETIES?

A self-reflexive study of Bali's local power–knowledge system, and of its links to those of the Indonesian nation state and the world at large, must begin with a general theory of representation. This is assuming that knowledge is constructed by a communicative process of representing, counter-representing, negotiating, conferring approval or rejecting others and their validity claims.

My own research in Bali has been dedicated to the marginal Mountain Balinese, and this work has raised specific questions about the power of representation and the agony of being represented. As an ethnographer living and empathizing with a people relegated to the shadowy recesses of an imagined paradise, by fellow Balinese and outsiders alike, I was perpetually reminded of the practical consequences of misrepresentation (see Chapter 8, this volume). This reality called for a moral response, but it also forcefully reminded me of problems of representation (if no longer a 'crisis') in anthropology and related disciplines.

The Western scholarly enterprise of studying and portraying other cultures has been cast into serious doubt by a growing awareness of the role of subjective bias in such representations, and of the negative practical implications of biased representations for those represented. In response to this challenge, Marcus and Fischer (1986) were among the first (in anthropology) to call for experimentation with innovative forms of research from a position of 'Anthropology as Cultural Critique'. This title of their book indicates a moot point. If Western researchers' knowledge of other cultures is subjective and has been in the service of Western power, then what foundation can there be for a more reliable and critical social science of the future?

One could, of course, altogether dismiss the proposal of adopting a critical stance in relation to cultures other than our own, by characterizing it as a disguised regression to paternalistic authoritarianism. Written from a position of power, by privileged academic subjects, all Western representations of non-Western cultures could be said to be doomed to become instrumentalized in the service of new and ever more insidious patterns of political domination. There is such a danger, but if we capitulate to it, the only remaining task for researchers, if any, would then be to 'deconstruct' the pseudo-scientific, Western power–knowledge structures of today, or better still, of an earlier age of colonialism, but without raising any alternative knowledge claims.

Recognizing the difficulty of writing anything at all about other cultures without constructing a further representation, and unwilling to stop writing altogether, Western scholars were indeed rather anxious, for a while, to undermine their narrative 'authority' as 'authors' by paying careful attention to their own style of writing. In keeping with a non-authoritarian, self-reflexive or post-modern style, the fully hyphenated new-age-ethnographer would simply 'channel' or 'evoke' the voices of others rather than 'represent' them (Tyler 1986). In its new conservatism and pseudo-realism, this approach did not resolve the central issue of representation. An authority overtly denied will resurge as an authority concealed, with the post-modern author safely hidden like an invisible conductor among the orchestra of others' appropriated voices.

In my own view, it is both unnecessary and unwise to dismiss the possibility of a constructive and critical role for social science, even if this involves taking a critical look at other societies, as this volume has done. The approach I wish to advocate instead can be spelled out by answering two central questions: Is the social science project of promoting cross-cultural understanding doomed to utter failure on account of the subjectivity of its practitioners? And further, can we ethically afford to abandon the pursuit of cross-cultural understanding as practitioners of social science in a globalizing world? My answer to both questions is a qualified but firm 'No'.

My initial response to the first, epistemological question is to concede that a particular piece of social research can never provide more than a partial and temporary interpretation of another culture, as experienced from the unique position of a particular historical subject. This scaling down of validity claims for social science is necessary in view of its own history, but it does not constitute a general admission of failure. It may well be a response with limited utility, however, unless the reasons for particular failures are addressed. In this I agree with Renato Rosaldo (1989), who argues that the survival of social science as a legitimate mode of inquiry rests on the assumption that some representations of foreign cultures are indeed better and more complete than others, even if all individual contributions must remain imperfect and partial.

Striving to produce better and more complete representations, however, does not require us to return to an objectivist position on the nature of truth. Rather, the epistemological challenge is to go forward, by grounding theories of knowledge in a fuller understanding of the structure of human 'subjectivity'. On the assumption that the content of subjective knowledge cannot be divorced from the means of its production, that is, from thinking, feeling and embodied human subjects, I am compelled to reflect briefly on the structure of human psychology and human interests.

Unfortunately, contemporary views on human interests and human subjectivity sometimes depart from a set of highly cynical assumptions. The somewhat dreary conclusion seem to be this: Representations of cultural others are always designed to serve the strategic interests of the representor, which necessarily and intrinsically differ from those of the represented. Representors are inclined to enhance their own power, wealth and status at the expense of these others. Human nature is intrinsically sinister, propelling us to try and dominate other individuals and peoples, and knowledge is but a servant of our interest in power. I am alluding here to popular understandings of Freudian and Marxist theory, but I am also thinking of the notion of the individual as a cold-hearted cost–benefit calculator that is espoused by liberal individualism and its many offshoots in contemporary economic theory. According to these viewpoints, human nature spells for the concealment of one's selfish motives and strategic interests from other individuals and groups, and even from oneself.

The purpose of this broad characterization is to expose covert negative assumptions about human nature and agency that, in my view, still seem to inform attitudes to knowledge in the social sciences to some extent. What I wish to criticize here is not a conceptual fault in any particular theory, which would be well beyond the scope of this concluding reflection, but to identify a general mood of cynicism, a lingering perception of the individual as a self-serving, independently calculating and knowing entity. Were we to accept this negative and limited position on human nature, we would have to confine social science to an epistemological limbo of subjectivism, wherein each subject is assumed to be essentially and insurmountably biased. In adopting a position similar (on this point) to the one outlined in great detail by social theorist Juergen Habermas (1984, 1997), I argue that this approach is mistaken in the tacit or explicit overemphasis it places on the sinister aspects of the knowing subject and, more importantly still, in neglecting the inter-subjective character and emancipatory potential of knowledge.

There is some truth in the portrayal of representation as an instrument of power, and of symbolic knowledge systems as a kind of instrument of legitimization. My own experiences with representation in Bali, however, did not leave me with the grim impression of a people operating as ruthless Machiavellian agents. Indeed, most theories of radical cynicism already evoke the shadow of their own nemesis. If a concern with power and self-interest were paramount to human nature, why would there be a need to legitimate power and conceal strategic interests, and what other human interest would explain this struggle for legitimacy? The marginal Bali Aga in particular reminded me that the relationship between power and knowledge is complex. As Habermas has argued on more theoretical grounds, the intrinsic empirical complexity is that people appear to have a communicative as well as a strategic interest in representing themselves and others.[2]

Knowledge can flow from power and can be used in a strategic manner further to disempower others, but it can also be based on free negotiation and encourage voluntary cooperation. Symbolic knowledge rests on a solid foundation of intersubjectivity, in that its construction depends utterly on communication and hence presupposes some degree of representational cooperation. From an epistemological perspective, the key to understanding power–knowledge systems is therefore not subjectivity but inter-subjectivity.

This argument also pertains to social science itself. Portrayals of other cultures and societies are not simply isolated, individual, and subjective knowledge claims. They too are positioned within a (secondary) inter-subjective field of representation, and sociological knowledge is contested and co-produced within this field. The subjective element in this and other fields of knowledge is not problematic so long as the content of representational knowledge is freely negotiated therein, under a condition of economic and political equity, and assuming full participation in the process of representation.[3] While these conditions may never be met completely in any actual social setting, this only reinforces the need for general and specific critiques of culture and knowledge. The recognition of this practical need informs my response to the second question above.

My response to the ethical question about representation is to argue that social scientists cannot at all afford to abandon the project of actively promoting critical understanding across cultures. Marginality studies, and studies of societies in a state of crisis (where inequalities are brought into relief as marginalized voices momentarily become more audible) illustrate very well why this is so. The subjective, temporary and partial nature of the knowledge we have to offer as individual researchers is evident and acknowledged. This does not absolve us, however, from a moral obligation to society as institutionally privileged social agents. Our difficulties in achieving a balanced and critical understanding of other knowledge systems must be evaluated in the context of their phenomenology as part of 'real world' scenarios. This is a world where representations are formed on first impressions, and where knowledge is often wielded as an instrument of domination with little concern for either truth or morality. Under these practical conditions, even a modest claim of relative impartiality for the knowledge produced by social science research may be sufficient to justify its practical application wherever this may help to alleviate human suffering.

The need for such a critical social science has never been greater than it is now. The problem of representation will continue to elbow itself to the foreground of discussions in the social sciences due to a profound transformation in the quotidian world these disciplines strive to comprehend. This is a world characterized by increasing economic interaction, cultural hybridization and mobility, wherein geographically distant societies encounter one another as participants in an ever tightening web of global interdependence. Unperturbed by any of the self-doubts of social science, however, the tendency to misrepresent and localize others on cultural grounds has by no means become a thing of the past. The opposite is the case.

At a level of popular discourse, the cultural, religious, racial or ethnic stereo-typing of others has become a dominant idiom of global politics and of many conflicts since the end of the Cold War, in Indonesia, Africa, Europe and elsewhere. Ironically, perhaps, the more tenuous the economic social and conceptual boundaries between different cultures or ethnic groups have become, the more vehemently have they been defended as lines of control. Such boundaries have been renegotiated at great cost, with outbursts of the most hideous interethnic violence bringing suffering to people in many parts of the world.

If it is accepted that knowledge can be legitimately co-produced under certain conditions and that the critical analysis of all kind of power–knowledge systems is an absolute, practical necessity in the contemporary world, this raises a final, methodological question: How is this general project of cultural critique to be applied to a specific situation?

My research in Bali has propelled me to apply a method of critical analysis to all power–knowledge systems, but with varying intensity depending on the material conditions, equitable or otherwise, under which they operate at a given time and place. In this I assume that representing and being represented by others are matters of universal strategic interest to all social agents. Every person has thus the potential to be a biased representor or a victim of biased representation in different contexts. I also assume that representational knowledge fulfils a second and equally general purpose, relating to the basic communicative (and hence necessarily cooperative) interests of human beings. A first answer to the question of where to direct the moral project of cultural critique is therefore: toward every form of representation and symbolic economy – but without lapsing into unwarranted cynicism.

An indiscriminate mode of critical inquiry is particularly relevant to situations where acts of mutual representation occur on a level playing field. In this situation no participant is positioned in advance as a likely victim of misrepresentation by factors outside the process of representation itself, because power and wealth are distributed rather evenly. Strategic interests remain important and biases must be anticipated. Nevertheless, specific claims are likely to be tested in an intersubjective process of relatively free argumentation. Rival claims must appeal to a shared conceptual and moral framework in reference to which their validity pretension can be assessed, rejected or confirmed. Apart from this need for communicative cooperation, participants would also be propelled to build mutually acceptable representations of one another in order to establish a foundation for practical cooperation and joint action. The representational system would tend to fluctuate between moments of compromise and cooperation, and times of more intense conflict and renegotiation. To a limited and varying degree, status struggles among different Bali Aga groups, or among other sectors of Balinese society with similar access to material resources, can be said to take place on such a relatively level playing field. Even under such favourable conditions, a proper account of any given knowledge structure, in its full historical actuality, must reflect the momentary balance among competing truths and the limited consensus on which participants base their collective and cooperative performances.

This general critical approach needs to be qualified in situations where the game of mutual representation is not played on a level playing field. How they are represented by others may be of universal practical concern to any group of people, in that social status is vested in the opinions of others. But variations in the intensity of this concern can be momentous. Where power relations are skewed, the knowledge structures of a symbolic economy may reflect, reinforce, or help to escalate political and economic inequities. In such a situation, the critique of knowledge may need to become skewed in the opposite direction. The relationship between marginal and privileged groups in Balinese society represents such a case, as I have discussed in reference to the Bali Aga (Chapter 8, this volume). Women in Bali, in some contexts at least, could also be described as systematically disadvantaged (see Kellar, and Nakatani, this volume).

While these and other disadvantaged groups may contest their misrepresentation in the narratives of the dominant stakeholders of a changing Balinese knowledge system, their negotiations issue from a position of political and economic disadvantage. In Gramsci's terminology, one could say that a hegemonic discourse of domination coexists with a counter-discourse of resistance. But it must be kept in mind that projects of 'hegemony' and 'resistance' are inconceivable unless there is some cultural provision for the mutual intelligibility of politically strong and weak validity claims. People in this kind of setting, therefore, are still communicating and expecting a degree of cooperation and acceptance from one another, even though there may be some hostility. Nevertheless, it would not be legitimate to endorse local knowledge structures that support a project of domination just because the oppressed may feel compelled to cooperate to some degree in the process of their own oppression.

A critical response to a local knowledge structure that is evidently in the service of power must be seen as an act of intervention and thus needs to be considered very carefully. A first step must be to determine the actual degree of disparity in political and economic power among the proponents of two competing discourses in a society. This assessment cannot be based simply on a textual analysis of the dominant discourse in the society concerned without checking its actual success or failure in achieving its aims. Rather than over-estimate the power of hegemonic discourses or fetishizing resistance, the assessment must be realistic. Resistance, for example, cannot be assumed to be a simple product of necessity. 'Resistance' or 'marginality' are terms to designate a particular stance that in one part is imposed and in another part may be embraced deliberately as a special source of symbolic capital.

A further issue to keep in mind is that knowledge and power are historically produced phenomena. With the advent of colonial rule and the subsequent establishment of a modern Indonesian state and following the fall from power of President Suharto, political and economic capital was partially redistributed in Bali. This was sometimes to the advantage but more often to the disadvantage of already marginal groups. The borrowed power and discourses of a modern Indonesian state and its administration system, especially during the Suharto period, delivered a degree of advantage to Bali's new political and economic elite that was unprecedented in the history of this island. The critique of a contemporary politics of representation must therefore be alert to significant historical changes, such as we are witnessing now.

Researchers may also encounter far more extreme situations, where struggles on an uneven political and economic playing field are not tempered by an element of regulated cooperation beyond the most basic requirements for communication. Knowledge may still be important in such cases, in that it may be used to 'justify' violence. However, the knowledge that enables a project of forceful and violent oppression tends to be more technical than it is cultural, and its critique no longer requires a special understanding of the cultures or identities involved. To justify a moral intervention on behalf of victims of systematic intimidation or genocide, for example, it is sufficient to know that they are human beings. Unfortunately, this kind of situation prevailed in East Timor until recently and, to a much lesser degree, in Bali as well.

Images of violent oppression and bloodshed in Bali are most strongly evoked by memories of colonial conquest in general, and of the *puputan* massacres of Balinese royal families in particular. These events must not be forgotten, given that the long-term effects of colonial rule are still felt today. Violence has not been the invention and prerogative of Western colonial powers, however, nor did it cease in Bali with Indonesian independence. There were perhaps more Balinese killed during the anti-Communist purge of 1965 that brought Suharto to power than those who ever fell victim to Dutch colonial aggression. Under his New Order regime there also have been other forms of violence. For example, many Balinese were forcefully dispossessed of their land and compensated very inadequately or not at all, in connection with tourism-related development projects in which family members and corporate allies of Suharto were deeply implicated. One legitimate and necessary form of intervention in such cases is to bring the concerns of an oppressed people to the attention of the world.

In keeping with these reflections, my proposal is to harness the critical potential of social science to address practical problems of representation – small and large, at home and abroad – in a multitude of social and historical contexts. This call for a critical and morally engaged social science may still seem problematic, but there are some important issues that ought to be considered in this context.

Taking the position of an unconcerned bystander to a struggle between others, particularly on an uneven playing field, is an act of passive complicity. For example, there is no neutral moral ground to walk upon for those who turn their back on an act of genocide. Even for violations on a comparatively moderate scale, the same principle applies. A second issue arises whenever we encounter a local cultural politics in which our historical predecessors have already intervened. In many cases, Western scholars have not been accomplices of colonial rule alone. In Bali, at least, they have also collaborated with the local elites who acted as their informants and cultural brokers, and have unwittingly supported local structures of domination. Presenting disadvantaged sectors of Balinese society in a more positive light, in an act of considered and explicit complicity, may help to balance the score. A third argument is that the analysis of strategic aspects in non-Western knowledge systems may help to define the problem of representation in more general terms than has been possible by a critique of Western power–knowledge alone. Such an analysis may reveal how other cultures have balanced strategic and cooperative interests in their societies. A critical analysis of non-Western knowledge structures does not necessarily imply that these are more in need of criticism than our own. On the contrary, critical analysis may reveal that Balinese or other local knowledge systems resolve differences of interest among participants in a rather effective and positive manner. Finally, I suggest that to deny the practical relevance of cultural difference to the shape of specific power–knowledge systems is to relinquish all hope of learning about our own social condition from others with whom we share a common humanity and common human problems.

These considerations are of central importance for an investigation of Balinese responses to Indonesia's national crisis. Insofar as this crisis has highlighted divisions, inequalities and simmering resentments within Balinese society, these need to be explored further and in a critical manner, for the sake of those involved and for the sake of advancing our general understanding of social change. And if Bali has escaped the more violent upheavals that have afflicted other provinces in Indonesia and have filled Western news headlines on many occasions over the last four years, this is an equally significant observation. Finally, Indonesia's crisis and vehement struggle for democracy must also be put into perspective by sparing a thought for another insidious, though less spectacular crisis in Western democracies.[4] Indeed, listening to my informants, as they began to envisage a new and more democratic Indonesian society of the future, especially in conversations just after the fall of Suharto, I had to admit to them that their ideals were by no means matched by our realities.

It may well be said that this volume falls somewhat short of fulfilling the criteria and aims of the project of a critical social science outlined above. It may also be said that some of the critique, particularly of the Suharto state, comes a little late, except insofar as the legacy of the New Order is still felt today. In acknowledgement of these evident limitations, I wish to express the sincere hope that neither Indonesians nor Indonesianists will ever again be muted to the same degree as they were at that time, and to remind us all that critical social science is not a project that can be accomplished by one individual set of contributions.

NOTES

1 Although its economy differs significantly from that of Indonesia, Japan is one of the other nations whose political leadership and financial structures came under severe scrutiny in the wake of the Asian economic crisis and, subsequently, the economic recession in the United States.
2 Among members of a species whose success has rested on an outstanding capacity for communication and social cooperation, individual self-interest is redefined in the context of belonging to a group, and the collective self-interests of groups are redefined in the context of their involvement in even wider spheres of social cooperation.
3 These requirements of free negotiation and full participation define an ideal case scenario for a field of intersubjectivity, and these requirements are rarely, if ever, met in reality. In the intersubjective field of social science itself, for example, a condition of completely free and equal global participation (of non-Western as well as Western scholars) has not been achieved as yet. Although there has been a significant trend in the direction of achieving such a condition, this process needs to be encouraged further.
4 The crisis I am referring to here shows itself in a number of symptoms: a decline of public confidence in the ability of elected representatives in two-party, same-policy political systems to effectively represent the interests of the public; low voter participation; growing political cynicism and apathy; the imminent decline of important democratic institutions such as independent universities, publicly-owned media and trade unions; and the general decline of politics in view of the economic dictates of a global market or the power of multinational corporations. Ironically, the current endeavour of Indonesians to build a new and democratic state comes at a time when the relevance of Western nation states and nation states in general is crumbling away in the wake of the privatization of public property and services, trade deregulation, and a global doctrine of economic rationalism.

REFERENCES

Habermas, J. (1984) *The Theory of Communicative Action (Volume 1)*, London: Heineman.

Habermas, J. (1997) *Die Einbeziehung des Anderen: Studien zur politischen Theorie*, Frankfurt: Suhrkamp Verlag.

Marcus, G. E. and Fischer, M. J. (1986) *Anthropology as Cultural Critique: An Experimental Moment in the Human Sciences*, Chicago: University of Chicago Press.

Rosaldo, R. (1989) *Culture and Truth: The Remaking of Social Analysis*, Boston: Beacon Press.

Tyler, S. A. (1986) 'Post-Modern Ethnography: From Document of the Occult to Occult Document'. In J. Clifford and G. E. Marcus (eds), *Writing Culture: The Poetics and Politics of Ethnography*, Los Angeles: University of California Press.

Vickers, A. (1989) *Bali: A Paradise Created*, Harmondsworth: Penguin Books.

Wiener, M. J. (1995) *Visible and Invisible Realms: Power, Magic and Colonial Conquest in Bali*, Chicago and London: University of Chicago Press.

Index

Page numbers in *italics* refer to illustrations, tables and maps.